W9-AKY-159

Software
Defect
Removal

Software Defect Removal

ROBERT H. DUNN
Manager, Programming Quality
ITT Advanced Technology Center
(Formerly with ITT Avionics Division)

McGRAW-HILL BOOK COMPANY

New York St. Louis San Francisco Auckland Bogotá
Hamburg Johannesburg London Madrid Mexico City
Montreal New Delhi Panama Paris São Paulo
Singapore Sydney Tokyo Toronto

Library of Congress Cataloging in Publication Data

Dunn, Robert H., 1929–
   Software defect removal.

   Includes index.
   1. Debugging in computer science.   2. Computer
programs — Testing.   I. Title.
QA76.6.D845   1984   001.64'2   84-4400
ISBN 0-07-018313-9

1234567890 DOC/DOC   8987654

ISBN 0-07-018313-9

The editors for this book were Stephen G. Guty
and Galen H. Fleck; the designer was Naomi Auerbach;
and the production supervisor was Reiko F. Okamura.
It was set in Century Schoolbook by Progressive Typographers Inc.

Printed and bound by R. R. Donnelly & Sons Company.

to Nancy *of all people*

Contents

Preface

Current economic conditions are such that a revolution is underway to improve worker productivity and product quality. To a large extent this has been brought on by foreign competition. In at least one field, however, productivity and quality were identified as major problems long before the success of imported subcompact automobiles, copying machines, and other products. Since the time of vacuum-tube machines, the practices by which computers are programmed have been undergoing a continuous revolution. Call it a rapid evolution if you will, but new methods and tools are developed at an astonishing rate; all to the end of improving productivity, quality, or both.

Apart from the more obvious pressures to improve programmer productivity, we have a Malthusian phenomenon to contend with. For the foreseeable future, at least, the number of programmers needed by our society will continue to outstrip the supply. Currently, growth of demand is 3 times that of supply. It is clear that this will not go on forever. The situation recalls the projections of some years ago for the dollar volume of the computer business. The programmer work force of the future, extrapolated from current growth curves, will no more exceed the total population than annual computer revenues ever reached the gross national product. If, in the future, we are not all to be professional programmers, it will not be for lack of programming applications. Rather, it will be because of alternatives to programming; most notably those arising from artificial intelligence. Also, the proliferation of personal computers suggests that computer programming will in time be a part of the job performance of many types of workers, not just professional programmers.

Nevertheless, we are stuck with the present, and if we are to improve programmer productivity — which we must — we will have to find vulnerable areas of programmer activity to focus on. None is more prominent than the time spent at the detection and correction of defects. Up to 50 percent of all programmer labor-hours is spent at this. It is hard to imagine an equivalent percentage of labor spent in removing defects from automobiles, books, bridges, cheeses, paintings, or anything else we produce.

If we can improve our processes for removing defects (unless an explicit distinction is made, I use the term to refer to both detection and correction), we will have made concomitant progress in improving program quality. Stories relating the effects of software defects are legion, and there is no need to repeat them here. What I think is worth mentioning is that we have no reasonable way to reckon the cost exacted by the effects of program defects. Intuitively, however, we know that low quality levels have resulted in too many hours spent at reconciling credit accounts, finding the several tons of frozen fish sent to the wrong warehouse, recovering the errant spacecraft, and placating the patrons waiting in line at the bank while someone tries to bring up the crashed teller network.

Software defect removal is not only an obvious candidate for our attention, it indeed does lend itself to improvement. A diverse number of techniques and tools have been developed to the end of finding and fixing bugs. Moreover, these span every phase of the software life cycle. Where once we had only testing, and not very efficient or effective testing at that, as our method of removing defects, we now have the means of removing defects starting as early as the requirements phase of software development. Once the software product has reached the code stage, we have a variety of approaches, both passive and active, at our disposal. If software producers are to extract maximum profit from this array, the weapons need to be utilized within the reference of a systematic program of defect removal. In turn, this means that the capabilities and limitations of each method, as well as any relations among the methods, must be understood. This is the purpose to which this book was written. My goal is to provide the software producer with enough information on each method — what it does, when it is best used, how it is used, and how it interacts or intersects with other methods — so that he can fashion an effective and comprehensive program of defect removal peculiar to his own applications and environment.* Section 1.4 grossly summarizes the defect removal methods that are discussed. Along with Section 1.8, it constitutes a road map to the rest of the book.

Beyond the methods that can everywhere be implemented today, I have included a few topics (for example, formal correctness proofs) that await further development before they can be considered for general implementation in commercial programming shops. However, discussion of these topics helps to provide deeper understanding of other, currently more practical, methods. Also, considering the rate at which software engineering technology evolves, one never really knows just when these new

---

* The prominence of women in the programming profession prompts me to draw the reader's attention to the practice, here and in later pages, of using masculine pronouns when referring to subjects of undefined gender. As so used, no implication of the subject's sex is intended, only consonance with familiar convention.

methods will have matured to the point of general utility. Indeed, some may have by this reading.

Some intersection with defect prevention was inevitable. I make no apologies for this. Although it resists codification into an implementable program of its own, defect prevention touches upon every aspect of software engineering, and certainly it bears as much on productivity and quality as does defect removal.

It is impossible for me to know the full extent to which the concept and preparation of this book were influenced by discussion with colleagues in industry, government, and academe. However, I do know that my association with the staff of ITT Programming Applied Technology, starting well before I joined them, had a major effect. I can also identify those people who were particularly helpful in reviewing manuscript drafts or, by sharing their insights, in enriching the book: Larry Doyle, Steve Dunn, Steve Guty, and Capers Jones.

May, 1983   *Robert H. Dunn*

Software
Defect
Removal

Introduction

To Err Is Human
To Find the Bug, Divine

In the Paleolithic Era of computer programming, when programs were small and rarely the product of more than a single mind, programmers discovered that they could not declare their programs to be complete until they had spent a fair amount of time removing the same bugs they had earlier implanted. Indeed, debugging was often the dominant activity, accompanied by various symptoms (grinding of teeth, pencil breaking, angry resetting of all computer registers to zero) of the programming debugging syndrome. Happily, the programmer's spirit was seldom defeated. Inevitably, if belatedly, the last known bug was fixed, the cue for a celebration. Sounds of joy were made; uninterested associates had listings of lovely output thrust under their noses; and computers were forgiven. A sign found in many computer rooms of the time reflected the growing awareness that too often programming was nearly synonymous with debugging: "The moment of truth is a working program."

When one considers that the subject may have been no more than the calculation of the constants of an equation fitted to a collection of observed data or the debit balance of each customer, the ceremonies which attended the first success seem extravagant. Still, like mathematical theorems, working programs have a certain beauty, and perhaps these early programmers were carrying on the tradition of Pythagoras, who is said to have sacrificed a hecatomb in honor of the beauty of his discovery that the square on the hypotenuse equaled the sum of the other two squares. Admittedly, few programmers have had hecatombs to sacrifice, and, anyway, sacrifices are out of fashion. Nevertheless, a working program remains an elusive thing of beauty.

The Neolithic Era of programming arrived during the early 1960s, with teams of programmers working on problems of greater scope and complexity. There were now tools to help cope with the new and greater problems: compilers, execution traces, and simple operating systems. However, programming continued to remain tantamount to debugging, or almost so. The principal difference was that programmers could point accusing fingers at each other rather than have to accept the sole guilt of failure to reason correctly. The rites of passage at the moment of truth were now marked by mutual conciliation and celebration.

Enter software engineering, with tools, techniques, and a disciplined approach to programming, and the modern era was established. Just in time, too, since the problems laid on today's programmers are a thousand-fold more sizable than the early ones, with the result that the ratio of bugs to problem size* is no worse than it had been. However, the bugs that are resident in new code are often so concealed within the involutions of the program structure that up to half of all programmer labor-hours are expended in their removal. While today's programmers celebrate a working program, their management fairly rejoices at the knowledge that further cost and schedule risk have finally ended. Therein lies the imperative for the application of software engineering not only to defect prevention but to defect removal as well.

1.1 Productivity and Cost

Programmer labor-hours are the one software measure that everyone understands. Defects per thousand lines of code (KLOC), failure frequency distributions, program volume, and many other attempts to quantify software attributes or behavior are subject to diverse interpretations or qualifications. But programmer labor-hours have to do with two related problems that are given grave consideration in many quarters: programmer productivity and programmer cost.

The growth of the software demand has matched the proliferation of computers, from programs for increasingly more powerful microprocessors to large systems for "super computers." If one includes consumer use of automatic cash dispensers, computer-controlled telephone switches, and the like, "by the end of the 1980's the typical working citizen of the United States will average more than five computer 'transactions' per day, every day, for life."[1]† The programming that makes these transactions possible will continue to grow at a rate far exceeding that of all other forms of labor. Programmer productivity is not only an issue for learned discussions by software gurus; it is a matter of major societal importance.

Inextricably bound to productivity is cost. As the nineteenth century

---

* A new ratio invented for this occasion and abandoned thereafter, or at least until such time as we learn how to quantify problem size.

† References are listed at the ends of chapters.

saw steel and electric power raise the standards by which people lived in the more advanced countries, and as the first half of the twentieth century was the era in which engines and electronics brought a new kind of affluence to nearly all, the second half of this century is destined to be remembered as the computer revolution: the welcome permeation of software-driven systems in yet untold aspects of our personal and business lives; assuming, of course, that society can afford the cost of the programming. Computer hardware costs are tumbling as rapidly as instructions per second and storage per cubic inch are climbing. If there is anything that can arrest what we like to think of as an inevitable trend, it is the cost of software. Consider but one buyer of software, the Department of Defense, which saw its costs for weapons systems software jump from less than $3 billion in 1980 to over $5 billion in 1982 and expects to be paying over $30 billion a year by 1990.

On a less lofty level, but one closer to home for the typical programmer, can the chief executive officer afford the programs to which his company is already committed or needs to undertake to expand or even to maintain its position?

> The 35 to 50 percent of programmer labor-hours now given to software defect removal represents the single most obvious target for improving productivity and reducing cost.

And this opportunity to save costs is distinct from improving the reliability and usability of the delivered product.

The implication that we should focus on defect removal should not be interpreted as an excuse to relax ongoing efforts at defect prevention. Quite clearly, every defect that can be prevented is one that will never have to be removed. Project planning disciplines, proven techniques of problem decomposition, structured programming, testable requirements documentation, complexity modeling, continual tracking of resource utilization, methodical updating of technology through the tracking of defect measurements, and software tooling must be maintained. Where these precepts of defect prevention are not in use, they must be introduced. It is unlikely, however, that we shall find a producer of large-scale software who has ignored them; for to do so is to generate so great a number of defects that we should not expect the producer to remain in business. In any case, defect prevention is quite another matter, and we shall return to our target of opportunity, the removal of the defects that for whatever reason eluded preventive measures.

1.2   Defects Defined

Programmers usually are quite willing to own up to the existence of bugs, problems, anomalies, quirks, eccentricities, peccadillos, or whatever. They seem, however, not to like the use of "defect," and they generally avoid it as though it had a pejorative ring to it. In fact, it does not and is certainly not used in that sense in this book. The usefulness of the word is its applicability to each phase of the software life cycle, something that cannot be said of the terms having greater currency.

Let us creep up on the definition by starting with its source: human error. The *IEEE Software Glossary* offers these definitions of an error and its consequences:

> ERROR: A conceptual, syntactic, or clerical discrepancy which results in one or more faults in the software.
> FAULT: A specific manifestation of an error. A discrepancy in the software which can impair its ability to function as intended. An error may be the cause of several faults.

A *defect* is either a fault or a discrepancy between code and documentation that compromises testing or produces adverse effects in installation, modification, maintenance, or testing.

Removal of program faults is generally more difficult than removal of documentation discrepancies, and the substance of the methods for defect removal that will be presented are mostly directed to the former. Documentation defects will not be ignored, however, since the mischief they can wreak can make a program prematurely obsolete, or, in the least, waste many hours of programmer time.

Before abandoning this business of software lexicology, we shall look at the definition of a software failure, a term that will be used later. As defined by Lloyd and Lipow.[2]

> FAILURE: A software failure occurs when a fault in the computer program is evoked by some input data, resulting in the computer program not correctly computing the required function in an exact manner.

Thus the causal 3-tuple: errors create faults that cause failures. Let us continue on this digression just a bit longer: When a program has evinced some minimum number of failures, people are likely to be disabused of the idea that they can *rely* upon it as they had expected. Herein we find a semantic justification for the term "software reliability" (not that so weak a definition allows us to do anything with it). More quantitative definition will be found in Chapter 10. For the moment, however, the right of "software reliability" to exist has been established, and — to the possible outrage of those who declare the term meaningless — it will be used informally for the intuitive and qualitative sense it connotes.

1.3   A Defect Taxonomy

We shall want to know more about the defects that require removal. Defect removal is the solution to a problem, and the more we know about a problem the better we can fashion a solution. There are two fundamentally different ways of viewing defects: in the large and in the small.

We shall leave the small for Section 1.6 and start with the large. In their classic paper,[3] Goodenough and Gerhart defined two principal classes of defects (which they called errors): performance and logic. *Performance* dealt with such matters as the adequacy of execution speed, while their four *logic* categories actually reflected the source of the fault. Combining these into three classes, we can succinctly and usefully fill a big picture frame:

REQUIREMENTS DEFECTS: Failure of software requirements to satisfy the environment in which the software will be used, or requirements documentation that does not reflect the design of the system in which the software will be employed.
DESIGN DEFECTS: Failure of designs to satisfy requirements, or failure of design documentation to correctly describe the design.
CODE DEFECTS: Failure of code to conform to software designs.

Now, ultimately, if not removed early, requirements defects will propagate to code. Still, putting the blame* where it belongs, these remain requirements defects. The message, to which we shall return later, is that there is much merit to removing defects as soon as possible after they have been created.

It is fairly easy for experienced programmers to relate each of the three classes to their own observations, but examples should prove useful to those who have yet to learn the awful truths of computer programming. Typical requirements defects include indifference to the initial system state, incomplete system error analysis and allocation, missing functions, and unquantified throughput rates or necessary response times. Among the many kinds of design defects, we have misinterpretation of requirements specifications, inadequate memory and execution time reserves, incorrect analysis of computational error, and infinite loops. Possible code defects include unreachable statements, undefined variables, inconsistency with design, and mismatched procedure parameters.

These examples are but a small part of the total defect space. From them, however, a pattern may be discerned. As we move from requirements to code, we can see that more detailed levels of hazard are encountered. This reflects the logical development of software: from concepts closely related to the problem but distant from the solution to those difficult to directly relate to the problem but more closely associated with the computer (or its software environment) on which the solution is finally implemented. Even as development descends through decreased levels of abstraction, so do defects.

---

* With apologies to egoless programming.

1.4   Defect Removal Taxonomy

Given an organized view of defects, we can attempt to get one for the means of their removal. The following classification of surgical techniques is a synopsis of the substance of most of this book:

Requirements reviews

Design reviews

Pseudolanguage processors

Code reviews

Static analysis

Proof of correctness

Structural tests

Functional tests

As an introduction to these, some brief definitions are called for.

Requirements reviews.   Requirements specifications are the subject of requirements reviews. These reviews focus on establishing *traceability* of the specifications to the system performance requirements. For an electronic office, such matters as the replication of current manual functions should, in one manner or another, be covered by the specifications. A specification for an operating system should specify the number of terminals to be supported, the computer resources to be managed, software packages to be supported, and the like. Typical of a specification for embedded* software we have real-time processing speed, statistical estimates of input data rates, and mathematical solutions to be formed. In short, requirements reviews are directed to the aspect of a system design that defines the role of a computer(s) in satisfying the overall system solution.

The second salient objective of a requirements review is *testability*. (There are other things to look for as well, but we'll wait for Chapter 3 to discuss them.) Each of the functions defined in a requirements specification must be testable. That is, each must be defined so completely, explicitly, and apart from other functions that specific test criteria can be established for the function.

While requirements reviews may seem to be directed at routing out defects in requirements documentation, such defects are often the symptom of defects in the system design itself. These are, of course, more grave.

---

* As used here, "embedded software" refers to the programs, documentation, and static data for computers intended for on-line operation with any combination of sensors, data collection devices, devices equipped for control by digital signals, displays, command consoles, and other elements of instrumentation systems.

As a simple example, it may well be that the accuracy of one circular degree specified for navigation system software is the accuracy required of the entire system and that those who wrote the specification either forgot about instrumentation error or (erroneously) assumed that the software designers would decide what the tolerable computational dilution of precision should be to arrive at a system error of one degree.

Design reviews. Design reviews are analogous to requirements reviews in that traceability to requirements specifications is a prime objective. For large systems, a single design review is generally insufficient. As we shall see in the next chapter, the development of large systems entails several sequential design stages, and each stage may be subject to review. If the design methodology is such that each stage is actually the paper implementation of the preceding stage (even as design in its entirety is the implementation of requirements), then each review looks for traceability of the subject design to the predecessor design phase.

Apart from traceability, none of the other important matters covered in design reviews stand out more than the attributes of the design itself: Is the design structured; is it feasible within the constraints of hardware resources; is it testable (usually, a comment on modularity); is it robust (will the program continue to perform even in the presence of violations of the assumptions in the specification); and so on. Again, these reviews are directed to design documentation, but they are more likely to reveal faults in the design than incorrect translations of that design to paper.

Design reviews, design inspections, and design walk-throughs are similar, but there are differences. These will be explained in Chapter 3.

Pseudolanguage processors. To a large extent, both requirements and designs may be documented in special languages that are a cross between programming language and natural language. Using rigid semantics and syntactical rules, but allowing considerable freedom otherwise (e.g., *if* the bond is in default, *then* credit zero), pseudolanguages tend to lend structure to the final software product as well as provide succinct and unambiguous direction for the next stage of implementation. To the extent that it is practicable to document requirements and designs in these machine-readable languages, it is possible to automate some of the aspects of requirements and design reviews. Processors for these languages can search for inconsistencies among the various sections, improper sequences of processing steps, interface anomalies, and the like. They can also provide various reports to present requirements and design data in forms that make defects more visible. These special language processors are discussed in Chapter 3.

Code reviews. As design implements requirements, code implements design. Here, traceability to design is easier to establish, since there is quite nearly a one-to-one correspondence between code segments and the elements of detailed design. Code, however, opens up new opportunities for programmer error: clerical mistakes, misuse of language semantics, incorrect syntax, and all the familiar ills that were the bugs best known to our Paleolithic forefathers with whom the chapter started. The objective of code reviews in this respect are obvious. Here too, however, we find variants of the review concepts: code inspections and code walk-throughs. All three are the subject of Chapter 4.

Static analysis. Requirements and design language processors operate on design and requirements documents without actually executing them. Similarly, static analyzers process code but do not execute it. Static analysis is the name given to a group of associated — and interrelated — software techniques for finding structural and semantic defects in code. To some extent, they automate code review processes, but they also are capable of finding certain kinds of defects that easily elude manual code-reading methods. Examples are calls to nonexisting procedures, improper software linkages, and subtle nesting faults.

Some static analysis reports, like those of pseudolanguage processors, are useful to those performing code reviews: lists of where data names appear and how variables are used, procedure linkage hierarchies, and program graphs. Static analyzers are specific to programming languages. An analyzer for Fortran is useless in a Cobol shop. We may also note that compilers and link editors often incorporate features of static analysis. Static analysis is covered in Chapter 5.

In Chapter 5 we also find a discussion of symbolic execution; it is included there because in many respects it is an evolutionary consequence of other static analysis capabilities and is certainly a structural one. Symbolic execution is the processing of code, step-by-step, by using algebraic input rather than real data values. The subject program thus appears to execute classes of data, rather than one specific datum at a time. The output is necessarily algebraic also, and in this form it may be compared to external specifications that are couched in algebraic terms.

As just described, symbolic execution sounds as though it were the greatest laborsaving device since the electronic calculator was invented. In fact, it compares more closely with the invention of the electric toothbrush in that, however effective it may be, its use remains time-consuming.

Proof of correctness. Perhaps even more labor-intensive is the technique of proving programs correct. Logicians may question the propriety of including correctness proofs in a book devoted to finding defects; but a correctness proof will fail when a defect is present, so the appearance in these pages of proofs is not at all unseemly. Defect removal starts with defect exposure, and correctness proofs do expose defects.

In a sense, symbolic execution may be said to be a means of proving correctness. If the algebraic output and the algebraic specification are identical, or can be made so with additional algebraic simplification, we can say that the procedure is correct with respect to its specification. As used herein, however, "proof of correctness" will principally refer to proofs in a formal system of logic. The best known technique is the inductive assertion method of Floyd,[4] given an axiomatic basis for interpreting the text of a computer program.[5] Assertions of the relations among variables are posited as a representation of the program. These assertions evaluate to boolean functions. Starting with assertions of the status of variables at a procedure's entry, and working through intermediate assertions to finally arrive at the exit assertion, one attempts to prove that the truth of each assertion encountered is implied by its predecessors. One can also start with the output assertion and work backwards.

These proofs are time-consuming, even error-prone, and are feasible only for single procedures. Still, they are intriguing, and they would seem to be of inestimable value for critical program elements — the security kernel of an encryption system, for example. The technique is discussed in Chapter 6, where we shall again find symbolic execution. Here symbolic execution is applied to code in which assertions requisite to a proof have been placed, thus using the power of the symbolic execution system to relieve some of the tedium and hazard of error of the mathematical operations.

Functional tests.   Is there a place in a modern software defect removal system for actually executing code? Indeed there still is, but we now know better than to simply consider testing as a monolithic activity. To start with, we define two inherently different kinds of tests: functional and structural. When we are finished testing, we should be able to see if code performs as we expect it to when installed in its ultimate operating environment or, as is frequently true, in representative cases of the several environments it is destined for. From these *functional tests,* or tests to external specification, let us work backward in time to functional tests of each program in a system of two or more associated programs, to the functional tests of major components of a program, and ultimately to very small elements of a program. I don't know who first applied the name "black box testing" to tests made to external software specifications, but the locution succinctly captures the idea: First, pour representative data into the input port of a software "box" of which we know (or pretend to know) nothing concerning its internal fabrication. Next, compare the data issuing from the output port to those which had been expected. Functional testing is the stuff of which Chapter 9 is concerned.

Structural tests. To many programmers, functional testing is the only kind to care about, and that rarely at levels below major components of a program. This is a regrettable throwback to the Paleolithic Era of software. The number of discrete states of which even the most simple programs or their major components are capable of attaining is so enormous that no number of test cases can ever cover more than the smallest part of the functional space. It is necessary to test also with regard to one's knowledge of the structure of the program, to view the program and its parts with the visibility afforded by a glass box, to fashion tests that plumb for defects in the mechanisms that one knows are there. This implies testing individual branch predicates and paths, and evaluating the truth of logical premises. Structural testing is discussed in Chapter 8.

Structural testing offers many opportunities to uncover latent defects that may escape functional testing. However, it is also true that functional testing can uncover defects that are transparent to structural tests. As a simple example, structural tests will not reveal requirements defects, but functional tests may.

Actually, structural and functional testing are not as mutually independent as this introduction suggests. Black box tests of program components are also structural tests at the program level. To best exploit both techniques, it is necessary to devise a comprehensive strategy for testing, the substance of Chapter 7.

Applying defect removal techniques. We have three classes of defects and eight techniques for their excision, as summarized by Table 1.1. Note that it is claimed that design reviews can catch requirements faults and that code reviews can find design faults. Although these reviews are not directed toward finding defects traceable to errors made in earlier phases, reviewers cannot totally erase from their minds the objectives of the earlier work. For example, in a design review for a payroll system it is observed that there is no provision for IRA deductions, nor was one included in the requirements specification. Nevertheless, an astute reviewer recalls having read in his newspaper that the client was one of the first companies to offer an IRA payroll deduction to its employees. A telephone call to the client confirms that this is a requirement. It seems that the decision to provide an IRA plan had been made after the requirements specification had been issued, and the need to modify that document escaped the thoughts of those who were involved.

It is quite obvious that Table 1.1 has no pretensions to profundity. It would, in the least, be surprising to find that requirements reviews could

Table 1.1   Defect Vulnerability

Excision techniques	Requirements defects	Design defects	Code defects
Requirements reviews	X		
Design reviews	X	X	
Pseudolanguage processors	X	X	
Code reviews		X	X
Static analysis		X	X
Proof of correctness		*	X
Structural tests		X	X
Functional tests	X		X

* Proofs can expose some design defects, but only at the lowest design level.

uncover faults laid to errors peculiar to the coding phase. Still, a certain pattern is evident: If we are to expose defects in requirements, we had better do so early. We shall not have another opportunity until many labor-hours have been spent in the design and coding that implement those defects, even in some of the testing. To a necessarily lesser extent, an analogous statement may be made of design defects.

1.5   The Importance of Timely Defect Removal

We are now looking at efficiency, or, if you will, productivity. This is worth further exploration. First, let us lump code reviews, static analysis, and proof of correctness into a single category: *passive tests*. Let us also make the reasonable assumption that requirements reviews and the use of requirements language processors take place prior to any significant amount of design and, further, that design reviews and the use of design language processors take place before code generation. Finally, we make the almost reasonable assumption that structural testing is completed before the start of functional testing or, at least, that most structural testing is completed at the time much functional testing (e.g., qualification) remains.

What we have accomplished with these consolidations and approximations is the following chronological sequence of defect removal opportunities:

Requirements reviews

Design reviews

Passive tests

Structural tests

Functional tests

The result of not catching defects at the earliest opportunity is shown in Figure 1.1, in which the earliest possible removal cost for each of the three defect types — requirements, design, and code — is normalized.

It may be noted that the cost of removing requirements faults is quantified for the passive and structural test phases, despite a lack of indication in Table 1.1 of such opportunity. Recall that the sequence of removal activities is only an approximation for convenience. There is always a need to return to requirements documentation during development, and any second reading — whether informally for clarification of some point or formally as a result of a directed change in the requirements — may expose an earlier defect. It is even possible that, at the first attempt to link-edit all the modules of a software system, one discovers that the amount of available program storage allocated during the requirements phase is insufficient. This should properly be considered a design defect, since design data should have provided early warning of the impossibility of stuffing 10 pounds of software into a 6-pound computer, but the result may well be a costly rethinking of the requirements.

In any case, the approximate average costs of delay charted in Figure 1.1 illustrate the importance of letting no defect removal opportunity go unturned.

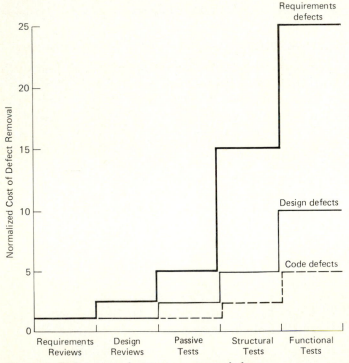

Figure 1.1   Defect removal costs versus removal phase.

What is it that drives the cost of tardy defect removal? "It" is several things. First among them is the loss of productivity concomitant to the implementation of a fault. A requirements defect propagated to the design phase results in designer labor expended on work that will have to be redone. If propagated to code generation, we have code, faithful to the design, that will have to be rewritten. Moreover, if not found until functional testing, the defect will result not only in design and code rework but in repetition of certain static, structural, and functional testing as well.

A second, although not quite independent, cost driver concerns nothing more than the number of persons involved with software production. At least until functional testing, and possibly even then, that number increases with time. The number of designers and coders is usually at least twice the number of requirements analysts (or system designers). Thus, more people are touched by the removal of a defect downstream from where it was caused than would be by a timely removal.

We have also to consider the nasty problem of defects masking other defects. This is especially true of design and code defects. The longer one of these remains in the system, the greater the mischief it causes if only because it may allow other defects to remain hidden. In a real-time system, for example, improper handling of data from an external instrument may have to await detection if the program has a second defect that causes it to always substitute, for real input, constants used for built-in system integrity tests.

When we think about defect removal efficiency, we usually do so in terms of either the number of labor-hours required to remove a defect or the percent of resident defects removed by a cleansing process.* What we have been considering is a more global connotation of efficiency, however, one that gets to the bottom line of programmer productivity. Like oriental rugs and Hepplewhite tables, defects get more costly with age.

Programmer productivity, of course, is affected by the choice of defect removal techniques as well. While we are severely limited in the number of techniques available for early removal of requirements and design defects, there are several applicable to detecting defects, regardless of source, at the code level. For a more detailed view of these, we shall need a defect taxonomy "in the small."

1.6   Defect Classes in the Small

Recall that our new taxonomy will consider faults that are found in code only. For this scheme, the origin is immaterial. Only the fact of a fault is important, and the categories result from partly subjective opinions of how defect attributes can best be divided into orthogonal sets. Orthogonality

---

* The latter will be redefined shortly as "efficacy of removal."

does not come easily, however, and the development of such schemes represents one of the more popular diversions for software engineers as they sit around warm stoves during the programming off-season. Or, at least it appears that way, since the literature abounds with a variety of imperfect schemes ranging from 3 to 30 classes of defects. The one that strikes me as the most sensible (and better than my own efforts at classification) is the one used by Lloyd and Lipow.[6] Its lineage may be traced to an earlier study,[7] and both sets of categories have since been used by several researchers. The taxonomy defines seven classes of defects:

Computational

Logic

Input and output

Data handling

Interface

Data definition

Data base

Lloyd and Lipow also have an "others" category, which, although indispensable in an imperfect system for classifying collected data, is not useful to the purpose to which we shall soon put the taxonomy.

Definitions of these classes are in order. Computational faults include incorrect equations or grouping of parentheses, mixing data of different unit values (adding days to weeks), or even performing correct computations on the wrong data. Although computational faults would seem to be easy ones to make, there are far fewer of them than logic defects.

Logic defects are, in fact, the most frequently found kind, and they appear in many forms. Among them are sequence faults (improper order of processing steps), insufficient branch conditions, incorrect branch conditions (how many times have the relationals in a conditional branch been reversed?), incorrectly nested loops, infinite loops, incorrectly nested *if* statements, missing validity checks, and so on.

Another of the frequent sources of failure is the group of input and output defects. These include input from or output to the wrong file or on-line device, defining too many data for a record size, formatting faults, and incorrect input-output protocols with other computers or communication devices.

Data handling is also among the more hazardous operations. Among these faults we find failure to initialize data before use, improper use or designation of indexes, mixing up the names of two or more data, and improper control of external file devices.

Typical interface defects are mismatching the parameter list of a procedure call with that internal to the procedure, using procedures as functions and vice versa, failure to override inadequate default parameters, and incorrect scheduling of other program units.

Data definition faults are relatively infrequent. Among them are incorrect type definitions (e.g., defining a real variable as an integer), improperly dimensioned arrays, and using subscript constants outside array bounds.

Data base faults are also one of the less-populated categories. Typical ones are incorrect data units and anomalies in data base initialization.

More on the application of defect removal techniques. Our new way of looking at defects is not without purpose. As we did for defect classes in the large, let us see how the removal techniques applicable to code apply to defect classes in the small. However, conforming to the greater level of detail inherent in the new classification scheme, it is appropriate to do more than just indicate applicability. Here, applicability will be labeled in the relative terms of high, medium, and low (Table 1.2).

To some, it may appear odd that functional testing — that is, testing to the external specifications — is not rated high for all types of defects. This is a consequence of the impossibility of testing all of the discrete states attainable by a program. This may be translated into the impossibility of testing all of the unique end-to-end paths through a program. Functional tests exercise each class of input, output, and function, but the specific data sets within the classes may not necessarily disclose all the latent defects that are there. More strongly, the likelihood that all these will be exposed in a large system is nil.

A disclaimer attaches to Table 1.2. Each of the seven categories is broad enough that we must recognize that within each there are specific faults for which a lower-ranked removal technique may be more effective. For exam-

Table 1.2   Defect Vulnerability

	Removal technique				
Defect	Code reviews	Static analysis	Proof of correctness	Structural test	Functional test
Computational	Medium	Medium	High	High	Medium
Logic	Medium	Medium	High	High	Medium
Input and output	High	Medium	Low	Medium	High
Data handling	High	High	Medium	Low	High
Interface	High	High	Low*	High	Medium
Data definition	Medium	Medium	Medium	Low	Medium
Data base	High	Low	Low	Medium	Medium

* Assumes proofs applied to single procedures only

ple, failure to check for division by zero is a logic fault, for which the table indicates structural tests are more effective than functional tests. However, for this specific logic fault, functional testing may be the more effective, since designers of structural tests rarely attempt to contrive test data that, after undergoing several mathematical operations, will combine to form a zero divisor.

It is tempting to rank the overall effectiveness of each of the five defect removal techniques by counting the number of highs, mediums, and lows. This will lead to fallacious results. Here is a demonstration: If we score each high as $+1$, each medium as 0, and each low as -1, the five techniques will fall into the following composite ranking:

Code reviews	4
Functional test	2
Static analysis	1
Structural test	1
Proofs	-1

It would appear that code reviews and functional tests alone might suffice. However, all is not so simple. Neither code review nor functional test is highly effective at finding logic faults, the category that may outnumber in defect count all the others. Moreover, code reviews that are highly effective are also highly costly. In one experiment with which I am familiar, the cost was equivalent to the cost of coding, although this is probably the extreme. For its part, functional testing is effective only when there is no untoward pressure to deliver the program when each functional class has successfully been executed but a single time.

Of the two middle-ranking techniques, most of the static analysis capabilities are relatively inexpensive to use once the tools have been acquired. Moreover, they provide output supportive of structural testing. Structural testing is very effective for finding the most frequently encountered faults: logic defects. Further, its low score partially results from its low rating in detecting the sparsely populated data definition class of defect. Indeed, overall, functional and structural testing are about equal in effectiveness.

Proof of correctness brings up the rear, and it is costly as well. Still, for highly critical program elements, one wants to do all one can to purge the software of any faults. Also, proof of correctness is highly effective for the important logic category.

In short, all five defect removal classes are important, and none should be overlooked in the quest for improving productivity and quality. Indeed, in Section 1.7 we shall take another view of the relative effectiveness of the techniques, one that takes into account defect population distributions and other influences. It correlates poorly with the simple scoring scheme of this section. Table 1.2 is enlightening, but quantitative abstraction of it is ill-advised. The real message of Table 1.2 is that there is a valuable role for every defect removal technique applicable to code.

There is another issue inherent to Table 1.2: passive defect removal versus active defect removal. Let us divide the five broad technique classes into two still broader categories, one of which we used in Section 1.5:

Passive defect removal	*Active defect removal*
Code reviews	Structural test
Static analysis	Functional test
Proof of correctness	

A defect is exposed by either of the two active methods when a failure occurs. The problem must then be diagnosed before the defect is located, a time-consuming process that may, particularly during functional tests, involve persons outside the programming group. It is common for a significant percentage of these diagnoses to be incorrect, with the result that the process must be repeated. Worse, although the fix may result in the program's passing the specific test that it had failed earlier, the revised code may still be incorrect, leaving a defect with a slightly reduced failure space. Experienced programmers are familiar with this problem of substituting one defect for another, a state of things that sometimes becomes the largest single cause of failure during the later phases of active test.

Passive methods represent a difference of kind. With the single exception of symbolic execution — and even that is arguable — passive defect removal does not find defects through failures. Passive methods directly disclose defects. Labor-hours are not wasted in often faulty diagnoses. There still is no assurance that the corrective action will be effective or immune to side effects, but at least there should be no question that the right defect is the one addressed.

1.7 Efficacy of Defect Removal

Before leaving this overview of defect removal techniques, we shall take yet another view of their relative value. In an attempt to quantify how well each satisfies its purpose, a new measure is introduced: the efficacy of removal (EOR).*

---

* As defined, this looks very much like a formula for efficiency. It should. It is. However, to use the word "efficiency" is likely to muddy the issue with thoughts of labor-hours expended per defect, quite another matter altogether and discussed — if not quantified — in the preceding section. On the other hand, I am the first to admit that "efficacy" is a word few of us feel comfortable with in ordinary conversation. Those who find it too bothersome may say "efficiency" — but to themselves. In any case, it will be mostly EOR for the balance of the book.

$$\text{EOR} = \frac{D_f}{D_f + D_r} \times 100$$

where D_f = number of defects found by the technique

D_r = number of defects remaining after the technique has been exhausted

The concept of EOR is far more important than the immediate use to which we shall put it: a tabulation of ranges.

	Range of EOR, %
Requirements review*	20–50
Design review*	30–70
Code review	35–85
Static analysis	20–40
Proof of correctness	50–100
Structural tests	20–70
Functional tests	20–70

These estimates derive from more than personal measurements. A number of sources (including Capers Jones of ITT, who, I believe, was the first to generate EOR estimates in this form) were consulted. The result is a set of ranges considerably greater than can be explained by the need to translate various EOR data into a particular classification scheme. These ranges are, in fact, the clue to the inference we must draw, the conclusion that is more important than the numbers themselves. *The extent to which techniques are fully employed and the production milieu in which they are used are paramount.*

As an example of the former, in Chapter 5 we shall see where static analysis can mean a number of things. An ambitious system can be very effective; a simple system merely helpful. Similarly, functional tests can include stress and boundary tests and copious amounts of random data, or they can be as simple as testing with one data set per input-function-output class. And so it goes. As in all things, there is no substitute for thoroughness.

With regard to production methodology and tools, certain of the procedures used to translate requirements into code lend themselves particularly well to the use of specific defect removal techniques. For example, decomposition approaches that enhance modularity also abet structural testing. The use of traceability tools, manual or semiautomated methods of

---

* The use of pseudolanguage processors is included here, rather than given separate entry, because in Chapter 3 the processors will be discussed as adjuncts to manual defect removal, notwithstanding their capability to find faults when used in isolation.

relating specific functional requirements to design and code elements and test procedures, has a favorable effect on EORs from design reviews through functional test. Finally, the methods used in the requirements, design, and coding stages will affect the distribution of defect types, and as we already know, each of the techniques for defect removal is more effective for some kinds of defects than for others.

1.8 A Quick Tour of the Book

Indeed, defect removal cannot be discussed outside the reference of production methods and tooled environments. Even the approaches to project planning have an effect. The means of problem decomposition, the choice of programming languages, the techniques of documentation—all of these, apart from their influence on defect production, also affect the latitude and to some extent the objectives of defect removal schemes. Thus, the next chapter will survey various development issues and approaches up to the point of active test. Although it falls far short of an encyclopedia of computer programming, it does attempt to provide a foundation for the chapters that will follow. With regard to the active test phases of a software project, a similar overview of testing will be embodied in Chapter 7, in which the issues that underlie the choice of a test strategy are discussed.

Section 1.4 contained a road map through most of Chapters 3 through 9. It may be noted that Chapters 3 through 6, which cover requirements, design, and code reviews, static analysis, and proof of correctness, are collected as Part 2 under the title Static Methods.

As noted earlier, Chapters 7 through 9 deal with active, or dynamic, testing. These lead off Part 3 which concludes with a chapter on defect data analysis. Such analyses are a useful mechanism for improving the productivity and quality of software development and defect removal processes. Since defect data include defects found by static methods as well as by active test, inclusion of this chapter in the section on dynamic testing may seem arbitrary. However, another aspect of defect data analysis provides help in answering the ubiquitous and difficult question of how one knows when enough testing (especially functional testing) has been performed.

Defect removal does not, alas, end with the delivery of software or the completion of installation tests. Large software systems nearly always start their operational life with some latent defects that somehow escaped the production removal process. Moreover, improvements made to the software or the addition of new functional capabilities may add more defects. Part 4 addresses defects during the operational life of software. Chapter 11 is devoted to configuration control, which may be viewed as the mechanism for managing software change, and Chapter 12 deals with the unique problems that attend the removal of defects from software in active use.

Before proceeding to the next chapter, we might pause to observe that despite the number of methods for defect removal that will be discussed, there is no magical way of ever assuring bug-free programs; at least, not for most of us:

> There's a wizard who treats with disdain
> Software testing of any known strain.
> He has said there's no cause
> For concern over flaws
> If you just know some legerdemaine.

1.9 Summary

1. Of all the activities that are required to produce computer software, removal of defects accounts for the greatest expenditure of labor-hours. It is the single most vulnerable target for the improvement of programmer productivity.

2. Defects result from human error in the requirements, design, and coding phases of development. The techniques for their removal may be thought of as falling into eight separate groups: requirements reviews, design reviews, pseudolanguage processing, code reviews, static analysis, proof of correctness, structural (glass box) testing, and functional (black box) testing.

3. Given this battery of techniques, defect removal can start as early as the end of the requirements phase. This is no small matter, for the cost of removal increases nonlinearly as the distance between the creation and the removal of a defect.

4. Although each of the defect removal methods that can be applied to code is effective, upon examination of the types of defects that are found in code it can be seen that no one removal approach is highly effective for all kinds of program faults.

5. Static methods (code reviews, static analysis, and correctness proofs) for finding faults in code directly expose defects. Dynamic testing requires that software failures be induced, with the concomitant requirement that each failure be correctly diagnosed to an underlying defect.

6. The effectiveness of any defect removal technique is very much the result of the thoroughness with which it is used and the production milieu in which it is employed.

References

1. Capers Jones, *Programming Productivity: Issues for the Eighties.* IEEE Tutorial, IEEE Cat. No. EH0186-7, 1981, p. 2.
2. D. K. Lloyd and M. Lipow, *Reliability: Management, Methods, and Mathematics,* 2d ed., published by the authors, Redondo Beach, Calif., 1977, p. 489.
3. J. Goodenough and S. L. Gerhart, "Toward a Theory of Test Data Selection," *IEEE Trans. Software Eng.,* vol. SE-1, 1975, pp. 156–173.
4. R. W. Floyd, "Assigning Meanings to Programs," *Proc. Symp. Appl. Math.,* vol. 19, American Mathematical Society, Providence, R.I., 1967, pp. 19–32.
5. C. A. R. Hoare, "An Axiomatic Basis for Computer Programming," *CACM,* vol. 12, October 1969, pp. 576–583.
6. D. K. Lloyd and M. Lipow, *Reliability: Management, Methods, and Mathematics,* 2d ed., published by the authors, Redondo Beach, Calif., 1977, p. 502.
7. T. A. Thayer et al., "Software Reliability Study." RADC TR-76-238, TRW, August 1976.

Chapter

2

An Overview of Development Methodologies

An alternate title for this chapter could equally well be Defect Implantation. Although additional defects will be introduced during testing and during modifications, the initial target of defect removal consists of the defects that result from development errors. The major thrust of software engineering has been the reduction of the number of defects generated in the requirements, design, and coding phases. The result is a diversity of methodologies to which the principles of defect removal must be adapted.

The distinction between defect removal and defect implantation is clear enough; that between defect removal and defect prevention less so. If a requirements defect has been removed before design has started, is this a matter only of defect removal or of defect prevention as well? It is both, of course, and a small matter at that. More subtle is the tracking of program storage estimates. As these are updated through the requirements, design, and early code phases, they would seem to be part of a defect prevention scheme aimed at avoiding a disastrously tardy realization that the available memory is incompatible with the mission of the software, the manner in which it was designed, the language in which it was coded, or any combination thereof. Yet, awareness of a monotonically growing program is often achieved only as a result of a series of defect removal reviews in which the latest sizing estimate is one of the many items examined.

At the extreme of subtle distinctions between defect removal and prevention, we have the indirect training received by programmers who participate in reviews and walk-throughs. We learn not only from our own mistakes but from those of others as well. Despite progress made in the development of programming methods based on mathematical foundations, it remains that programmers acquire their professional skills through one form or another of apprenticeship. Participation in defect removal is one of the more effective learning processes.

As we look at contemporary practices for software development, we should recognize that these have evolved in response to the problem of defect generation. Defect prevention is itself the subject for a lengthy book, certainly too broad a topic for a comprehensive treatment here. Still, the methods and tools for development that we shall briefly survey represent the current state of *thoughtful* software management. We shall not waste time on programming approaches of the genre (at an extreme) in which the boss calls in a lead programmer and says, "See what Pearl in accounting wants and write some code for it." In such a milieu, the one that needs systematic defect removal the most, we are unlikely to find any interest in the subject.

Beyond the emphasis on software engineering, the discussions that follow will be restricted to the aspects of development methodology that directly affect defect removal practices.

2.1 Software Attributes That Affect Defect Removal

We start with a lengthy digression: the intermediate and end products of software rather than software fabrication. Four features of software have a marked effect on both the latitude and the direction of the defect removal process. Moreover, the first two are criteria by which software engineers often assess the success of a development process. The four are complexity, modularity, source language, and documentation techniques.

Complexity.   There are techniques for measuring program complexity, and we shall encounter them in Chapter 7. For the present, let us be content to consider complexity in a qualitative (but intuitive) sense. Software complexity has to do with the perplexing interaction between the elements of software: source statement segments, procedures, major components, data structures, and even stipulated performance characteristics. Many, perhaps most, instances of software complexity arise from the inherent complexity of the task being dealt with. That is, the problem may have many parts to it, and some of these may be difficult to solve in software. For example, the programs that drive the microprocessors or minicomputers embedded in large military systems are nearly always complex. Other examples that quickly come to mind are graphic computer-aided design packages, telephone switch programs, and data base management systems.

We encounter excessive software complexity when the software solution seems disproportionately intricate with respect to the problem. There are times when programs can appear to be more simple than the problem. An example is Wirth's elegant recursive solution[1] to Gauss' eight-queens problem. However, we do not normally expect complex problems to give rise to less complex solutions. Contrarily, we have come to expect all too often that the solution is more marked by labyrinthine logic paths and involuted data structures than the problem would seem to warrant.

More to the point, complexity in code makes it harder to remove defects. It usually makes defect detection more difficult; it always makes the success of the correction problematical. At the level of individual procedures, structured programming is the universal antidote for complexity. Lack of structure militates against the use of certain static analyses and compromises structural testing. Complexity in design reduces the ability to trace design to requirements and confounds the diagnoses of test failures. It also tends to hide inconsistencies among the elements of the design and the logic faults within those elements. Excessive complexity in requirements documentation makes it more difficult to design test cases that will disclose the possibility that the resulting code does not satisfy the requirements.

Accordingly, as part of the defect removal process, requirements specifications, designs, and code are all judged for excessive complexity. Independently of this, successful development techniques attack complexity for the purpose of preventing defects.

Modularity. Of all the weapons used to attack complexity, perhaps the most notable is modularity. The division of a program into articulated modules, each with a well-defined purpose, each self-contained, and each maximally independent of other modules, provides a hostile environment for the intrusion of defects. The precepts of modularity also apply to the design of individual data sets. For example, it should not be necessary to repeatedly refer to one file for data, only to have several of the fields represent pointers to other files for data that remain constant between fetches.

Apart from its encouragement of error, lack of modularity makes it costly to design test drivers and stubs, difficult to fashion an incremental integration scheme, and tedious to fill in data structures for testing. With regard to individual procedures, poor modularity adds perplexity to code reviews. A weak modular structure also compromises the ability to trace design back to requirements or to devise functional test cases for individual modules and groups of modules.

In Section 2.2 we shall survey problem decomposition methods. The prime goal of these is a modular structure.

Languages. Among the several ways in which the language of source code influences defect removal, the greatest is that wrought by the level of language: assembled or compiled (or interpreted).

Programs written in compiler languages can be debugged at five times the rate of their less-advantaged siblings. To be understood by independent testers and reviewers, assembler language programs require more detailed documentation; at the very least, much more annotation. Assembler languages open up a level of hazard, hidden by most compiler languages,* to programmer error, that of register and bit manipulation. While this relates to defect prevention, it also bears on the creation of new defects during correction processes. As noted earlier, structured programming is important to static analysis, structural testing, and correctness proofs. Some compiler languages support structured programming. No assembler programs do. Finally, unless interpretive simulators or emulators are provided, assembler language places greater restrictions than does compiler language on the number of computers on which testing can take place.

In short, programs written in compiler language lend themselves more easily to defect removal than do programs written in assembler language.

Given that one's mission is to remove defects from a compiler language program, the choice of language has further effect. Languages having the Böhm-Jacopini canonical constructs (other than sequence) of *if-then-else* and *do-while,* or their derivative forms, are the ones in which structured programming is feasible. Languages with strong data typing (e.g., Pascal) permit compile time detection of many misuses of variables. Further, the stronger the typing, the more likely that software interface faults in the data domain may be found by static analysis. Finally, it should be relatively difficult for defects to remain hidden for long in highly recursive languages (e.g., LISP). On the other hand, finding the bug may require more ingenuity, since its effect affects its effect.†

It is rare for a language to be specified with verifiability as the main objective. For the most part, such languages have served chiefly as interesting experiments leading to further language design. Concurrent Euclid (CE)[3] is an exception. The constructs of CE, although increasing the difficulty of writing code, abet verification while enhancing reliability and understandability. Consider the following properties. For each CE procedure, the programmer must provide a list of the variables that the procedure has access to. To reduce hazard, certain restrictions were imposed on the data structure and other features of Pascal that underlie CE; for example, functions are not allowed side effects, a restriction enforced by rules governing parameter, variable, and procedure importing. Array pointers are so closely tied to the objects in the arrays ("collections" in CE) that

---

* There are exceptions; C, for example.
† A statement inspired by a definition in the *Devil's DP Dictionary:* "Recursive *adj. See Recursive.*"[2]

they appear as subscripts, allowing the proof techniques used for arrays to be applied to pointers. Aliasing, which confounds correctness proofs as well as the programmers trying to track down a bug, is banned.

As have other "verifiable languages," CE has been used little outside its place of origin (University of Toronto), where it was the language in which its own compiler and UNIX-like operating system were written.

Forms of documentation.   In much the way languages do, the written expression of software requirements and designs affects defect removal. Recalling that a defect was defined as either a fault in the program or a discrepancy between code and documentation, it is obvious that the clarity of specifications influences the likelihood of finding defects in the documentation itself. The intelligibility of requirements documentation is also a factor in the success with which design data may be traced back to requirements. Analogously, the clarity of design specifications bears on the capability of correlating the design to the specified requirements and, iteratively, code to design data.

Thus, the documentation techniques will influence the manner in which reviews of requirements, designs, and code are conducted. Beyond that, documentation in pseudolanguage will permit partial automation of traceability records and the use of pseudolanguage processing for defect removal.

Requirements documentation.   For defect removal, the most prominent attribute of a requirements specification is its *testability,* the quality that defines how well criteria can be established to demonstrate conformance of the end product to the specification. We tend to think of testability in terms of the individual functions defined by the requirements documentation. The obvious influence of testability on testing is actually the less important of its consequences. More significantly, it really defines how accurately the specification can be interpreted by those who will implement it, the software designers. We shall deal more with testability in the next chapter. For the present, we return to the forms of presentation of requirements specifications.

The most familiar specification is that written almost entirely in natural language. It describes the functions that must be performed, the hardware resources available to the program (memory space, disk space, and so on), hardware devices to be controlled, input, output, exceptions, limitations, constraints, response time, external constants, input data rates, accuracies, and a description of the initial system state; each is described as it applies — if it is applicable at all — to the type of problem. That is, the information contained in specifications for, say, embedded software, compilers, and data base management systems will vary in many respects.

Presented as voluminous prose, requirements specifications are both costly to prepare and tedious to use. While the difficulty of using such specifications falls mostly on the designers who must learn from them, it is equally unwelcome to those who must review the specifications or those who will subsequently attempt to match them to design documentation. Also, documentation of this form is not a natural by-product of a systematic analysis of the systems problem. More structured forms of documentation are.

Among the structured forms, perhaps the best known is hierarchy plus input-process-output (HIPO). Used mostly as design documentation, HIPO has also found considerable application at the more abstract level of requirements specifications. As the name suggests, HIPO lends itself to hierarchically structured problem decomposition. Figure 2.1 illustrates the expansion of HIPO modules in an accounts receivable system.

The references to specific files in the illustration betray a common problem in specifying what one wants a program to do, a problem not peculiar to HIPO. As soon as one refers to a file or a major function as though it were a program component, one has stepped beyond the line that separates requirements from design and has begun to specify *how* as well as *what.* When specifying updates of current software, this is entirely reason-

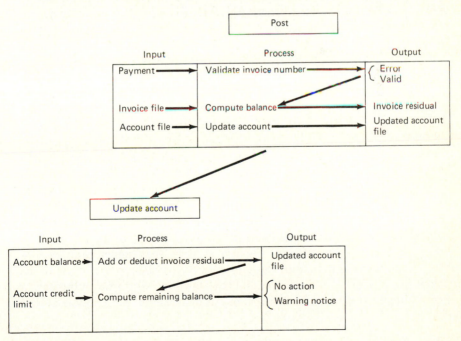

Figure 2.1 HIPO

able. For new programs, however, carried to an extreme, the system designer specifying the role of software in the system may end by designing a system without ever really defining its external characteristics. This not only causes a problem that will emerge when it is time to test to external specifications but may also confuse the designers who, rejecting as inefficient design details in the putative requirements document, erroneously infer their purpose.

> I suspect that the reason so many requirements specifications are as much design documents as they are anything else derives from the more concrete substance of design. Design deals with objects: program units, files, tables, and maybe hardware features. Requirements are at a more abstract level, one with which most of us are less comfortable. Then too, if the person preparing a requirements document has sufficient programming experience, it is nearly impossible to avoid thinking in terms of a software structure that can implement the requirements.

A graphical system distantly related to the concept of HIPO is SADT.* SADT, which stands for structured analysis and design technique, is a methodology for designing total systems: hardware, software, people, and their interrelation. Like HIPO, more than a documentation method, it is a technique[4] for analyzing requirements within the reference of a formalized system of diagrams. As with HIPO, each SADT information block may be iteratively expanded as the functional analysis leads to more acute definitions of the required processing. Unlike HIPO, SADT defines requirements independently of whether they will be implemented by people, hardware, or software. Placing requirements definition at a more abstract level than implementation should bear favorably on the previously discussed problem of specifying structure rather than function. As we shall see, both HIPO and SADT extend to design as well as requirements, which — among other advantages — lends continuity to the overall decomposition process.

Data flow diagrams are another graphical means of documenting software requirements. Since they closely resemble the signal flow diagrams that electronic systems engineers have used for many years, one might expect them to apply mostly to embedded software. However, they serve other types of programs equally well. Figure 2.2 illustrates the application of a data flow diagram to the same problem addressed by Figure 2.1.

As used in the illustration, the circles (bubbles) depict processes or transformations of data, and the arcs connecting them portray the paths taken by the data. I believe it was Tom DeMarco who first published[5] a hierarchical use of data flow diagrams. In his scheme, each bubble can be

---

* SADT is a trademark of SofTech Inc.

expanded into a data flow diagram of its own, thus giving the analyst a tool to document the process of stepwise problem decomposition — much as we have seen with HIPO and SADT.

The essential concepts of data flow diagrams are to be found in diagrammatic approaches to top-layer functional decomposition and to the depiction of time-based functional, decision-making, and operational sequences. At a more specific level, these apply to program design as well. Enos and Van Tilburg[6] wrote of the use of functional flow diagrams for dividing a system into major functions and processes, functional sequence diagrams to relate system functions on a time scale, action sequence diagrams to describe detailed sequences of actions defining the interfaces of operators, subsystems, equipment, and software, and operational sequence diagrams for illustrating data flow from acquisition through processing and on to output.

Other forms of documenting requirements, generally used together or in conjunction with graphical approaches, are data dictionaries to describe information external to programs (these may also be structured, rather like BNF language specifications), various tabular arrangements of information, truth tables, decision trees, and structured English and its derivatives.

Structured English (or whatever the tongue of one's choice) uses the control primitives of structured programming to define alternative, repetitive, and sequential operations but permits natural — if terse — language for describing predicates and objects.

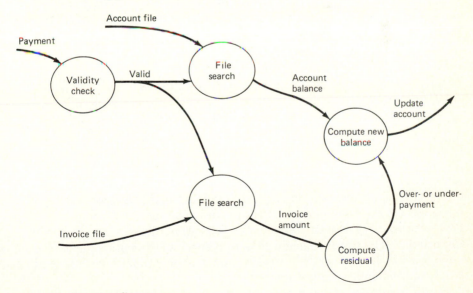

Figure 2.2   Data flow diagram.

```
if credit exceeds balance by less than $1000 then issue warning
Update account file
```

The absence of adjectives and adverbs, except when incorporated in an object name (favored_credit_risk), reduces both wordiness and ambiguity. The incidental loss of linguistic grace is a small price to pay for the precision that results. Ambiguity may be further reduced by defining all objects in a data dictionary.

The crispness of structured English sounds downright Proustian when compared to more formal languages particularly designed to specify software requirements. Like SADT, which may be thought of as a graphical language, most requirements languages are more than documentation media; they are the tools to support specific analysis regimens. Davis[7] provides a taxonomy for these languages. *Axiomatic languages* incorporate the precepts of formal logic systems found at the programming language level and first developed by Hoare.[8] We shall return to Hoare's work in Chapter 6. Languages based on *operational models,* of which there are very few, behave according to the rules of well-defined hypothetical machines. Davis' third category is "other," which includes the problem statement language (PSL) of the ISDOS project,[9] the requirements statement language[10] (RSL), and PAISLey,[11] each of which we shall refer to shortly.

Axiomatic and operational languages lend themselves to verification along the lines of the proofs of executable programs (Chapter 6). Among the axiomatic languages are ALPHARD,[12] which supports abstract data types, SIMULA,[13] which traces its roots to ALGOL, and AFFIRM,[14] which has perhaps even greater suitability to the level of software structure than to requirements but is not peculiar to that level. The Vienna definition language,[15] a metalanguage for defining programming languages, is an example of the operational model.

None of these languages for the specification of software are designed for use by the layman. Only a programmer, or a systems designer with programming experience, is a candidate for fluency in them. Moreover, most are fairly remote from specific applications areas. For example, RSL is based on finite-state machines, which precludes modeling the environment. PSL, based on data access concepts, has gained considerable acceptance for data processing applications. It cannot, however, specify the time order in which things must happen, so it is fairly ineffectual for real-time purposes. On the other hand, PAISLey is designed specifically for embedded software, where event sequences in the time domain are of major importance. The closer a language is to a specific applications area, the greater will be its readability — the sine qua non for manual defect removal from requirements specifications.

Formal requirements languages may be processed by other programs to provide structural and consistency checks and synopses useful in requirements reviews. In Chapter 1 we referred to these programs as pseudolanguage processors, although, in fact, axiomatic languages as a class are true languages even if they are not executable in the sense of programming languages.

Although requirements languages (other than PSL and RSL) are seldom used at present — and then chiefly by their inventors, which gives them an experimental cast — we may expect that acceptance of them will increase. Their remove from natural language will continue to restrict their use to persons familiar with the use of programming languages. Thus, we should expect that they will be used less for the performance definition of software systems than for the subsystems or components of those systems. That is, given the overall requirements in some other form, program analysts will use formal requirements languages to specify the major parts of their portion of the whole.

Design documentation. We start with noting that there exist design languages much like those requirements languages that are the means for expressing the results of specific analysis methods. For example, AXES is the design language that supports the higher-order software[16] (HOS) model of software development discussed in Section 2.2. Indeed, we shall see that documentation protocols, whether textual, graphic, or both, are integral parts of several of the well-defined design methodologies. Here, however, we shall look at documentation techniques that can be applied more or less independently of the development approach.

With regard to more general design languages, any number of these have been developed by software development units for their own use. An early one was MCAUTO'S™ pseudocode dialect of PL/1.[17] It used the control primitives of structured programming (extended to include the *do-until* and *case* constructs) while allowing the text of statements to be couched in natural English. This sounds much like the structured English used for requirements specifications. The principal difference is that program design languages must accommodate specification of software interfaces and internal data representations. Thus, we find in the text of documentation in design languages such features as procedure call references with parameter lists and data structures.

The advantages of program design languages over more traditional documentation techniques are several. Since program flow must be structured at design time, the code that implements the design will more easily be structured also. In fact, a coder would have to work at writing unstructured code. The design documentation is quite readable and relatively unambiguous. Design language statements, if used as the annotation for the source code of the executable program, permit clear correlation of code to design, which greatly simplifies the work of establishing traceability in code reviews and in verifying consistency between design documentation and code. Also, analogously to requirements specified in requirements languages, designs in program design languages are machine-readable and thus can be processed for structural and consistency checks and for reports useful during design reviews.

The proprietary Program Design Language[18] of Caine, Farber & Gordon, Inc. is in fairly wide use. In addition to supporting the rigorous specification of processing algorithms, it permits the definition of all external and internal interfaces, validity conditions, procedures and their calls, global data, and control blocks. Going one giant step further, verifiable axiomatic program specification languages offer new horizons for defect removal. The experimental Gypsy system,[19] for example, a system with intersecting specification and code level programming components, allows consistency between elements of the design and between the program and its specifications to be verified.

As noted earlier, HIPO probably enjoys greater use for design documentation than for requirements. Its attractiveness derives from its use as a vehicle for documenting a top-down decomposition process. Each input-process-output chart can be used to describe processes performed by hierarchically subordinate input-process-output charts. As one designs to the HIPO model, it is natural to think in a top-down manner. (I find that true of program design languages also, although this feature of pseudocode is seldom touted.) Apart from its use as the documentation convention for a specific design methodology, HIPO is in use in a number of software development facilities simply as a documentation tool.

HIPO is not well suited for depicting control flow. It does well at graphically replacing much of the text that forms a part of traditional program documentation, but it is weak at showing how transformations should be performed. Thus, HIPO seems most compatible with problems that involve standard computational operations, typically transactional processing. For any software application — certainly for any single process application (concurrency might be a problem) — HIPO is useful for portraying the hierarchical structure of program models, a structure examined in top-level design reviews.

SADT also provides continuity from requirements documentation through design documentation. SADT shares the HIPO problems related to detailed design, but the methodology of SADT and its rigorous formula for diagrammatic depiction of the results are well suited for top-level design documentation. It is claimed[20] that SADT diagrams support the decomposition processes of structured design, the Jackson approach, and the Parnas approach, all of which will be found in the next section, even though each has its own concepts of design documentation.

The most familiar graphical documentation technique is the ubiquitous flowchart. Constantly denigrated because of its lack of any inherent structure, its weak compatibility with iterative decomposition approaches, its resistance to modification, and its reliance on reams of supporting text, the flowchart lives on, disdainfully indifferent to the protestations of its detractors. One reason for its hardiness is that general management knows what flowcharts are and often demands them as evidence of thoughtful design. In general, outside the software community, conventional wisdom has it that flowcharts are synonymous with program documentation. For example, documentation specifications written into U.S. defense systems contracts have demanded flowcharts, along with narrative description, as the chief ingredient of design documentation. The management rubrics learned at a software symposium of a decade ago sometimes die hard.

One approach to contractual compliance used by software engineers bent on more usable design documentation practices is to employ one of several programs that generate flowcharts, after the fact, from source code. The line printer rendition of these is difficult to read (admittedly, a subjective opinion), and it is necessarily encumbered by the same cryptically named operands as the flowcharting program finds in the source code. The major design intelligence communicated is through comments inserted in the source file and copied out to the printer. As trying as it may be to make sense of them, these diagrams seem to satisfy the contractual requirements of buyers of software who dictate the use of flowcharts, leaving the software development people free to use more structured forms of documentation.

In 1972, I. Nassi and B. Shneiderman published a technique for structuring flowcharts.[21] The Nassi-Shneiderman (N-S) technique employs rectangular symbols for each of the structured primitives and their derivatives; Figure 2.3 illustrates three of them. These symbols (along with those for *repeat-until, case,* and other iteration forms) are combined by placing them adjacent to each other as in Figure 2.4, which computes an honor roll of the student(s) having the highest grade point average. The absence of connecting lines protects the structure from being compromised by meandering branches.

N-S and other innovative graphical representations of program design that embody the precepts of structured programming may have mounted a strong attack, but their impact on the traditional flowchart remains small. The days of the flowchart may be numbered, but many of the people who review detailed design specifications continue to have to wrestle with what for all the world look like the maps of the New York City subway system, except that the mystifying transfer stations of the maps are replaced by uninformative predicates such as $I > J$.

Apart from program logic, other aspects of design are usually documented. A plan of the system is of inestimable help to reviewers of the

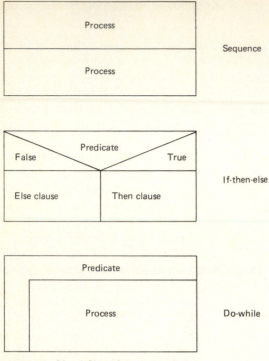

Figure 2.3   Nassi-Shneiderman symbols.

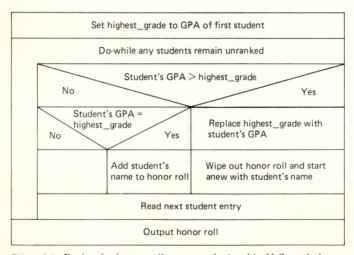

Figure 2.4   Design for honor-roll program depicted in N-S symbols.

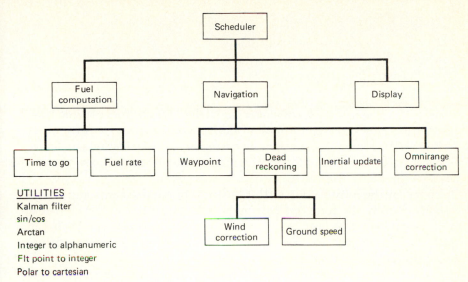

Figure 2.5 Structure chart.

design. The most common portrayal is a graphic representation of the hierarchy of program elements. Figure 2.5 shows one manner of illustrating this.

Program structure charts, such as the chart of Figure 2.5, are sometimes referred to as family trees, the term used to describe the depiction of the interrelations among the drawings used to define a manufacturing process. Not all hierarchical architectures are tree structures, of course, but have some modules subordinate to more than one other module. In Figure 2.5 all such modules are segregated as utilities. If not documented in pseudocode or in the language specific to a given design system, the function of each module, its inputs and outputs, and any limitations or constraints are usually specified in a companion document.

The hierarchy can also be shown in various textual formats. For example:

```
SCHEDULER
  FUEL_COMPUTATION
    TIME_TO_GO
    FUEL_RATE
  DISPLAY
  NAVIGATION
    DEAD_RECKONING
      WIND_CORRECTION
      GROUND_SPEED
    WAYPOINT
    INERTIAL_UPDATE
    OMNIRANGE_CORRECTION
```

```
UTILITY PACKAGES
  KALMAN_FILTER
  SIN/COS
  ARCTAN
  INTEGER_TO_ALPHANUMERIC
  FLT_TO_INTEGER
  POLAR_TO_CARTESIAN
```

Finally, we have tabular presentations of data arrays, records, and files, all of them nearly always a part of design documentation. Also, other matters (limitations, assumptions, constraints, global constants, memory budgets, and so on), if not found as comments to pseudocode, are given in text.

To repeat the introduction to this business of requirements and design documentation, the form exerts a major effect on the conduct of defect removal reviews. However, the documentation schemes are rarely chosen with reviews in mind. They derive from custom, style preference, external demands (customer requirements, for example), or as a means of supporting specific development methods. In the following section, we shall see variants of several of the representative documentation methods that have just been described. Each variant is peculiar to a specific design method.

2.2   Production Methodology

What exactly is it that design documentation communicates? Quite simply, the intermediate and end results of a problem decomposition process. We shall look at several systematic approaches used to translate requirements into designs. Schematically, these may be thought of as the columns of a two-dimensional array descriptive of production methods. The rows of the array have to do with the order in which elements of the problem are reduced to detailed design and finally to code. Having discussed these matters, we shall end this section with an increasingly used regimen, *prototyping,* that in several respects is a complete production methodology of its own, although it need not be used independently of the others.

Problem decomposition.   Problem decomposition is a fancy name for how one gets from here (a definition of requirements) to there (design detailed to the point that the coding process is one of direct translation). Borrowing a term from Bergland and Gordon[22] (who use it to cover other aspects of software engineering as well), we might refer to the methods of problem decomposition as software design strategies.

Although one can design programs without a conscious strategy — and in fact I suspect that this is the most general case — to give the issue some focus, it is helpful to briefly survey several of the more deliberate methods that have been developed. Of these, none seems to have gained greater notice than *structured design* based on the decomposition strategies of L. L. Constantine. First published[23] in 1974, it has since been described in greater detail by Yourdon and Constantine.[24] Identifying the characteristics of module coupling (that is, the factors that cause module interdependence), module cohesion (the quality of self-sufficiency), and modular architecture, structured design proceeds to offer two top-down approaches toward attaining minimum coupling and maximum cohesion. Each starts with a data flow diagram to depict the problem being attacked. Each ends with a structure chart. The first of these, *transform analysis,* is an information flow model in which modules are developed and organized hierarchically according to whether they pass information upward in the program structure, downward, or are best characterized as transformers of information. The result is a modular structure with control concentrated at the top and intermediate levels, the actual work being performed toward the bottom of the structure.

The second method is that of *transaction analysis,* which is applicable to data flow that splits into discrete paths or to systems in which input data are manipulated by multiple processing states. In essence, the rules of transaction analysis divide functions into subfunctions of the same hierarchical rank.

To these two methods Myers[25] adds a third process, expressly directed toward achieving *functional decomposition.* Apart from its more rigorous meaning within the framework of Constantine-Myers structure design, the divide-and-conquer philosophy of functional decomposition is in wide use. Stated simply, at the top level, major system functions are identified as modules. Each is then divided into a set of subfunctions (modules), each performing as unique a role as can reasonably be fashioned, and so on until modules no longer seem capable of being divided into smaller parts. The process is iterative, sort of an extension of Wirth's stepwise refinement[1] to the program architectural level. Early steps are often redone as work on their descendants exposes poor decisions made earlier or advantages to be gained by combining modules. Any rework of this kind has no effect on the hierarchical siblings of modules that are respecified, so the process is quite manageable.

Functional decomposition is compatible — even a vehicle for — Parnas's "information hiding" approach.[26] Underlying the Parnas concept is the recognition that top-down design is a descent through levels of abstraction. One of Parnas's goals for program specifications is that the user is provided all the information needed to properly use the program, but nothing further. Another goal is that the implementer of the program must be provided all the information needed to develop it, but nothing more. In particular, the implementer of a subprogram should be given no information about the calling program. Iteratively, these goals form the guidelines applicable to each hierarchical level of development. Specific implementation of the Parnas approach results in module interfaces of minimum information content and the "hiding" of the design details within modules that may be altered without affecting their external behavior. Many applications of this method result in data structures segregated in separate modules. Parnas's ideas are widespread. The tenets of information hiding are now found in the heuristic procedures followed by many designers who reject the use of formal design strategies.

Quite different from the Parnas approach is that of Jackson,[27] who fashions his methodology about a very visible data structure. The process used is a rote one requiring little creativity from the designer. Rote processes tend to break down in the face of complexity, and the Jackson data structure approach is more applicable to the components of a large program than to the entire program. The Jackson approach starts with the definition of data structures. These are decomposed hierarchically by using graphic tree notation or text in the manner of a data dictionary. (Quite formally, Jackson has used BNF to describe the structure.) The notation provides primitives for sequence, iteration, and selection. Working backwards from the output to the input of the data structure, the operations that correspond to the structure are listed. Since the operands of the individual operations are data objects, this scheme lends itself to direct expression of the allocation of operations in pseudocode. For example,

```
Transaction_file sequence
  Open transaction_file
  Read transaction_file
  Report_body iteration until transaction_file.EOF
    Total: = 0
    Subtotal: = 0
    Account_key: = Invoice_field
        .
        .
        .
```

Since the module boundaries are defined by elements of the data structure, one expects the process to result in modules of high cohesion. The Jackson approach has met with considerable success in producing well-structured designs in business applications, which typically are file-oriented.

Very similar to Jackson's method is that of Jean-Dominique Warnier. In the United States, Warnier's work is best known through the extensions made by Kenneth Orr. The most striking aspect of Warnier-Orr is the use of a unique set of graphics to depict every step of the procedure. The repeated use of the same set of graphics provides an attractive continuity. Incorporating symbology for boolean relations, structured programming primitives, recursion, and concurrency, the graphics are used for depicting input and output, requirements definition, system design, program flow, and data flow. Operations may also be illustrated by using an "assembly line" diagram, of which Figure 2.6 is an example. Warnier-Orr diagrams have been used as the detailed design documentation for programs translated into a diversity of languages, including Cobol, Fortran, PL/1, Assembler, Basic, and RPG II.[28]

Higher-order software (HOS) is the name given to an approach[16] to software development incorporating its own system of tools, the integrated software development system (ISDS). The design language AXES, noted in the preceding section, is processed under ISDS. HOS is a more formal system than the others that have been remarked; it contains decomposition rules that stipulate the allowable relations among modules and between program logic and data. Moreover, the HOS model has six axioms that govern the decomposition approach. These restrict the control and calling domains of a module, define each module's access to variables, and restrict a module's control of data. The decomposition techniques require the designer to work within the reference of the functions to be performed by the system, with each function decomposed into one of three axiomatically correct structures. Although this would seem to imply that the resulting architecture is a unique consequence of the set of functions, there is in fact considerable room (and need) for the designer's discretion.

Allusions have been made to the fact that most design is probably accomplished either as a random process reminiscent of the Paleolithic Era of programming or as a combination of several of the systematic processes. Some personal experience may illustrate the latter. In my earlier experience in application programming, my staff and I followed an informal procedure that in retrospect seems to embody several of the concepts of the methods just described.

We preferred to start with data by organizing information into struc-

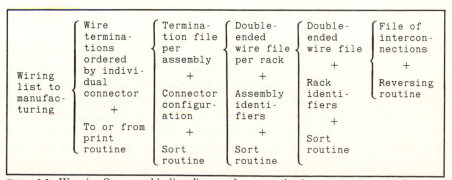

Figure 2.6   Warnier-Orr assembly-line diagram for generating interconnection wire list.

tures that seemed to bear congruency with the transformations that, seen even at the earliest stages of design, were obviously going to have to be made. We next sketched data flow diagrams that the data structure gave rise to and then iterated the two steps through whatever number of cycles were required to achieve a visceral feeling that the problem had been reduced to a minimum — or near minimum — number of processing steps. This approach, which had been arrived at without much analysis and with no research (my first computer programs predated the evolution of software engineering), is no more than an extrapolation of the techniques I had used as a systems engineer for the design of complex hardware systems.

With the data structure established, and with a crudely drawn road map of the transformations that would be made upon the elements of the structure, we were ready to name the elements of the program that would implement the transformations. Again, this technique was borrowed from the apportioning of systems problems to individual hardware elements. We followed both top-down and bottom-up methods, as we now call them; top-down in the sense that we wanted iteratively to resolve the data flow bubbles into some sort of hierarchical order, but at the same time bottom-up because the diagrams made obvious the existence of certain processing kernels. In proceeding through the system, certain functions (e.g., trigonometric computations) would be identified for inclusion in a utility package. Somehow or other, the software structure that emerged looked as though it were meant to solve precisely the problem to which it was directed. More importantly, the members of the structure were each assigned conceptually simple tasks to perform. That certain modules would be quite large relative to others — perhaps in ratios of as much as 20 to 1 — never bothered me (and still doesn't). We knew we had a sufficiently decomposed system when the function of each of its elements could be described in just a few words. Further, other than utilities, each element naturally lent itself to an uncontrived single-entry–single-exit form, although when I started designing software, I was unaware of the significance of this. Another test we applied to the soundness of the structure was whether it appeared that the individual modules could be debugged without a disproportionately complex software test fixture. This, too, was a transfer of hardware systems technology.

The method just outlined can scarcely be considered scientific. Still, it is interesting to observe that the translation of a systems engineering methodology into the language of software employed a mixture of several of the currently used decomposition procedures. Even in the light of today's knowledge, few software systems are decomposed by using one technique exclusively. We are much smarter, and certainly more conscious of what we are doing and why we are doing it, but management seldom attempts to legislate programming style to the extent that a single systematic methodology must be religiously followed in detail. Management may, however, specify the form of the incremental documentation products of that methodology and the sequence of their release.

This quick walk* through design methodologies suggests that a single method for timely removal of design defects cannot at once be rigorously formulated for universal application and be specific to the implantation of defects. Accordingly, Chapter 3, which deals with requirements and design reviews, addresses fundamentals rather than specific rote procedures.

Implementation strategies. The design methods that have been described are, for the most part, top-down. Not all design is performed systematically, however, which leaves the door open for bottom-up approaches as well. Not that bottom-up has to be inferior to top-down; it may even be preferable for some systems. For example, a scientific program may have as its central problem computational accuracy or number-crunching efficiency, in which case it is certainly reasonable to start attacking the system where the anticipated problems lie — at the lower hierarchical levels. Moreover, if reusable modules are a management priority, considerable bottom-up thinking will have to be incorporated in the design process.

Even in a top-down design regimen, one questions the purity of the designer's thoughts. From the start, the designer, unless very inexperienced, has probably had inklings of what shape the lower-ranking modules might take.

We see, then, top-down, bottom-up, and combinations of the two. Since top-down strategies are sufficient to illustrate the points that need to be made with regard to defect removal, we shall start there; later we shall note special circumstances attending bottom-up. We shall leave for Chapter 7 comparisons of top-down and bottom-up test strategies and concentrate here on the production cycle exclusive of matters unique to testing.

Generally, designers have the freedom to decompose their system one hierarchical tier at a time across the breadth of the program structure or, alternatively, at some point in the process, to devote all their effort to only one part of the system. Figure 2.7 freezes the decomposition process for each of these two cases. The "even-descent" approach lends itself to stepwise refinement of global data structures; the "plunging" approach lends itself to earlier implementation of some system functions. Of course, the plunging approach will produce early results, other than detailed design data, only if accomplished by immediate coding of the modules at such time as the set corresponding to an external function is completely designed.

---

* Sprint may be the more appropriate word. More leisurely surveys are found in Ramsey, Atwood, and Campbell,[29] Bergland,[30] and Griffiths.[31]

The top-down methodology employed by the chief programmer team (CPT)[32,33] management approach (anticipating Section 2.5) not only plunges but also has each module coded and tested (with subordinate modules stubbed) before work on the subordinate modules proceeds. Many consider this the definitive form of top-down production.

Even when early capability of part of the system is not a goal, a plunge to the waters of the lowest hierarchical tiers offers the quickest descent to procedures that are the kernels of the computational problem. Thus, to a large extent asymmetrical development also accommodates the goals of bottom-up development.

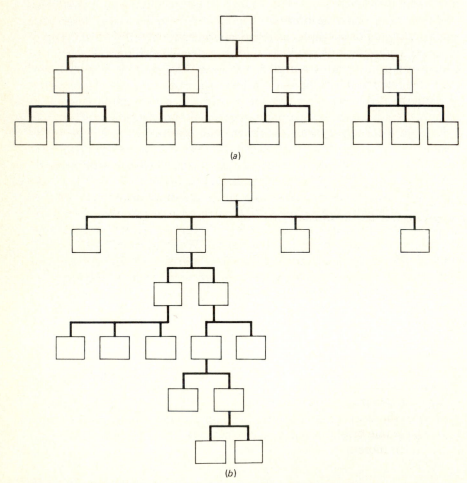

(a)

(b)

Figure 2.7 (a) "Even-descent" top-down decomposition. (b) "Quick-plunge" top-down decomposition.

A development plan directed to the purpose of providing increments of capability — plunging first to one function, then to another, coding and testing each when it is designed — results in a series of system *builds.* (Sequential builds may also be planned for an even-descent implementation, but the consequences of this are fairly unimportant except for providing incremental baselines to assist library control.) A systematic approach to determining the functions to be implemented in each build starts with the identification of each function that can perform some operationally useful purpose and also be individually tested. The sequence in which these functions are to be implemented determines the order in which modules are designed, coded, and tested.

A moderately formal method[34,35] for accomplishing this recognizes the functions, the implementing modules, and the test cases applicable to each function as a system *thread* identified in terms of functional stimulus-response pairs. The procedure is to first build a logically complete system; one that, in the least, can accept input data, do some processing of it, demonstrate that the data have been operated on, and cycle through the control mechanism. Threads are then added, each by each, in successive builds. With the modules, whatever their hierarchical arrangement, identified as members of one or more threads, the implementation sequence of the threads implies the implementation sequence of the modules.

However it is implemented, any methodology employing incremental functional builds means that there is not one design review for each predefined design stage (say, a top-level design review and a detailed design review), but several. The time for design reviews is before the design is implemented. Top-level design reviews should be held before a significant amount of detailed design has been accomplished, and detailed design reviews should be held prior to any code generation. When incremental builds are employed, each module in the group to be coded must be reviewed before coding takes place if the full benefits of the review are to be realized. Working backwards, the structure of the modules that will enter into the new build and the data the modules process must be reviewed before the modules are individually designed.

Similarly, a set of code reviews should take place for each build. Going on in time, we see that there will be several periods during which new code is tested. These points may be obvious, but I have encountered persons involved with the management of computer software who assume that all reviews at the ith stage applicable to the system will be planned to occur within the same brief interval of time; this even though the planning also indicates an incremental build strategy.

Opposite to the strategy of incremental builds, or the expanding system model, we have the philosophy (one hesitates to honor it with the word "strategy") of the lockstep development of a software system. Here no coding takes place until all design is complete; no testing starts until all the code is written. Presumably, the idea is to avoid rewriting code if the design decomposition process failed to produce a set of sufficiently independent modules. The cost of this security is high. The lockstep production method fails to offer any management options if schedules are jeopardized by unforeseen contingencies. Also, it precludes the opportunity for early validation of the implementation of critical functions.

Most of these remarks on implementation strategies hold true for the bottom-up model as well. The major difference is that greater emphasis must be placed on finding defects in the top-level design. If the functions and interrelations of lower-ranking modules are not correctly identified at the onset, the modules will never work in concert.

Prototyping. The prototyping approach to production must be considered as a separate case. Although it may embrace any decomposition method and any implementation strategy, prototyping is more comprehensive in scope.

It is quite possible for someone to know that he wants a software system to perform a service yet be uncertain of exactly what it is that the system should do. For example, a chain of bookshops knows that it is buried under paper in an attempt to keep up with warehouse inventory, store inventories, back orders, and changing wholesale and publisher prices. It decides that it needs an electronic "paperless" office. But what exactly does that mean? The chain goes to a major computer manufacturer who advises that the problem is similar to one solved last year by a chain of fast-food franchises just across the state line. Buoyed by that pronouncement, the chain buys the same computer that had successfully been used for tracking frozen meat patties, only to subsequently discover that the problems of frozen meat patties and those of remaindered books are only superficially similar.* At the recommendation of the computer manufacturer, the bookshop people invite a software house to propose the development of the system software for its electronic office system.

By now, the paperbound chain knows a little more of what it wants, but it is still unable to precisely define its requirements. The best it can say is that it wants the system to provide the same information currently available to each office in its headquarters. The software house recognizes that there are other matters to attend to: cross-checking of information by context rather than clerical intuition, prompts for data entry appropriate to keyboards rather than paper forms, procedures for system recovery, and so forth.

The consultants could, of course, write a requirements document based

---

* Taste excepted.

on what they think the system needs to do, but the bookstore chain would probably have trouble understanding the full import of the information contained in the specifications.

Here is where prototyping comes in. For its own guidance, the software house minimally documents its understanding of the requirements and then proceeds to develop the system without the customer's verification of that understanding. Well, not the whole system. Certain elements invisible to the customer (e.g., system recovery from power failure during file updates) are left out. On the other hand, for this application, the user interface is completely spelled out.

The programming language selected for this model system is a very high level language (VHLL)* capable of the simple expression of complex computer processes; APL, perhaps, or a list processor such as LISP or SNOBOL. Execution time efficiency is of small concern. What is important is the speed at which the system can be defined in executable form.

The prototype is installed on the customer's system, and its employees go through the motions of entering representative data and making inquiries. In a few days the bookshop chain is ready to say that the system looks pretty good, "Except you didn't quite get it right here . . . and here . . . and here, and also, we think that now that all the data is in one place, we would like this . . . and this . . . and this." The changes are duly made, and the evaluation is repeated. After several iterations, the customer says that he is satisfied, at which point the software house can begin to design in earnest; that is, with efficiency, maintainability, and robustness as goals apart from meeting operations requirements.

Prototyping may be used outside the bookshop marketplace as well — indeed, any time the user is unable or unwilling to prepare a definition of the requirements. The details that are not included in the prototype system will differ, of course, from application to application. The all-important inquiry screen and report formats of business applications are of little consequence to embedded systems, where temporal sequencing, of no concern to our bookshops, may be paramount. Neither of these is essential to the prototype of a compiler, but the precise interpretation of the language specification is, and exception handling — ignored for the electronic office — is completely modeled. (Interestingly, a prototype compiler for Ada was written by the Courant Institute of New York University in its set-oriented

---

* The term "very high level language" has also been applied to the languages previously referred to as pseudolanguages in the sense of specification languages. Further, VHLL has been used to denote certain other languages apart from those we usually consider to be programming languages. The VHLLs most suitable for prototyping are probably those defined by Wulf[36] as set-oriented languages, functional languages, and applicative languages. Also, powerful simulation languages such as Simula.

language SETL. In 1982 this prototype was being evaluated in 150 user locations.)

In summary, prototyping is a methodology that uses a VHLL to create a mostly (perhaps fully) functional and executable (if inefficient) version of a program. For production, the program will at least be recoded in a more efficient language, and it may be redesigned as well. That is, in a single step one may use prototyping not only as a model of requirements but also as a model of the final system. This last may lead to problems. Prototyping is still a technique of sufficient youth that I can state only as an opinion that an attempt to at once prototype requirements and system design will compromise either the speed of prototyping or the quality of the design or both. On the other hand, there is one redeeming consideration: the design will certainly be consistent with the requirements.

Depending on whether the prototype is to model both requirements and design, the prototype code will be the major part of the requirements and design documentation subject to defect removal reviews. What these reviews must focus on are omissions ("Okay, the prototype doesn't cover input validity checks, but where *are* these specified?"), feasibility of implementation within response time constraints (if any), interfaces to other systems not tested with the prototype, and computational accuracies not modeled by final algorithms; indeed, any aspect of system performance not totally verified by the model's execution.

2.3 Traceability

In Chapter 1 the point was made that an important aspect of defect removal hinges on tracing designs and code back to requirements. We can do this in two ways: by comparing each software product to the product of the preceding phase of development (verification), and by comparing it to the operational — or at least to the software — requirements definition (validation). Validation is often thought of as the last phase of development testing, when we formally evaluate the code against the functional requirements. However, well before that point, paper products and code can be measured against the requirements. Although the advantage of doing so is obvious, it is commonly recognized that at these intermediate points it may be difficult to relate the product to the requirements. For example, what has the design of an obscure sort routine to do with the performance of an air traffic control system?

Various methods have been used in attempts to assure a continuum of traceability to the functional requirements. While these essays have been largely for the purpose of guiding project planning and development, the techniques used are also invaluable for defect removal. In the most simple schemes, each module and group of modules that functionally devolves from a single aspect of the requirements specification is marked on the structure chart or some other document with the applicable paragraph number of the specification. This number appears also in the prologue of the source code for the modules. Unfortunately, so simple a scheme is weak when the functions, even if testable, intersect, or when the module configuration departs sharply from a tree structure.

The ultimate system for traceability would account for each transformation of data. Against the identification of each module we would need to place not only each applicable part of the requirements document but also a summary of the pertinent performance information (limitations, computational error budgeted to the module, and so on) distilled from the applicable specification paragraphs. As an example, let us take the module:

Time-order sort   Paras. 16.2.7.1.4.5, 16.2.2.19

Sort key is ETD. Order is earliest
ETD first, modulus 2400 hours.

Note that the definition of input, output, or even of the process is unnecessary, since these may be found in the specifications for the module. All that appears, beyond the applicable paragraphs, is that information that is required for evaluation of how well the module performs its function.

A traceability document with this amount of information is a very painstaking undertaking. It is rarely attempted. It can be successfully completed only when the decomposition has resulted in strong module cohesion and weak module coupling and when those preparing the traceability document have the judgment to determine the minimum information that should be stipulated.

The Computer Sciences Corporation has developed a traceability technique[35] that stops short of actual performance details but does correlate decomposition elements with specified system functions. The technique is wedded to the thread-at-a-time production methodology described in Section 2.2. The system functions are assigned to discrete, but interconnected elements, or threads. A thread may reference one or more paragraphs of the system requirements specification. The symbol for a thread, shown in Figure 2.8 both schematically and with an example applicable to air navigation, is disarmingly simple. To be used, the system must account for the relations among threads. The permissible forms established by Computer Sciences Corporation for their connections are given by Figure 2.9.

The use of the diagrams as an aid to verifying consistency of top-level design with requirements is apparent. Beyond that, however, Deutsch[34] illustrates how the diagrams can carry through to validating the specifications for functional tests of the completed system.

Decomposition graphing lends itself to partially automated validation of traceability if the requirements are specified in a formal language. The U.S. Army Ballistic Missile Defense Advanced Technology Center's requirements statement language (RSL),[10] remarked on in Section 2.1, has

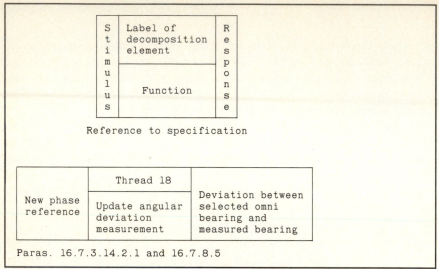

Figure 2.8 Basic symbol of system verification diagram.

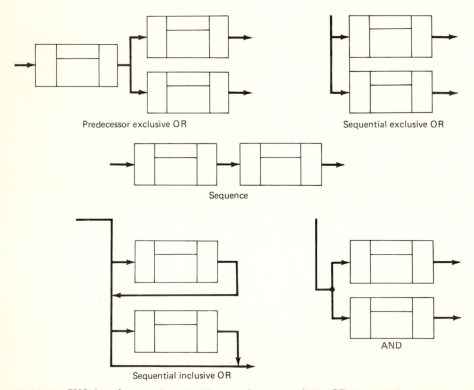

Figure 2.9 SVC thread connection primitives: predecessor exclusive OR, sequential exclusive OR, sequence, sequential inclusive OR, AND.

been incorporated in a comprehensive requirements analysis concept that includes traceability. The software requirements engineering methodology (SREM)[37] calls for the development of a network of stimulus-response functional elements, similar in some respects to system verification diagrams, and a detailed requirements specification in RSL. The RSL specification is entered into the data base of the requirements engineering and validation system (REVS), where a static analyzer checks for consistency and completeness. Timing, accuracies, and other requirements of each of the network paths entered in the REVS data base are tied to the functional requirements from which they can be extracted by REVS for subsequent test case design. These may also be validated earlier by using real algorithms rather than functional models.

There are various tabular ways in which one may relate requirements to the products of each phase of development. For example, a two-dimensional table may have one row per requirements specification paragraph and one column per identified module. If the module is specific to the satisfaction of the requirement, the intersection of row and column is given a check mark. (A sparse population of marks is more indicative of low coupling than is a dense population, but this cannot be relied on.) The table is useful during design and code reviews. Later, the columns may be given over to paragraphs of a test specification. So used, the table directly shows any requirements that will not be validated by functional testing. It will also indicate possible test redundancy. When requirements specifications place several functional requirements in one paragraph, the rows of these *traceability matrices* must contain a bit more information than just a paragraph number.

It should be evident that the scheme needs some alteration when the requirements are largely specified by means other than natural text. For example, for several of the methods discussed in Section 2.1, paragraph numbers are not the most relevant identification of functions.

Although their construction and maintenance may be time-consuming, traceability mechanisms afford a source of quick reference during defect removal processes. A return on investment is a reasonable expectation.

2.4   Software Development Environments

As do so many software terms, "development (or production — I see no real difference) environment" means different things to different people, with the several interpretations mostly a function of what one is familiar with. To some, "environment" implies a virtual machine at each programmer's disposal. To others, an environment is a collection of software tools (editor, compiler, linker, maybe some test tools) used by a programmer. There are software engineers who insist that any respectable environment must have a *cohesive* set of tools; at least to the point where they all operate on pseudocode and executable code files organized in a data base system. More demanding people feel that "environment" implies that the tools complement each other; no overlaps, no gaps.

Well, all of these are environments. A development environment comprises the software that surrounds a programmer as he develops and, perhaps, tests his program. Sitting at the CRT, the programmer has interactive* control of the system, and draws upon its resources much as a chemist reaches for flasks and reagents. (Note that an analogy to an artist and a palette of oils was *not* made.) The software development environment is so integral a part of the programmer's professional life that henceforth in this section "environment" will be used synonymously with "software development environment." Elsewhere in the book, "environment" may embrace programmer workspace, management attitudes, air quality, and so forth, but in this section its use is restricted.

There can be little question that the best-known environment is UNIX,† a time-sharing system with an associated toolbox.[38] UNIX, written in the language C originally for support of C programming, is an example of an open-ended environment; one that each user may choose to augment with additional tools, including compilers for various languages. In some cases, the additional capabilities have been organized into a kit of related tools, of which the Programmer's Workbench (PWB)[39] is the most widely installed example. Although the file control capabilities of UNIX are adequate for most library control requirements, PWB is more powerful and better suited to projects in which several programmers are likely to need access to the same source code. PWB's library control features include the capabilities to recreate a module as it had existed in any previous version and to manage multiple concurrent versions. These file control functions are auditable; that is, they provide visibility for those configuration management checks that are essential to the assurance that defect detection leads to defect removal and not to the reintroduction of old defects. PWB's test drivers for the generation of repeatable tests offer yet another feature valuable for defect removal operations.

A strong environment tends to standardize the development process. Since UNIX is open-ended, even to the point of allowing programmers to define their own system commands, it has fostered the development of many homegrown environments tailored to the local establishment of desired programming practices. PWB started this way, as did the more recent Microprocessor Software Engineering Facility (MSEF)[40] of SofTech, which is similar in scope to PWB.

---

* This, at the very least, if we are to consider contemporary program development practices.

† UNIX is a trademark of Bell Telephone Laboratories.

Despite the diversity of environments, certain structural properties are common. At the core of each is an interactive command interpreter (time-shared if not installed on a microcomputer dedicated to a single programmer), a file manager, a text editor, and the basic production tools of assembler (and, generally, compiler) and link editor. Additional capabilities may include those useful through various development stages. Examples are requirements language processors and traceability tools, design language processors and discrete system simulators, source code managers and code analysis tools, stub and test driver organizers, test coverage analyzers, and test data generators. When placed in a data base management system, with interfaces to provide compatibility of one tooled function with another, these tools result in systems that not only abet productivity and quality but become the foundation for many of the procedures for defect removal.

For the most part, the various tools of an environment, while operating on common data with whatever interfaces are necessary, remain articulated in their application. Greater cohesion is the natural consequence when an environment evolves in accordance with common concepts. An example of an especially well-integrated environment is Interlisp,[41] designed for the support of programs written in the LISP language. Interlisp is integrated to the extent that it is possible to invoke the use of one tool from within the context of another.

It has been noted that a strong environment tends to standardize the development process. Going a step further, environments have been built to support specific production methodologies. SREM,[37] the requirements analysis and specification system referred to in the preceding section, may be viewed as an environment. Another example is Grumman Aerospace Corporation's SOLID,[42] which includes tools for requirements analysis, top-down design, test planning, configuration management, staffing and resource planning and control, code control and documentation, and test progress tracking. The Ada* Programming Support Environment (APSE) will also have tool capabilities applicable to specific methodologies covering all phases of the software life cycle. The underlying philosophy tying methodology to APSE has been given by Lt. Col. Druffel, the first director of the Ada Joint Program Office: "We will not realize the full potential of Ada until we are able to define a software development methodology complete with management practices which can in turn be supported by automated tools."[43]

The Ada environment recalls the pattern set by UNIX/PWB. Its kernel, KAPSE, is the operating system. Unlike UNIX, it has no tools of its own, but it contains primitives, I/O facilities, and data types available to the tool

---

* Ada is a registered trademark of the Ada Joint Program Office, U.S. Government.

set. "Minimal APSE," or MAPSE, includes the command language interpreter, configuration manager, editor, compiler, debugger, and linker-loader. To these basic capabilities will be added an array of tools applicable to a particular project or programming facility, creating a complete APSE.

There also exist environments directed to formal verifiability. As we saw in the earlier discussions of specification languages, most of these remain experimental in the sense that they have been used only by their originators. Gypsy,[19] referred to in Section 2.1, is more than a language system; it is an environment. There are others as well, but their direct impact on programming methodology remains indirect outside their host facilities.

Whatever the software development environment, the practices used for defect removal will depend on the capabilities of the environment for assisting defect detection and for controlling code and support libraries. Defect removal processes will be shaped even more strongly if the environment enforces a specific methodology.

2.5   Management Methods

Thus far we have been dealing with technology. We have also to consider aspects of the management of technology that affect defect removal. It may be remembered that software engineering — the theme that underlies all current research toward improving software productivity and quality, especially for large systems — has two interlocking components: technology and management. Indeed, the two are so interwoven that it is often difficult to distinguish one from the other. The fundamental reason is found in the complexity that attaches to the functions performed by large software systems.

> Given the complexity of the problems to be solved by large software systems, effective software management is nothing less than the management of complexity.

The approaches to managing complexity have direct effect on procedures for defect removal. One of these approaches nearly always is the division of the development process into discrete phases.

Phases and milestones.   Phases and milestones have previously been alluded to. A typical* scheme is to divide development into the following sequential stages:

Requirements analysis and specification

Design

Code and unit test

---

* But by no means unique.

Integration

System test

These may be further divided. Design may consist of discrete top-level, intermediate, and detailed design phases. Integration may have several plateaus of discrete system builds. Tests of the full system may resolve to individual tests of tasks or mainline programs, tests of tasks and programs operating in concert, integration of embedded software with system hardware, qualification tests, installation tests, and so on. The fragmentation method will reflect the size and type of system being developed, to some extent the decomposition process, and to a lesser degree the capabilities of the software development environment. It is also a matter of style. However the stages are defined, the purpose is the same: each task is marked by a starting place (one or more documents, one or more code files) and a conclusion (another set of documents, another set of code files). An alternative name for the conclusion is *milestone,* a point at which tangible results can be examined, the project reappraised for technical and planning purposes, and another phase initiated from an established baseline.

Each of these milestones is attended by defect removal procedures enumerated in Chapter 1 but not identified in terms of management plans. The inference to be drawn is that the principles of defect removal, the substance of the succeeding chapters, should be linked in some fashion to the milestones identified in the management plans. This serves two purposes: providing a clean running start for each phase and affording management insight into the true progress of the project.

Functional divisions. It is not only the phases of development that are likely to be fragmented; the project staff is also divided into various functions. Not unlike the functional decomposition of Section 2.2, the personnel working on large development projects invariably are split into several discrete functions.

The mainstream of software development is composed of requirements analysis and specification, design, coding, and testing. Although there is great diversity in the manner in which these tasks are divided among functional groups, Table 2.1 illustrates a popular breakdown used for embedded software projects. In the table, P indicates primary responsibility and S indicates support responsibility.

To whom do we assign responsibility for defect removal? To all. Each of the three development groups has the capability of removing defects from its own work. However, as we shall see in the next two chapters, apart from the use of tools from the software development environment, a more effective defect detection process takes place when functional groups collaborate. In certain cases, and inversely proportional to the power of the development environment, defect detection is most effective when the chief

Table 2.1   Assignment of Tasks to Worker Categories

Task	Development groups			Test groups	
	Systems engineering department	Senior design staff	Design group	Software test group	Systems test group
Requirements analysis and specification	P	S			
Software top-level design		P			
Detailed design		S	P		
Code and unit test			P		
Software integration		S	S	P	
Software qualification tests				P	
System integration	S	S			P
System qualification tests					P

P = primary responsibility; S = support responsibility

responsibility for finding defects is given to persons other than the originators of the faults. This, of course, is the argument for separate test groups,
but we see it also — as an example — where the only opportunity for timely
removal of requirements defects is a requirements review. Here, the persons who will have to implement the requirements, the senior design staff,
will be the ones most likely to find inconsistency and incompleteness.
Thus, apportionment of the work not only permits development of specialized skills but also supports the work of defect removal.

The well-publicized chief programmer team method[32,33] leaves all design
decisions in the hands of the chief programmer. Supported by a few assist-
ants to do detail and clerical work, the chief programmer is all functions
rolled up into one. For large projects, CPT clearly requires that CP be a
programmer hero, and his backup person only slightly less so. Since heroes
are in short supply,* CPT is more talked about than tried. When CPT is in
use, that use precludes profiting, during reviews, from the diverse views of
persons from different functional divisions.

Quality assurance.   A number of things happen during project development.
They happen in different rooms, at the hands of different people, when

---

* Moreover, I wonder how many of those who have earned the rank care to play vice-hero
for a year or so.

different tools are used, and in the attempt to meet different milestone deadlines. An independent group, one that maintains its objectivity by having its own reporting channels to general management, can help keep track of events and assure that standards are being adhered to. This is the basic role assigned to software quality assurance (SQA). SQA may be called upon to perform three related functions:[44]

A management tool for control and visibility

A representative of the user community

An agent for the improvement of productivity, reliability, and maintainability

The first of these militates against the counterproductive tendency to relax standards for the completion of each task when one is confronted by difficult schedule constraints. As an example, a report by the development people that top-level design is complete is misleading if the design is not completed according to local standards. Without verified documentation that covers all elements of what has been accepted as such, top-level design will simply flow into detailed design and considerable opportunity will be left for major design flaws to develop. SQA, by participating in the top-level design review, perhaps leading that review, can certify its proper completion.

As a representative of the user, SQA takes an active role in all defect removal procedures, in some cases as an auditor, in others as the leader. Depending on management's philosophy, SQA's charter may be a major one for some phases and a minor one for others. For example, SQA may only examine a programmer's work folder to certify that unit test was successfully conducted, but may act as the lead function for reviews or the use of certain analysis tools. In some companies, the responsibility for qualification tests has been separated from the software or systems groups and given to SQA.

From the point of view of long-term profit, perhaps SQA's most important work is its collection and analysis of defect data to the end of improving productivity, reliability, and (for defects found during the operational period) maintainability. Historically, the software community has taken a cavalier position toward the collection of such data, not to mention analysis of what it does have. However, this is a traditional quality control function that, adapted for software, results in the identification of the parts of the development process that need strengthening and in the measurement of the effect produced by the introduction of new tools and techniques.

Not every software development facility has an SQA operation. Facilities that do not should give serious thought to having one.

Configuration control.   Requirements documentation, design documentation, various code files, test data files, and test result files are all subject to change from the time of their initial generation. To provide stability, modern programming practice calls for the formal release of documentation and source code, with the release occurring at least as early as the time "ownership" of the materials passes from the originator to a user. For example, in many facilities programmers may do whatever they wish with their source code up to the time the test team is ready to integrate the code into the system. At this point, the code is released via formal notification processes that, in effect, say that the code has been judged ready for integration. "Readiness," a matter of internal standards governing defect removal at the level of modules or procedures, is normally attested to by someone other than the programmer, say, by the lead programmer and possibly a software quality engineer as well. It is at this time that the master of the source file is placed in the library.

Once under control, changes to documents, code, and test files are made to the masters of each only with the approval of a change control board, although for development tests (e.g., integration) working copies of the code files may be the de facto masters on a day-to-day basis. The mechanisms for this are described in Chapter 11. For the present, we are concerned only that (1) a change control board is usually found in software development organizations and (2) the changes made to all masters are generally made by *librarians*.

Anticipating Section 2.6, where we shall distinguish between defect detection and defect removal, a tacit function of change control boards and librarians is to ensure that a defect, once removed, stays removed and, moreover, is not replaced by another spawned in the ambiguity of knowing which code was actually tested, the data set used, or the requirement or design feature to which the test was directed.

Independent verification and validation.   Most often seen and heard in its abbreviated form IV&V, independent verification and validation has become a shibboleth by which Defense Department people involved with programming management recognize each other. By the early 1980s, it had attracted interest in industry as well. IV&V is verification and validation performed by persons outside the programming organization. Who they are and what they do will be revealed shortly. But first let us define verification and validation.

If IV&V is rarely heard, or even written, in other than the short form, it is because verification and validation have nearly become an inseparable pair, with the inevitable reduction to V&V. I once heard an eminent software authority speak on the subject for 30 minutes, mentioning V&V many times, but not once saying either "verification" or "validation." This remark is not directed at the speaker's style. The problem is that we are beginning to forget how to separate V from V, with the consequence that the contribution of each to defect removal is often overlooked.

Like a good vaudeville team, verification and validation are complementary. Each can evoke laughs (well, defects anyway) on its own, but they are most effective in concert. Verification and validation were defined parenthetically in Section 2.3. With slightly more explanation, we have:

> VERIFICATION: Procedures that attempt to determine that the product of each phase of the development process is an implementation of a previous phase; that is, that it satisfies it. Thus, the design of the components of a system are examined to see if they meet the external characteristics specified for them in the top-level design.
>
> VALIDATION: Procedures that attempt to determine that the product of each phase of the development process will lead to satisfaction of the most abstract requirements set: the specified operational requirements for the system of which the software is a constituent or, if that is not applicable, the software requirements specification.

This definition of validation differs slightly from another common interpretation, one that restricts the validation process to the final product, where, indeed, it is a distinct test stage. That validation is most conspicuous when applied to the fully integrated program does not preclude some usefulness at earlier stages. Certainly, kernels of design that bear a one-to-one correspondence with elements of the prime requirements set can be examined with respect to the function they are to implement. For example, if the prime specification for a process control system includes the requirement that viscosity be measured to an accuracy of 1 millipoise, the equation and its numerical approximation for relating viscosity to observed pressure may be scrutinized to see if the computational dilution of precision is consistent with a 1-millipoise accuracy. As we go through the various techniques of defect removal, we shall see many opportunities for validation of intermediate software products.

It may appear that verification and validation are each opposite to defect removal. V and V are* trying to show that something is right and defect removal that it is wrong. If the people performing V and V work take the notion that they want to prove compliance, their efforts may well produce a poor harvest of defects. And this notion is not at all unnatural if these are the same people who designed and coded the program and then debugged it to their own satisfaction. (Of course, this applies equally to precode phases.)

---

* Note the plural "are." Admittedly, the chance that this will start a new fashion in software engineering locution is slim.

Thus, independent verification and validation: V and V performed entirely by persons who make no direct contribution to development. IV&V teams pore over software requirements specifications and try to relate these documents to each of the prime systems functions. They also look for inconsistencies within the specifications and deviations from any standards of documentation. In much the same manner, they closely examine design documentation at all levels. They perform independent inspections of code on a statement-by-statement level. They prepare functional test plans and design test cases applicable to each function of the highest level specification available.

A pretty neat job. It is also expensive: up to 30 percent of the cost of development. The reason for the high cost is that the development community is excluded. This means that the IV&V'ers cannot immediately learn why a questionable construction was used; they cannot be helped to understand a difficult data structure by an answer or two from its designer. The IV&V team must grapple with each element by itself, document (even informally) its suspicions, and await a response by the developers. In the process, a few red herrings may inadvertently be spawned that will also divert the energies of the developers into a documented answer. (These cost implications do not apply to independent test teams, since they need no understanding of the structure of the program components for which they design functional tests.)

One way to get many of the benefits of IV&V without the full cost is to eschew employment of a complete IV&V team in favor of using SQA in collaboration with development people. We shall see this in the following chapters as it applies to most of the defect removal processes. At the other extreme we have the military services, who for many projects employ IV&V contractors having no corporate connection with the project developers.

2.6   Defect Removal versus Defect Detection

This topic is not quite germane to a chapter on programming methodologies, but since we began with remarks on the distinction between defect removal and defect prevention, it is appropriate to end by distinguishing between defect removal and defect detection — especially since with the next chapter we launch directly into the waters of defect removal.

Most of what constitutes the procedures of defect removal are the steps taken to detect defects. Flaws nestled in the convoluted folds of computer programs and their paper precursors are so well hidden that the natural, and proper, emphasis is on their detection. Still, it does little good to find a defect if it is not fixed, and many unproductive programmer-hours have been spent in searching anew for defects previously detected or in searching for new defects that replaced old ones.

Let us start with a classic example of improper defect removal. Figure 2.10 represents a one-dimensional array for which a procedure, ROTATE, is designed to circularly shift a set of contiguous entries one place to the right.*

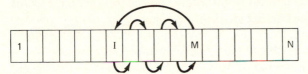

Figure 2.10

```
procedure ROTATE (VECTOR,I,M)
TEMP: = VECTOR(M)
while M> I loop
  VECTOR(M):= VECTOR(M — 1)
  M:= M — 1
end loop
VECTOR(I):= TEMP
return
```

During dynamic test, incorrect processing resulted when ROTATE was called from the following code:

```
    .
    .
    .
call ROTATE (STRING,A,B)
if STRING(B)= LASTCHAR exit
    .
    .
```

Unknown to the author of this code, the utility routine ROTATE had, of course, reset the value of B to that of A. Diagnosis of the failure revealed this to the programmer, who then changed the calling code to compensate for ROTATE's disrespect of a calling parameter:

```
    .
    .
    .
K:= B
call ROTATE(STRING,A,K)
if STRING(B)= LASTCHAR exit
    .
    .
    .
```

---

* The programming language used here and throughout the book is not a real one. Rather than presume the reader's knowledge of any one specific language, except where stated to the contrary, the examples are given in programming terms that should be readily decipherable to most programmers. Indeed, no attempt is made to be consistent with the language of these examples, but just enough semantics and syntax are contrived each time to illustrate the point of interest. This example, while clearly derivative of Algol, does not need *begin* and *end* block delimiters or variable specifications to make the point, nor does it ever have to be compiled.

This worked for the case that failed. However, sooner or later another unsuspecting programmer was bound to run into the same problem. The only real removal of the defect would have been to rewrite ROTATE to substitute a local variable for the formal parameter M.

Faulty defect removal processes are likely to occur when defects compound other defects. The true defect, partly masked by another, is improperly fixed if touched at all. Nor must the covering defect be a software fault; hardware bugs also are capable of masking software bugs. A variant of this is particularly irritating to programmers of embedded or systems software. Many a programmer, convinced that a failure that really resulted from faulty hardware was attributable to the program, has proceeded to change the program to correct the symptom and has thereby inserted a compensating defect in the software.

Side effects present subtle difficulties. For example, the following is noticed some months after a program has been placed in operation, and a correction is made.

```
call ANYPROC(X,Y)
call GETVALUE(Z)
call ANYPROC(X,Y)
C:= X * Z/G.
```

Unknown to the maintenance programmers, the development people had deliberately left in the redundant call to ANYPROC, a remnant of an earlier version. As it happens, ANYPROC increments the global variable G on each call, and the redundant call was really a defect compensating for the defect of not explicitly incrementing G in the program text. The maintenance programmer, in correcting what appeared to be a cosmetic defect, removed one of the calls with the result that C was then computed incorrectly.

Then we have the phenomenon of defects that, once extinguished, rise phoenix-like from their ashes to be seen again. How? One forgets to reenter a patch. The source code is modified to correct a fault, but the library of relocatable modules is not updated with the recompiled procedure. After an interruption, testing is resumed, but with the program loaded from the disk bearing the previous version. These are all problems of configuration control, treated in Chapter 11.

At the core of the defect removal–defect detection issue is the question of how one knows that a defect is removed. We may note that this problem has little to do with defects found by any of the static methods, since in almost all cases there can be no question of where or what the defect is. For those defects found by dynamic test, however, detection of the presence of a defect is no assurance that the defect will be removed. Moreover, after the repair has been made, in the desire to continue dynamic testing as quickly as possible, static defect removal procedures are usually neglected. Structured programming and functional modularity strongly encourage correct diagnosis and accurate repairs, but they provide no guarantees. Meticulous regression testing is certainly a help, especially for problems related to configuration control, but there are no guarantees here either. For example, regression testing offers no immunity to the effects of intermittent hardware performance defects.

We shall return to this problem again in Parts 3 and 4, where the likelihood of removal will be equated with the fidelity with which detection processes are reapplied to the mended program. Admittedly, this begs the question, but let the distinction stand: Defect detection followed by debugging is not necessarily defect removal.

So much for philosophical digressions. The following chapters contain a number of examples of defects. The reader who chances to recognize some of these as his own should take no offense. The author has been guilty of most as well, although not recently:

> When my programming style was austere
> In the rate that I erred I'd no peer.
> I got rid of the curse
> By designing in verse,
> Though I must say my code looks quite queer.

2.7 Summary

1. Although the procedures for defect removal are frequently intertwined with those for defect prevention, they generally are distinguishable. Even the best of the modern development methods that focus on defect prevention do not obviate the need for defect removal processes prior to active test.

2. The actual methods used for defect removal, as well as the likelihood of their success, are strongly influenced by four attributes of software: complexity, modularity, the language of the source code, and the form of documentation.

3. With regard to requirements documentation, the most important quality for defect removal (as well as for development) is testability, the goal of a number of documentation methods. These include natural language text, HIPO and various other graphical approaches, structured English, and more formal specification languages. Each bears on how requirements may be reviewed, and all but the voluminous prose approach may be interwoven with the analysis of the system-level problem.

4. There is also a diversity of techniques for documenting design, and

once again these bear on the practices for removing design defects. Among the methods are flowcharts and other graphical depictions of control flow, HIPO, program design languages and more formal specification languages, structure charts, and the (mostly graphic) conventions attending certain systematic decomposition methods.

5. The most conspicuous aspect of production methodologies is the decomposition process used for program design. There are various organized methods that have proved successful. Included among them are structured design, information hiding, data structure approaches, and higher-order software. Pastiches comprised of parts of these systematic processes can be surprisingly workable. Whatever the method, removal of design defects must conform to the unique products of the iterative stages.

6. Defect removal must also be keyed to the implementation strategy in use. Top-down, bottom-up, and combinations of the two define the scope of defect removal activities at discrete points. Incremental functional system builds further demand iterations of the entire defect removal scheme.

7. Prototyping, an iterative approach that embraces the requirements, design, and — in a sense — coding phases, exerts a unique and challenging set of influences on defect removal.

8. Techniques that trace individual functional requirements through all stages of development may profitably be used in the search for defects that reflect noncompliance with the end use of software. Graphical, tabular, and textual means exist for documenting traceability.

9. The tools used in programming may shape the defect removal process as much as the documentation techniques, decomposition methods, and implementation strategies. The more powerful the software development environment, the more standard will be the development process and the more tightly coupled to development will be defect removal.

10. For several reasons, management approaches to project development generally call for sequential stages, each terminated in inspectable products. Defect removal activities may conveniently be directed to these products.

11. Among the divisions of the staff employed in project development we are likely to find independent test teams, software quality assurance specialists, and configuration control specialists; each group making its own contribution to defect removal. Independent verification and validation (IV&V) teams also are used, although cost limits the extent of this practice.

12. Most defect removal activities are really those of defect detection. Unfortunately, exposing the existence of a fault does not necessarily mean that the fault will be properly removed or, indeed, that the defect was properly identified. Regression testing and iteration of defect removal procedures help confirm, but cannot guarantee, successful removal.

References

1. Niklaus Wirth, "Program Development by Stepwise Refinement," *CACM*, vol. 14, April 1971, pp. 221–227.
2. Stan Kelly-Bootie, *The Devil's DP Dictionary*, McGraw-Hill, New York, 1981, p. 111.
3. R. C. Holt, "A Short Introduction to Concurrent Euclid," *Computing Surveys* and *SIGPLAN Notices*, ACM, vol. 17, May 1982, pp. 60–79.
4. D. T. Ross and K. E. Schoman, Jr., "Structured Analysis for Requirements Definition," *IEEE Trans. Software Eng.*, vol. SE-3, January 1977, pp. 6–15.
5. Tom DeMarco, *Structured Analysis and System Specifications*, Yourdon, New York, 1978.
6. J. Enos and R. Van Tilburg, "Software Design," *Computer*, February 1981, pp. 61–83.
7. Alan M. Davis, "The Design of a Family of Application-Oriented Requirements Languages," *Computer*, May 1982, pp. 21–28.
8. C. A. R. Hoare, "An Axiomatic Basis for Computer Programming," *CACM*, vol. 12, October 1969, pp. 576–583.
9. D. Teichroew and E. A. Hershey III, "PSL/PSA: A Computer-Aided Technique for Structured Documentation and Analysis of Information Processing Systems," *IEEE Trans. Software Eng.*, vol. SE-3, January 1977, pp. 41–48.
10. C. Davis and C. Vick, "The Software Development System," *IEEE Trans. Software Eng.*, vol. SE-3, January 1977, pp. 69–84.
11. Pamela Zave, "An Operational Approach to Requirements Specification for Embedded Systems," *IEEE Trans. Software Eng.*, vol. SE-8, May 1982, pp. 250–269.
12. M. Shaw et al., "Abstraction and Verification in ALPHARD: Defining and Specification of Iteration and Generators," *CACM*, vol. 20, August 1977, pp. 553–563.
13. O. Dahl, "Simula — An ALGOL-based Simulation Language," *CACM*, vol. 9, September 1966, pp. 671–678.
14. David Musser, "Abstract Data Type Specification in the AFFIRM System," *IEEE Trans. Software Eng.*, vol. SE-6, January 1980, pp. 24–32.
15. P. Wegner, "The Vienna Definition Language," *ACM Computing Surveys*, vol. 4, March 1972, pp. 5–63.
16. M. Hamilton and S. Zeldin, "Higher Order Software — A Methodology for Defining Software," *IEEE Trans. Software Eng.*, vol. SE-2, March 1976, pp. 9–32.
17. P. Van Leer, "Top-Down Development Using a Program Design Language," *IBM Systems J.*, vol. 15, no. 2, 1976, pp. 155–170.
18. Stephen Caine and E. Kent Gordon, "PDL — A Tool for Software Design," *Proc. 1975 Natl Computer Conf.*, vol. 44, AFIPS Press, Montvale, N.J., 1975, pp. 271–276.
19. R. Good, R. Cohen, and L. Hunter, "A Report on the Development of GYPSY," *Proc. 1978 Annual Conf.*, ACM, pp. 116–122.
20. M. E. Dickover, C. L. McGowan, and D. T. Ross, "Software Design Using SADT," *Tutorial: Software Design Strategies*, IEEE Catalog No. EH0149-5, 1979, pp. 309–321.
21. I. Nassi and B. Shneiderman, "Flowchart Techniques for Structured Programming," *SIGPLAN Notices*, vol. 8, ACM, August 1973, pp. 12–26.
22. Glenn Bergland and Ronald Gordon, *Tutorial: Software Design Strategies*, IEEE Cat. No. EH0149-5, 1979.
23. W. P. Stevens, G. J. Myers, and L. L. Constantine, "Structured Design," *IBM Systems J.*, vol. 13, 1974, pp. 115–139.

24. E. Yourdon and L. L. Constantine, *Structured Design,* Prentice-Hall, Englewood Cliffs, N.J., 1979.
25. G. J. Myers, *Composite/Structured Design,* Van Nostrand Reinhold, New York, 1978.
26. D. L. Parnas, "A Technique for Software Module Specification with Examples," *CACM,* vol. 15, May 1972, pp. 330–336.
27. Michael Jackson, "Constructive Methods of Program Design," reprinted from *ECI Conference 1976* in *Tutorial: Software Design Strategies,* IEEE Cat. No. EH0149-5, 1979.
28. Kenneth Orr, "Introducing Structured Systems Design," *Tutorial: Software Design Strategies,* IEEE Cat. No. EH0149-5, 1979, pp. 72–82.
29. H. Rudy Ramsey et al., *An Analysis of Software Design Methodologies,* SCI, Technical Report 401 of the U.S. Army Research Institute for the Behavioral and Social Sciences, August 1979, available through NTIS as ADA081319.
30. G. D. Bergland, "A Guided Tour of Program Design Methodologies," *Computer,* October 1981, pp. 13–37.
31. S. N. Griffiths, "Design Methodologies—A Comparison," *Tutorial: Software Design Strategies,* IEEE Cat. No. EH0149-5, 1979, pp. 189–213.
32. J. D. Aron, report given at Conference of the NATO Science Committee, Rome, October 1969. Report printed in J. M. Buxton, P. Naur, and B. Randell, *Software Engineering: Concepts and Techniques,* Petrocelli/Charter, New York, 1976, pp. 188–190.
33. F. T. Baker, "Chief Programmer Team Management of Production Programming," *IBM Systems J.,* vol. 11, 1972, pp. 56–73.
34. Michael Deutsch, *Software Verification and Validation: Realistic Project Approaches,* Prentice-Hall, Englewood Cliffs, N.J., 1982.
35. Kurt Fischer and Michael Walker, "Improved Software Reliability through Requirements Verification," *IEEE Trans. Reliability,* vol. R-28, August 1979, pp. 233–240.
36. William Wulf, "Trends in the Design and Implementation of Programming Languages," *Computer,* January 1980, pp. 14–22.
37. Mack Alford, "A Requirements Engineering Methodology for Real-Time Processing Requirements," *IEEE Trans. Software Eng.,* vol. SE-3, January 1977, pp. 60–69.
38. D. M. Ritchie and K. Thompson, "The UNIX Time-Sharing System," *CACM,* vol. 17, July 1974, pp. 365–375.
39. Evan Ivie, "The Programmer's Workbench—A Machine for Software Development," *CACM,* vol. 20, October 1977, pp. 746–753.
40. R. Eanes et al., "An Environment for Producing Well-Engineered Microprocessor Software," *Fourth Internatl Conf. Software Eng.,* Munich, 1979.
41. Warren Teitelman and Larry Masinter, "The Interlisp Programming Environment," *Computer,* April 1981, pp. 25–33.
42. Louis Fabiano and Joseph McCarthy, "SOLID: The Software Life Cycle Development Environment," *Proc. Natl Aerospace Electronics Conf.* (NAECON '81), 1981.
43. Lawrence E. Druffel, *Ada Joint Prog. Office Info. Bull.,* May 1982, p. 4.
44. Robert Dunn and Richard Ullman, *Quality Assurance for Computer Software,* McGraw-Hill, New York, 1981, pp. 212–215.

Static Methods

3

Requirements and Design Reviews

As the title indicates, the thrust of this chapter is on review processes during and immediately following the requirements and design phases of software development. Reviews, we know, are not the only means of uncovering defects during the "paper" stages of development. The use of requirements and design language processors is independent of any reviews. Pseudolanguage processors can detect anomalous processing sequences, interface inconsistencies, redundant and inconsistent data definition, improper control structures, and forgotten branches. These fault detection capabilities are used mostly during the preparation of specifications. By the time the specifications are ready to be used by other than their originators, the remaining defects are those not visible to the processor. This is rather like the compilation procedure. We don't need to consider how we will use compilers to remove compile time defects; the compilers will be quite insistent that we do so if we want binary output. Admittedly, pseudolanguage processors produce summary reports even though faults have been found, but their clear presentation of these faults amounts to much the same thing. Thus, with regard to formal defect removal programs, our principal interest in these pseudolanguage systems is our use of them at review time.

All of this is getting ahead of ourselves a bit. Our melancholy subject is that of defects, and we would do well to know a bit more about requirements and design defects.

3.1 All about Defects

The number of kinds of defects is limited only by our powers of invention, and it would be fruitless to attempt a delineation of defects that is at once comprehensive and rigorous. However, we can certainly look at the more common generic types.

Requirements defects.   These are the defects that originate during the requirements phase and exist in the tangible output of that phase: the requirements definition (specification), whatever its form.

Failure to reflect a more abstract specification.   If a higher-level specification exists, the software requirements definition must be viewed as the functional allocation to software of its part in the overall solution. Requirements specifications are defective to the extent that the eventual programs do not complete a satisfactory composite solution. For example, a classroom computer for programmed instruction in seventh-grade mathematics has a defect if it employs (specified) word problems having to do with investment options for pensions and the percentages of Medicare payments. Generally, defects of this kind are a superset of several of the classes that follow.

Omitted functions.   In analyzing a higher-level specification, one of its requirements may not have been translated into a requirement within the applicable specifications of the next lower level of abstraction, one of which is the software requirements definition.

Higher-order requirement improperly translated.   A function may not have been forgotten; but in its apportionment to software, something may have been lost in the translation. Let us take another hypothetical example in programmed instruction, this one a system ordered by a Canadian city. The board of education specified that the system be capable of either English or French as the interactive language. The software specification that ensued had it as a "bilingual capability." Guess what happened when implementation of the specification was assigned to the contractor's Miami office.

Software requirement incompatible with the operational environment.   This is one of the most common requirements defects, since it covers a great many cases. A typical one for an embedded program is the stipulation of an input data rate less than that which will actually be encountered owing to random events.

Incomplete requirements.   Incomplete, that is, not in the sense of omitting a function, but in not stipulating all that one needs to know about it. For example, the embedded program of the preceding defect class may have the correct input data rate specified, but the response time to each datum may have been omitted. If the only operational requirement is that output be at no slower rate than input, no harm is done. Frequently, however, it is the interval between each stimulus and its response that is crucial.

Infeasible requirement. Now the response time has been stipulated, but there is no way it can be achieved given the amount of processing required and the speed of the computer.

Conflicting requirements. The response time for each of several asynchronous inputs, each individually attainable, has been specified. In combination, however, the response times are not attainable. An example of a very different kind relates to conflicting specification domains. The probability of correctly recognizing a pattern of data, as in the enhancement of photographs, is a function of the amount of data processed. For real-time pattern recognition, accuracy is clearly inimical to response time, and it is possible to place requirements on the two that are pairwise incompatible.

Incorrect specification of resources. The amount of computer available for the program may be overstated. Of course, no matter what is defined for memory size, disk storage, the number of I/O ports, or whatever, the programmers will want more.

Software specification incompatible with other system specifications. A typical example, again for embedded programs, is the requirement that two successive signals input from an 8-bit register be distinguished if their amplitudes differ by more than one part in 1000.

Wrong or missing external constants. Since constants are easily changed in a parameterized program, this is not a costly defect unless initial detection takes place late in the testing phase — or worse, in operation, as did the incorrectly specified radius of the earth for an early space-tracking program.

Incorrect or missing description of the initial system state. Program designers will assume a quiescent or zero-valued state unless the state is specified otherwise. This problem is generally confined to embedded software: The external environment may be far from at rest at start-up, and program initialization may have to be driven by status registers.

Incorrect error allocation. The statement, "The accuracy of the solution shall be within ± 1 milliradian," will be read as a bound on computational dilution of precision. Unfortunately, specifications often contain only the maximum permissible *system* error, that which includes instrumentation error, rather than the error size allocated to computer processing.

Incorrect input or output descriptions. These are relatively minor but common. Moreover, they waste an inordinate amount of test time. Included here are incorrect formats, scaling, status bit polarity, and the like.

All others. The author's escape clause. Actually, the preceding categories will account for nearly all requirements defects.

Design defects. The number of kinds of defects that arise during design are as many as those found in requirements documentation. Here are a few.

Omission or misinterpretation of specified requirements. This broad category may not always result from designer error. Sometimes the problem lies with an unclear or ambiguous requirements definition. In either case, the design will be the first place where the fault is irrefutably a fault.

Inability to operate on the full range of data. At the most detailed level, we have a trigonometric routine capable of correct operation only in the first quadrant. At an intermediate level, we have a lexical analyzer that does not handle the full character set. For an equally unlikely, if recognizable, top-level design defect, we have a compiler design that does not provide for nested loops.

Infinite loops. We usually think of infinite loops as a phenomenon of code. However, they exist in design also. Figure 3.1 illustrates one. The design ignores the possibility that synchronization between sender and receiver may not be achievable. Endless loops that encompass events or acts outside the domain of the program are not always so evident from inspection of the design as this one. A misleading error recovery message to a data

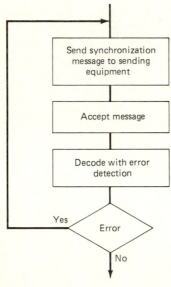

Figure 3.1 Infinite loop.

```
do until no error
    Send synchronization message to sending equipment
    Accept message
    Decode with error detection
endo
```

entry operator can result in a sequence of operations that ends only when a coffee break terminates the operator's persistence in attempting to get the data accepted as (seemingly) directed.

Incompatibility with hardware resources. Reviews have uncovered the planned use of more I/O channels and tape and disk units than exist, more real memory than is available, and more registers than those in the computer. Other design faults of this class include the indiscriminate use of special (e.g., index) registers and the use of nonexisting stacks, real-time clocks, and other architectural features.

Incompatibility with software resources. Designers may assume that operating system or library features have capabilities other than or beyond those with which they are actually endowed. For example, in a multitasking system, an optimistic designer may interpret the executive command "suspend (t)" to mean that all processing is halted for t seconds — an easy way of designing a time-out — when, in fact, the command suspends all tasks scheduled to be invoked in the next t seconds.

Unacceptable processor load. In real-time applications and interactive multiterminal systems, excessive execution time is a damaging source of defects. In this regard, the absence of credible execution time estimates to accompany the design is itself a defect if processor load is a material issue.

Incorrect analysis of computational error. Although few designs fail to account for the round-off and truncation errors of a single operation, the effect of such errors when cascaded is sometimes ignored. We see also the failure to choose a numerical approximation consistent with the accuracy objective. For example, the use of a library routine to fit a parabola to collected data may be the easiest way to determine the curve's parameters; but if the routine is a least-squares fit and the critical error is the maximum deviation, the design would be the better for using a Chebychev approximation. In the same vein, programs requiring random function generators should be so designed that the behavior of the random function matches that required.

Incompatible data representations. The input is in pounds and the program processes kilograms. The design reverses the sense of discrete binary inputs. Internally, one module talks statute miles per hour and its mate responds with knots. Similarly, we find inconsistencies in scaling and word lengths.

Nonexisting or inadequate error traps. Good designs check the validity of input. These checks are frequently absent or are of insufficient scope to properly protect the program. Beyond the obvious validity tests of numerical and character field entries, designs often must be concerned with checking the sequence of input. This is especially true of keyboard input. It is also poor design if the module that traps an error does not contain the recovery mechanism. Passing error handling to a peer module reduces its structural independence.

Failure to handle exceptions. Designers frequently are so caught up in the solution to the main body of the problem that they forget to handle unique conditions even when the conditions are specified in requirements documentation. The essence of this problem may be seen in a chess program in which the pawn-moving apparatus ignores en passant captures. Inadequate attention to exceptions is properly a subset of the first category, omission or misinterpretation of specified requirements, but it is enough of a problem to warrant separate notice. The greater the number of independent discrete inputs that influence a single chain of processes, the greater the likelihood of faults of this type. Akin to exception handling, of which reaction to invalid data is really a subset, is the care taken for boundary conditions. Of these, failure to initialize is the most common.

Weak modularity. This may not result in a performance failure, but it is a defect in the sense that it encourages the subsequent production of faults, reduces the likelihood of comprehensive testing, and is antithetical to successful maintenance.

Inexpansible control structure. Again, we have a design defect that may not result in failure but may sharply reduce the usefulness of the program. An executive control system comprised exclusively of in-line logic or daisy chain call sequences to determine which routine should next be invoked does not easily lend itself to the addition of further functions. Although it must be recognized that multitasking schedulers and table-driven executives may impose a significant overhead burden, they are invaluable at modification time not only during the operational period of a program but, of more immediate interest, during integration and evaluation phases as well.

Control structure ignores processing priorities. Almost every real-time or multiterminal system has priorities. An instrumentation system may have to accept data from an external register before the next input overwrites it. A time-sharing system frequently designates one terminal as that having priorities over others. Many systems have much more complicated time-dependent sets of functions. Apart from processor load considerations, failure to satisfy specified priorities is a defect.

Detailed design does not conform to top-level design. This would seem self-explanatory. In preparing for reviews, however, we should remember that frequently the problem is that the top-level design was modified but the changes were not documented during the period of detailed design.

Failure to conform to standards. An omnibus category with deviations from the precepts of structured programming at the design level as the classic example.

It may be noted that design defects seem to fall into three categories:

- Noncompliance with requirements or higher-level specifications
- Faults intrinsic to the design apart from design traceability to higher specifications
- Documentation defects

Only the first of these is the object of verification; it is defined in Section 2.5. Although verification may incidentally find defects of the other two categories, it is not directed to that purpose. Design reviews conducted as part of a comprehensive defect removal program treat all three categories equally. This is a specific instance of the more general distinction between the objectives of verification and those of defect removal. An even more prominent one is found in active testing, where verification is much the same as in functional testing, to the exclusion of structural testing. In short, verification (and validation also, for that matter) may not be equated to the more powerful regimen of comprehensive defect removal.

3.2   Verification and Project Control

There is a productive aspect of verification that attaches to, yet goes beyond, the business of tracing the results of one phase to the output of its successor. Simply put, if development does not proceed in an orderly, step-by-step fashion, there can be no verification. To proceed with design, other than the initial steps, before requirements are established is to court disaster. So too for each of the other phases save the first. Thus, reviews, which include verification practices, can also serve as project control mechanisms, up to and including code reviews, to ensure that criteria are properly met for terminating the zeroth iteration (and possibly later ones as well) of each phase. Similarly, phase entry criteria (when may the next task be given an unrestrained go-ahead?) may be based on the results of the review of the predecessor phase.

To many, the most vexing software problem has been that of project control. Project management people can do worse than to look to reviews as control mechanisms during the paper stages of development.

3.3   Pseudolanguage Processors

As was implied by the introductory lines of this chapter, if a requirements or design language processor is incorporated in the programming development environment, we may assume that, at the time of the applicable review, one of the documents presented is an error-free listing of requirements or design, that is, one in which all defects identifiable by the processor have been correctly removed. One of the first items to be considered at the review is this listing, and the first item to appear on a review checklist is affirmation that no defects are listed.

The listing serves other purposes as well, however. Depending on the processor capabilities, related information appearing throughout the "specification" can be collected, digested, and summarized. Structure can be made evident by functional cross-references, procedure-calling hierarchies, and the places where references to global data or external devices appear. To illustrate, let us consider the reports available from a program design language processor. The example design is to satisfy the following requirements:

For assigning drivers from a pool of itinerants, a local delivery service needs a calendar of the workdays in each year.* Workdays are all those save Saturdays, Sundays, and holidays. The calendar is to be placed in a file for subsequent use, and it must also be printed with each month's dates on a separate page. Since the drivers are not on a regular payroll, vacations do not need to be considered.

The design for the program and the reports generated by the design language processor appear in Figures 3.2 through 3.10. The design language used for this example is a composite of the features I most like of the three design language processors I have available. (Indeed, not content with that exercise of literary privilege, I have added a couple of refinements that none offer.) For illustration, all output that is presented exactly as input (except for indexing and pretty printing) is in lowercase and all analysis results are in uppercase.

Several matters are worth noting. Underscoring the first (and only) letter of a word is the designer's way of identifying it as a data reference. In line 1 (of those numbered by the language processor) of Figure 3.3, we see *holidays* clearly used as a data representation, but declared neither at the system level nor locally. This is a matter of the designer's discretion. There is no need to declare data as potential referants if their only use is immediate.

Both *print* and *mainline* have local variables named *date*, but because these were declared locally, the processor did not declare them to be available to the system. The use of the term "system data" to cover global data, files, and passed parameters weakens the ability of the processor to find certain inconsistent uses, but it does permit greater latitude in writing flow

---

* Precisely why one would need a 12-month calendar for the assignment of itinerants is another matter. But then, systems do get overspecified in real life, if not as frequently as they are underspecified.

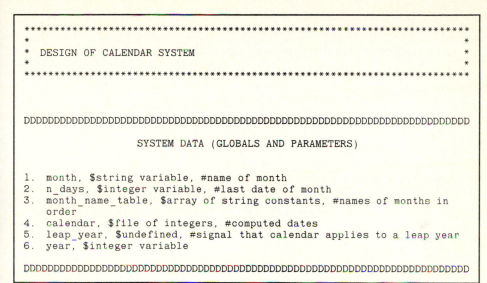

```
**************************************************************************
*                                                                        *
*  DESIGN OF CALENDAR SYSTEM                                              *
*                                                                        *
**************************************************************************


DDDDDDDDDDDDDDDDDDDDDDDDDDDDDDDDDDDDDDDDDDDDDDDDDDDDDDDDDDDDDDDDDDDDDDDDDDDD

                    SYSTEM DATA (GLOBALS AND PARAMETERS)

1.  month, $string variable, #name of month
2.  n_days, $integer variable, #last date of month
3.  month_name_table, $array of string constants, #names of months in
    order
4.  calendar, $file of integers, #computed dates
5.  leap_year, $undefined, #signal that calendar applies to a leap year
6.  year, $integer variable

DDDDDDDDDDDDDDDDDDDDDDDDDDDDDDDDDDDDDDDDDDDDDDDDDDDDDDDDDDDDDDDDDDDDDDDDDDDD
```

Figure 3.2

statements. It may be that an ideal environment would be one in which fault suppression control statements could be used for the initial entry of the design, followed by subsequent refinement of the design with the fault diagnostics enabled. Given this, one could eventually define procedure calls and assignments with the rigor that would allow the detection of further instances of inconsistent data use. The example permits automatic detection only of inconsistencies between *declared* system and local data and, moreover, without regard to whether the system data are parameters, are global, or are external records or files.

Let us digress just a bit to expand on the concept of a design language processor that can be adapted, through the use of control directives or pragmas, for statement forms of stepwise decreased abstraction. It is certainly possible to envision an integrated design system that culminates in the source code for the executable program. To this end, several suggestions have been made that the most appropriate design language for Ada programs is Ada itself. Ada currently has an inherent feature that lends itself to top-level and intermediate design stages: procedure specifications can be compiled separately from procedure bodies. What remains is for APSE* to include levels of forgiveness for violation of statement forms (including those in the specification) and data reduction capabilities from which the structure of the program may be inferred.

---

* See Section 2.4.

```
                           CALENDAR SYSTEM

PPPPPPPPPPPPPPPPPPPPPPPPPPPPPPPPPPPPPPPPPPPPPPPPPPPPPPPPPPPPPPPPPPPPPPPP

        local data
          holiday_table, $array of integer variables, #date of each holiday
             0101..1225
          day, $string variable, #name of day
          day_name_table, $array of string constants, #sun..sat
          date, $integer variable, #day of month


        **

1.    input holidays and year and build holiday_table
2.    set month to jan, date to 1, and initialize day
3.    do until 12 months have been processed
4.      invoke numbday procedure to compute n_days
5.      do until n_days
6.        if day not = sat or sun
7.          then check month and date in holiday_table
8.          , if not in table
9.             then add date to calendar
10.         endif
11.       endif
12.       increment day by circularly shifting day_name_table
13.     endo
14.     date:= 1
15.     increment month using month_name_table
16.   endo
17.   invoke print procedure to print calendar by month

PPPPPPPPPPPPPPPPPPPPPPPPPPPPPPPPPPPPPPPPPPPPPPPPPPPPPPPPPPPPPPPPPPPPPPPP

FAULTS:  NONE
SYSTEM DATA USED:  CALENDAR, MONTH, MONTH_NAME_TABLE, N_DAYS, YEAR
PROCEDURES CALLED:  NUMBDAY, PRINT
```

Figure 3.3

Continuing with our example, so far as the *processor* is concerned, the manual input of system data specifications (Figure 3.2) is optional. Except for the assistance it received in the definition of data types, the processor's own summary of system data (Figure 3.7) was produced from the references within the procedure bodies to the data items (words with the initial letters underscored) that were not declared as local data. Thus, we have a useful check between what the designers intend to be shared data and that which is actually designed into the system. Of course, if the designers do not bother to underscore the first letter of data items, the check cannot be made. Reviewers should look to see if the designers had been derelict in making their references to data explicit; which carelessness diminishes the value of the pseudocode and its reduction.

The structure information presented in Figures 3.8 and 3.9 can uncover procedures written but not used or called for but not designed. These

```
                        CALENDAR SYSTEM

PPPPPPPPPPPPPPPPPPPPPPPPPPPPPPPPPPPPPPPPPPPPPPPPPPPPPPPPPPPPPPPPPPPPPPPPPP

      procedure numbday
      local data
        none

      **

1.    if month = sep or apr or jun or nov
2.      then set n_days to 30
3.      else if month = feb
4.        then invoke leap_year_calc
5.          if leap_year
6.            then set n_days to 29
7.            else set n_days to 28
8.          endif
9.        else set n_days to 31
10.     endif
11.  endif

PPPPPPPPPPPPPPPPPPPPPPPPPPPPPPPPPPPPPPPPPPPPPPPPPPPPPPPPPPPPPPPPPPPPPPPPPP

FAULTS:  NONE
SYSTEM DATA USED:  LEAP_YEAR, MONTH, N_DAYS, LEAP_YEAR
PROCEDURES CALLED:  LEAP_YEAR_CALC
```

Figure 3.4

```
                        CALENDAR SYSTEM

PPPPPPPPPPPPPPPPPPPPPPPPPPPPPPPPPPPPPPPPPPPPPPPPPPPPPPPPPPPPPPPPPPPPPPPPPP

      procedure print
      local data
        last_date, $integer variable, #previous entry from calendar
        date, $integer variable, #day of month

**

1.    initialize month to jan
2.    do until 12 months have been processed
3.      print month
4.      last_date:= 0
5.      do until next date from calendar less than last_date or until end
              of file
6.        print date
7.        set last_date to date
8.      endo
9.      back up calendar one entry
10.     increment month from month_name_table
11.  endo

PPPPPPPPPPPPPPPPPPPPPPPPPPPPPPPPPPPPPPPPPPPPPPPPPPPPPPPPPPPPPPPPPPPPPPPPPP

FAULTS:  NONE
SYSTEM DATA USED:  CALENDAR, MONTH, MONTH_NAME_TABLE
PROCEDURES CALLED:  NONE
```

Figure 3.5

```
                          CALENDAR SYSTEM

PPPPPPPPPPPPPPPPPPPPPPPPPPPPPPPPPPPPPPPPPPPPPPPPPPPPPPPPPPPPPPPPPPPPPPPP

     procedure leap_year_calc
     local data
       none

**

1.  if year divisible by 4 and not divisible by 100
2.    then report leap_year
3.  endif

PPPPPPPPPPPPPPPPPPPPPPPPPPPPPPPPPPPPPPPPPPPPPPPPPPPPPPPPPPPPPPPPPPPPPPPP

FAULTS:  NONE
SYSTEM DATA USED:  LEAP_YEAR, YEAR
PROCEDURES CALLED:  NONE
```

Figure 3.6

```
                          CALENDAR SYSTEM

********  SYSTEM DATA  *********
```

DATA ITEM	DECLARED AS	PROCEDURE	LINES WHERE CITED
CALENDAR	FILE, INTEGER	MAINLINE	10
		PRINT	5, 9
LEAP_YEAR	UNK, UNK	NUMBDAY	5
		LEAP_YEAR_CALC	2
MONTH	SCALAR VAR, STRING	MAINLINE	3, 8, 16
		NUMBDAY	3
		PRINT	3, 10
MONTH_NAME_TABLE	ARRAY CONS, STRING	MAINLINE	16
		PRINT	10
N_DAYS	SCALAR VAR, INTEGER	MAINLINE	6
		NUMBDAY	2, 6, 7, 9
YEAR	SCALAR VAR, INTEGER	MAINLINE	1
		LEAP_YEAR_CALC	1

Figure 3.7

```
                          CALENDAR SYSTEM

          *********  PROCEDURE LINKS  *********

          MAINLINE CALLS    NUMBDAY, PRINT
          NUMBDAY CALLS    LEAP_YEAR_CALC



          LEAP_YEAR_CALC IS CALLED BY    NUMBDAY
          MAINLINE IS CALLED BY
          NUMBDAY IS CALLED BY    MAINLINE
          PRINT IS CALLED BY    MAINLINE
```

Figure 3.8

```
                      CALENDAR SYSTEM

            ********  FLOW STRUCTURE  ********

            1       MAINLINE
            1.1        NUMBDAY
            1.1.1        LEAP_YEAR_CALC
            1.2        PRINT
```

Figure 3.9

```
                      CALENDAR SYSTEM

            ********  SUMMARY  ********

            FAULTS FOUND:  0
            LINES OF SYSTEM DATA SPECIFICATIONS:  6
            LINES OF LOCAL DATA SPECIFICATIONS:  4
            NUMBER OF FLOW STATEMENTS:  43
```

Figure 3.10

reports also serve as a road map to the logic of the system and a check against the intended structure. A program design language listing used in a top-level design review can be expected to show many procedures called for but not yet in the system. They will be there at the final design review, though.

3.4   The Greater Issue of Quality

Defects of the kinds listed in Section 3.1 are, at least within the context of this book, the primary subject of requirements and design reviews. Still, having assembled a group of people for the purpose of uncovering clear-cut defects, it would seem short-sighted not to consider other aspects of software quality. Admittedly, not all matters inimical to quality are likely to be corrected, especially if the designers are working to a tight schedule. For example, a specification so poorly organized that it is difficult to understand without its author's coaching degrades from the maintainability of the consequent program. Given that success in meeting the schedule for program delivery is a confessed risk, the specification will not be revised— at least not until sometime after the program is operational. Nevertheless, even if no greater purpose than that of education is served, reviews should be mined for profits beyond the detection of defects.

The "other" aspects of quality that can be brought into the scope of reviews include

Testability

Readability

Thoroughness of analyses

Reliability (apart from the effect of defects)

Usability

Complexity

Maintainability

Expandability

Potential for reuse

To a large extent, each of these quality aspects* is compromised by defects. The immediate interest, however, is in the attributes in which a causal relation to defects either does not exist or is hard to establish. Testability, for example, regarded in some quarters as the preeminent business of requirements reviews, has to do with more than defects of the types enumerated in Section 2.1. Testability is not easily defined. The usual definition having to do with the capability of establishing criteria for measuring test success strikes me as too donnish to really get the idea across. I rather like the example of the circa 1914 Army specification that reads something like this:

> The contractor shall deliver a flying machine capable of lifting two men having an aggregate weight of at least 300 pounds for a distance of 10 miles and at an altitude of at least 1000 feet. The flying machine shall be of sufficiently simple construction that a properly trained mechanic can repair it within a reasonable amount of time.

The first sentence is testable. The second is not.

Even if each function is accurately and completely specified and the several functional descriptions are consistent, it may be difficult to establish testing criteria in the presence of a weak separation of functional performance characteristics or of descriptions that are overly intertwined with those of external operations or equipment. Testability arises during design reviews also, mostly as it relates to modularity. A weak modular structure may not necessarily exhibit defects that can be associated with expected performance, but it is a potential source of grief and should be corrected. If nothing else, intermodular binding will add to the cost of constructing test scaffolding for unit and integration testing.

The ability to correctly understand requirements and design documentation is also of obvious importance. As long as the authors remain accessi-

---

* Often referred to as the "ilities" of programming.

ble to those whose own work must be based on that documentation, readability would seem a secondary matter — at least compared to the others. Even here, however, misinterpretations may occur without the reader's awareness; that is, without the reader's knowing that the author should be consulted. In any case, the originators of documentation have been known to become unavailable through transfers, resignation, and illness. Also, when development is distributed among several geographically dispersed sites, access in fact is not always what it appears to be on paper. Finally, poor readability exerts a profoundly unfavorable effect on the capability to maintain and modify a system.

A review is an excellent opportunity to detect inadequate analyses. While looking at a new technique for identifying and classifying sources of electromagnetic energy, I once expressed concern that it was so great a departure from previously used methods that I needed further explanation of how its inventor (a highly creative and able designer) knew it would work. His answer: "Actually, I don't know with certainty, but given the information available to the computer for this project, it's the only way I could think of to do the job." When I asked if he had modeled the complex algorithm, he responded that, indeed, he had intended to do just that, but when time permitted. I knew that time would never permit prior to system integration, demand schedules being what they are, and with a promise to explain things to his supervisor, I got the designer's agreement to make the necessary simulation his first priority.*

Reliability is mostly a matter of sparse defect population, but in an operational sense there are other issues as well. One looks for built-in defenses against invalid data, against operator errors, against faulty equipment. Even with regard to defects, there is at least one aspect not included among Section 2.1's defect types: How much reusable code does a design call for? Previously used modules have the benefit of the test of time to add to one's confidence of low defect count.

A host of questions can be raised with regard to reliability: Does the downloading of ROM data get verified? Are all transactions recorded in a backup audit trail? Can the program get hung up waiting for an interrupt or status flag? These and their like are grist for the review mill.

The confirmation of usability is largely covered by the search for defects and by the other aspects of quality. Still, especially in a requirement review, one tries to relate the program to its operational environment. I have been told of a review for an operating system in which it developed that to

---

* The denoument is not germane, but to avoid a dangling anecdote, I report here that the method actually proved to be successful. However, after tinkering with the model, the designer was able to come up with several improvements that reduced the complexity of the design.

meet the specifications for the time available to each of several packages that were likely to be run concurrently on the system, the console operator would have to reallocate workspaces or priorities every few minutes.

Complexity is closely correlated to several of the other quality attributes, both as a consequence and as a cause, but is noted separately to make certain that reviews cover structured programming, and, indeed, all facets of good design practice.

Maintainability also has been touched upon. Beyond matters previously discussed, reviews should be concerned with the organization of files with respect to error-free periodic backup, design information available to ease the incorporation of new functional features, the updating of installation-peculiar data, and so on.

Potential for reuse is almost never considered, but if we are willing to gain from the reuse of modules from other systems, we should be equally willing to design (and document) so that our designs may be used by others. 'Tis more blessed to give than to receive.

It would be marvelous if we could measure all of these attributes not solely and directly related to out-and-out defects, if, that is, we could ascribe a score of some sort to maintainability, reusability, and the others. Except for reliability and complexity, for which good beginnings have been made and to which we shall refer in Chapters 7 and 10, we software engineers have yet to find a way to intelligently quantify the "ilities." Others have, but their counts of *goto* statements, ratios of documentation pages to lines of code, statistics on module sizes, and so forth, while interesting for research purposes, have little merit as indexes of quality. If we could specify what we want in software by simple measures (bigger than a breadbox but smaller than a refrigerator) there would be fewer questions of what software engineers mean by "software quality." Unfortunately, we cannot. For the time being, at least, quality remains qualitative.

3.5 Assumptions, Limitations, and Constraints

Assumptions that underlie the definition of requirements and the design of programs, limitations of operating range implied by requirements and design specifications, and operational constraints inherent in these specifications are rarely true defects. However, they have much to do with the quality of the final product. Careful systems analysts and designers often remember to document their assumptions and the restrictions embedded in their specifications. But more often than not they are not documented either because the author of the work did not realize an assumption was made or simply forgot to record it or because the limitation or constraint was not considered important or the author was unaware that it was implied. Analysis tools and verifiable specification languages will not necessarily reveal them — rarely, in the case of assumptions — and so we must look to reviews to expose them, document them, and weigh their acceptability.

Assumptions in requirements specifications frequently arise from uncertainties in the operational environment. A system to control the heating and cooling machinery for a factory, one that will add or shed loads in a manner that will smooth peak power requirements, will have to account for maximum and minimum use of fabrication machinery and worker population. These will have to be assumed if the information is not available in past records. For an air traffic control system, the entry to the control sector of new aircraft may be specified in the system specification in terms of average and maximum rates, but the actual frequency distributions (gaussian, Poisson, and so on) and their variances may have to be assumed in the allocation of functions to hardware, software, and operators. Any interactive system assumes the operator's level of comprehension.

Assumptions arise at design time also. An accuracy specification may be assumed from the wording of requirements documentation to apply to the average of many computations, when in fact it was intended to apply to each. Enough disk space may be allocated for an assumed daily archiving of an EDP transaction audit trail; failure to stipulate it may lead to problems when some users choose to archive weekly.

Limitations and constraints most often arise from compromises, or trade-offs as they seem most often to be called. Any convergent closed loop that involves a computer and external instrumentation results in a compromise of solution speed and accuracy. (Of course, this is also true of iterative numerical solutions, such as Runge-Kutta root solving, but speed is seldom critical to these solutions.) Requirements documentation may specify either accuracy or speed, with the other left as a limitation of the program and a constraint on the use of the system.

Restrictions are even more commonly implied by designs. The number of depositors for a bank passbook savings accounting system may be an explicit limitation in the requirements specification and the design, but the resulting program may also limit the number of daily transactions for each. Many years ago I designed a system to provide solutions to the classic traveling salesman problem. The algorithm used was an iterative one in which chains of various "cities and routes" were created as interim steps. There was no presumptive way of knowing how long any chain might get, but it was clear that if one, two, or maybe three chains grew to sufficient size, their storage requirements would prevent other chains from maturing in the iterative process. In the documentation of the program, I bounded the number of "cities" and "salesmen," but I neglected to stipulate those storage-related constraints on the input topology that would assure convergence to an optimal solution. Later, after complaints from several users, I had to revise the design so that users could tune the system to their requirements. Had the original design been properly reviewed, I might have been spared the rework.

There is no application that fails to evoke implied assumptions, limitations, and constraints in the requirements and design phases. Examples can go on endlessly. Ferreting these out during reviews is often of equal importance to exposing defects. An unacceptable assumption or restriction may not easily be removed after the fact.

3.6   Planning Aspects of Reviews

We have also to consider another issue not directly related to defects. Reviews provide a useful medium for encouraging sound management practice. If done at no other time, a requirements review is a good time to review the design-code-test plan; assuming, of course, that the software designers have been keeping sufficiently close tabs on the progress of requirements definition to gauge the scope of the project and to do some preliminary analyses. Unless development standards change little from project to project, a requirements review is none too early to make certain that a software development environment has been selected and that any work required for its availability has been started. At the requirements review we would also expect to see a preliminary test plan, or, for stand-alone software systems, a test plan for qualification. Interestingly, the act of thinking out how the satisfaction of requirements can be validated often results in the discovery of defects within the requirements as specified. Thus, persons whose corporate competence is directed to defect removal have grounds for insisting that test plans be available concurrently with requirements documentation.

Design reviews, and especially top-level reviews, are the time to confirm that the hardware, software, and personnel resources for each stage of development testing have been identified and that steps have been taken toward their development or acquisition. Staffing plans, if not reviewed elsewhere, should be available for examination. Unrealistic planned buildups are only slightly less common than estimates modest to the point of diffidence. Closer to the subject of defect removal, the development test plan should be reviewed to see what defect removal operations are planned and to confirm that detailed pretest planning will conform to standards. Configuration control plans should be available early also; in fact early enough that requirements and design documentation can be placed under control directly they have been approved.

3.7   The Review Process

It is convenient to think of a review in terms of three phases: preparation, the review meeting, and follow-up. The review meeting is, of course, the review proper. However, considerable attention must be given the phases that flank it if full value is to be received. We proceed chronologically.

Preparation. Before the review meeting can be held, several matters must be attended to: scheduling the time and place of the meeting, determining its participants and notifying them, and distributing the material to be reviewed.

Disposing of the most simple first, the room scheduled for the meeting should have a table (or tables) large enough to accommodate all the paperwork that each person will need. Admittedly, this is a most pedestrian matter, but documents and listings that slip from laps or have to be stacked about one's feet are not conducive to efficiency. Recall, too, that it is not just the results of the subject development phase for which space must be available; documentation from previous phases and handbooks or binders of standards must also be at the ready. In short, software reviews are paper-intensive, and there needs to be room for all the paper.

The time to conduct the review is bounded by two constraints: the meeting cannot take place until the work being reviewed has been documented, and it must take place before the ensuing phase has progressed beyond its initial steps. The latter constraint reflects the definition of timely defect removal as that which militates against costly rework.

The first of these constraints does not imply any measure of formalism to the material reviewed. As long as it is readable and has enough organization to be followed, it can be used. This comment is relevant mostly when the substance of the material must also be presented to a customer as evidence of progress. Submissions to a customer usually entail editorial changes, reformatting, proofreading, and reproduction. This may take two or more weeks, depending upon the extent to which the documentation is machine-readable. Waiting for more cosmetic documentation may compromise the constraint of timeliness.

Each of the participants should receive a copy of the review material sufficiently in advance of the meeting to give it careful study. The results of this study should be:

- A list of things the reviewer does not understand
- A list of what the reviewer believes may be defects
- General comments concerning other matters pertaining to overall quality and planning

The participants should use checklists similar to, if not identical with, those that will be used during the review meeting.

Determining the dramatis personae of a review will depend on the review in question and the policies in force that govern task responsibilities. Here is a ground rule useful for deciding the groups or functions that should be included: Attendance should include at least one representative each of:

- Those whose earlier work provided the basis for the work about to be reviewed.
- Those who performed the subject work.
- Those who will be responsible for the phase of work that will be performed in response to the documentation under review. (They may be considered the immediate users.)
- A function independent of any of these groups but cognizant of the entire development process. Software quality engineers fit this category very neatly.
- Those responsible for the final form or integrity of development documentation. Librarians, technical editors, and configuration management representatives are typical candidates.

All this may seem a bit complicated, so we shall take an example that follows a previously published model.[1] The example is based on the following premises, which use the development groups identified by Table 2.1.

1. The software will be embedded in an instrumentation system being developed under contract.
2. Systems engineering (SYST) defines the software requirements and plans hardware and software integration and system test.
3. The senior design staff (SENDES) performs the top-level design and plans all software development tests.
4. The design group (PROG) is responsible for detailed design, code, and unit test, including unit-level test documentation.
5. The software test group (SOFTST) performs software integration and software qualification tests, including the preparation of test specifications and procedures for them.
6. The systems test group (SYSTST) has the primary responsibility for systems integration, including hardware and software integration and systems qualification tests, and prepares the test specifications and procedures for these tests.
7. The librarian (LIB) is responsible for seeing that the final form of documentation conforms to documented standards and for keeping track of updates to interim and final documentation.
8. Quality assurance (QA) enforces development standards, both administrative and technical, and sees to it that traceability to the systems requirements is verified.
9. The customer (USER) hopes all these folks are talking to each other.

Table 3.1   Casts for Conducting Reviews

	SYST	SENDES	PROG	SOFTST	SYSTST	LIB	QA	USER
Requirements review (incl. system test plan)	X	X			X	X	X	Optional
Top-level design review (incl. software test plan)	X	X	X	X	Optional	X	X	
Detailed design review (incl. unit test specs.)		X	X	X		X	X	

This is our cast of players — a typical assortment of assigned roles — who will move on and off the review stage in accordance with Table 3.1.

Table 3.1 implies that test documentation will be reviewed at the same meetings in which requirements and design specifications are reviewed. They may, in fact, be reviewed separately, at a small cost in efficiency. (The content of the reviews of pretest material is deferred until Part 3, where it can be more closely associated with other issues pertaining to active testing.)

Top-level and detailed design phases, as defined, must be regarded as the bracketing design phases for large systems. Several intermediate stages may be required, each terminated by a review. Since the descriptions of intermediate design stages are subject to considerable diversity — a function of the application, size, and design approach — Table 3.1 ignores them. It must be understood, however, that intermediate design reviews borrow from top-level and detailed design review particulars. Large systems may also require more than one stage of requirements reviews, say, an overall review concentrating on interfaces to the outside world and a second review (or series of reviews) for each major component of the system.

Each group may be represented by more than one person, especially the first four groups. However, the total number must be kept small so that no participant is tempted to shirk responsibility. Also, preparation time is costly. Fagan[2] recommends only one person in each of four roles (designer, coder-implementer, moderator, tester) for design "inspections."* At the other extreme, the military agencies may marshal a cast of thousands (well,

---

* "Inspection" is an often used synonym for "review." I prefer not to use it. Once a year the state of New Jersey inspects my car and declares it safe (or, with equal likelihood, unsafe pending adjustments). Once a year a mechanic, approved by the Federal Aviation Agency and about to enrich himself at my expense, inspects my airplane and confirms that it is still airworthy. My new tennis racket was inspected by No. 17. I rather think of inspections as wheel pulling, cable stretching, lamination counting operations attended by dark scowls and followed by red tags. By contrast, we *review* books, concerts, and plans for urban rehabilitation, each, like our software products, the result of laborious cognitive processes. And in the process of these reviews, we are forced to make decisions supported not by gauges that read "pass" or "fail," but by judgment.

as many as 200 anyway) for a preliminary design review or critical design review. Actually, except for keynote and plenary sessions, these are really concurrent sets of reviews. Each meeting is rarely attended by more than 20 people, so perhaps the number 20 is a fairer representation of the upper limit. In my own experience, more than 10 persons has seemed awkward (and usually leaves one or two on the periphery of the discussion).

One more item remains: who actually calls for the review? A valid case can be made for making nearly any one of the participants the review muezzin. However, it is doubtful that one can improve on the practice followed by ITT Avionics Division. There the originator of the material is charged with the responsibility for calling for its review. Giving the originator the initiative dispels any suggestion of the author's being pulled, dragging and screaming, to an inquisition. (At the risk of seeming to ape a familiar rubric of parlor psychologists, I have observed that the more capable the system engineer or software designer is, invariably the more eager he is to have the review over and done with — I suspect so that he can immediately move on to another task.) Of course, if the originator neglects to call for the review, software quality assurance is always there with a reminder.

The review meeting.   Very good then. The review has been called, the documentation has been distributed and studied, and the participants have gathered to make common cause in a room with sufficient table space to spread out the material. Who presides? A likely candidate to chair the meeting is the software quality assurance representative. Chairpersons of business meetings are the ones who most often take on the job of distilling the proceedings into some sort of record, and software quality engineers are going to take their own minutes anyway, simply because they are software quality engineers. Also, they neither feed nor are fed by the work reviewed, with the consequence that of the technically cognizant persons who participate in reviews, they are likely to be the most objective. As an alternative, the person calling the review may also serve as chairperson.

Presumably, each of the participants understands that the function of the review is to avert future problems. The originator knows that defects detected in the review will largely go unnoticed by any but the attendees, but defects caught during, say, system integration will reflect with high visibility on their source. This is not to say that the chairperson and other participants should be indifferent to sensitivity. The meeting may be directed to the subject material and not its authorship (following the tenet prescribed by Weinberg[3]), but the subject clearly is the reasoning and faculty of one or more persons. Whether or not these are noble and infinite, they are very personal matters. The more that discovered problems are voiced in the manner of a helpful friend (the most appropriate attitude in any case) or as probing questions, the smoother will be the meeting. And although there is abundant opportunity to display one's trenchant wit, to do so also betrays an attitude that may derail the productivity expected of a review. Above all, reviews are not adversary proceedings.

One must not overdo the issue of sensitivity. Most reviewers have enough common sense to infuse their participation with the proper spirit, and most reviewees have the sense to realize who stands to profit the most. Indeed, experience indicates that the most capable people are never defensive about their work. Even those who are numbered among the less productive professionals are rarely defensive — and then mostly about suggestions that would greatly increase their workload.*

We return to the proceedings: the first item of business is for the author(s) to update the material under review. To say that a review occurs at the end of the requirements phase or each design phase is somewhat idealistic. In the real world, requirements and designs (save at the most detailed level) are usually released when most — say 95 percent — of the work is complete. The remaining 5 percent may take weeks to finish as one awaits the customer's further pondering of a minor point, the results from simulations of algorithms, the arrival by mail of the interface logic for a peripheral device, or whatever. To avoid delaying further progress, the documentation is released with a few TBDs — information to be determined. Some of these may have been completed in the week or so between the final preparation of the documentation and the meeting. Moreover, their resolution may have affected other areas erroneously thought to have been settled. Finally, closing the file on a phase of development does not always end the designer's thought process, and last-minute improvements are not at all uncommon.

Written updates are, of course, preferred over those given orally. It may be annoying to have one's carefully annotated stack of listings replaced with a new one ("There's at least one line changed on almost every page, so I thought I'd just give you all a new set."), but this may be the price to pay for working with up-to-date specifications.

The second item of business is to confirm that all features of the pseudolanguage processor have been exercised and that the listings provided have no faults flagged. Alternatively, the author can explain away the faults that are reported. In a large system it may be necessary to violate certain design rules, such as leaving out a design component because of information TBD.

Most of the time spent in the review meeting is that given to manual

---

* Only once have I observed a designer so defensive that the meeting became argumentative. This was a temporary (as it transpired, very temporary) employee who had done so sloppy and incomplete a piece of work that there was nothing for it but to recommend that most of it be scrapped and started anew.

detection of faults. I have experimented with two formats for this. In the first, each participant in turn goes through his list of questions and suspected defects. The author responds to each one by enlightening, agreeing to clarify, agreeing that the work is at fault, explaining why the reviewer is mistaken, or asking that the matter be deferred for more thorough consideration. Any discussion that a point initiates is likely to draw in others as well, and the dynamic interchange often produces a synergism that would be denied were each review a private one-on-one meeting between reviewer and reviewee.

The second format seems even more successful at encouraging such synergism. Here the author explains the work in a coherent, logical way. It may be as simple a matter as following an all-text specification paragraph by paragraph, or it may require the author's synthesizing bits of computer outputs, drawings, and verbal descriptions one step at a time. Whatever is required, the originator "walks through"* the work, with the reviewers interrupting at appropriate places with their prepared comments or with thoughts evoked on the spot by the author's explanation or the comments of others. The only disadvantage to this format occurs when the originator is unskilled at communicating concepts and the material is not a monolithic homogeneous specification. Until the skill of explaining one's work is developed by exposure to several such reviews, the chairperson must be prepared to help guide the process (one reason the author is not the chairperson of choice).

Whatever the format, the purpose is to flush out defects, questionable practice, and inadequate planning. Perhaps a point can be solved simply by the addition of a few clarifying words. Perhaps the specification of a requirement or a piece of design must be redone. The important thing is to find the problems, not to try to solve them at the meeting. An appropriate action item in the minutes is "Para. 6.12.2: Angela will clarify the measures to be taken upon repeated entries of invalid passwords," not "Reword Para. 6.12.2, from the third sentence on, so that the requirement will be respecified to call for disconnecting the terminal, alerting the console operator, and recording the event, including start and stop times, on the master transaction file." Or, "The design ignores the requirement for degraded mode operation if either computer fails," and not a new piece of design conceived at the meeting.

One reason meetings should avoid trying to solve problems is that design by committee is often inferior to that which, in a more leisurely and contemplative way, would be reached by the person having the primary responsibility. A second reason is that these tend to be expensive solutions.

---

* This, of course, is the essence of design walk-throughs, described in Section 3.9.

Six persons are not likely to solve problems faster than one, but the solution will be six times as expensive. Finally, there simply is not enough time. Reviews should be held to about two hours at a maximum. The work is tiring, and efficiency decreases after the second hour. Indeed, reviews are often divided into several closely spaced sessions, each of a reasonable duration. Given this, it is important to spend all the available time and energy on the detection of problems and the determination of their disposition.

Still, it would be doctrinaire to proclaim that the record of the review may contain no solutions. Suppose a requirement has it that a message is to be output to command console A, and the design outputs it to command console B. Obviously, the action item is "Change the output so that it is received by command console A." Unfortunately, few defects are corrected by the very context of their identification, as was this one; yet many are of sufficiently restricted scope that immediate solution remains a reasonable action. The gray area is vast, and the chairperson's discretion must be used again and again. This is especially true of detailed design reviews, when elder statesmen — now senior designers, test planners, or quality engineers — tend to seize upon any opportunity to once again grab a design problem in their teeth and run.

The EOR (recall its definition in Section 1.7 as a measure of the effectiveness of a defect removal process) of any review will be enhanced greatly by each participant's use of a checklist. Checklists are useful both before the review meeting, when the material is studied, and during the meeting.

One of the last actions at the review meeting is to negotiate agreement on the action items to be assigned. "Negotiate" is probably too strong a word, since one rarely experiences much controversy over the action items. Nevertheless, the time to determine if there is any dissension concerning previously discussed correction requirements, agreement to which is often tacit, is while the issues are still fresh in everyone's mind.

Finally, the more troublesome business of attaching priorities to action items must be tackled. To minimize the time spent discussing priorities, their number should be kept small and each priority condition should be defined simply. Simple descriptions give rise to an occasional loophole, but the minutes of the meeting are a working paper, not a legal document. As an example, one might have the following priorities:

1. Until corrected or until missing information is supplied, further work affected by this item must be suspended.*

2. Until satisfactorily resolved, further work affected by this item cannot be completed.*

---

* If possible, deadlines should be assigned to these.

3. May be resolved at the next issue of the documentation or at the completion of the next phase of work.

Follow-up.   Directly after the meeting, the chairperson should prepare the minutes of the meeting. Alternatively, the job can be delegated to another participant, but one rather likes this important work to be undertaken by the person who is given responsibility for the review's EOR. Each of the other participants will have notes on any action items of personal responsibility, but the minutes are the official chronicle of required corrections and further analyses, the log that should be audited in the days or weeks to come to ensure that defect detection has resulted in defect removal.

The format for the minutes may be simple: identification of each element of documentation (preferably by name and library control unique identifier), date of the meeting, names and functions of the attendees, and the items requiring correction. To each correction item should be attached its priority and the name of the person or function to whom it is assigned. The person named is not necessarily the author of the work reviewed. Occasionally, completion of an action item may require additional information to be supplied by one of the other participants. For example, the acceptability of an assumption or restriction may require analysis by those responsible for a higher-level specification.

Each action item must be closed out at some time. It is not enough to simply identify what needs to be done; defect removal means doing it. The person responsible for confirming the resolution of problems is a function of organization particulars. If there is a quality assurance function, its representative is the obvious candidate. Whoever is appointed, many action items may require technical concordance beyond that of the official auditor. The person charged with responsibility for closing the book on problems will often have to check with at least one other member of the review team. It may even be necessary to call for a second review if among the action items there are any of sufficient magnitude (e.g., an area of major redesign) or of special consequence (e.g., analysis of a critical constraint of questionable acceptability). Regardless of who called the original review, should it appear prudent to call for its iteration, the person responsible for officially closing out action items should take the initiative of recalling the participants. The mere number of action items, however, should not be a criterion for rereview.

3.8   Checklists

As has been noted in the preceding section, checklists are invaluable aids to reviews. A checklist should reflect the generic type of software being developed, the software development environment, and the actual reviews used.

The three checklists that follow are necessarily general in their content — boilerplate, if you will. The assumptions underlying them are that a single top-level design review is sufficient and that no intermediate reviews are required prior to a single detailed design review for each coherent collection of procedures. In fact, intermediate design reviews, and perhaps even more than one level of requirements reviews, may be appropriate for large systems. When the assumption of a single requirements review and no intermediate design reviews does not hold, the following checklists will have to be adapted — and probably expanded — to suit applicable standards.

Requirements reviews

Is the output from the requirements language processor complete and fault-free?

Are all hardware resources (available memory, and so on) defined?

Have applicable response times been defined?

Have minimum reserves of processor load and memory been stipulated?

Have all hardware and external software interfaces been described?

Do all data interfaces identify sources and sinks, formats, ranges, and scales?

Have external software linkages been defined?

For real-time systems, are input rates given either as fixed numbers or, when necessary, as statistical estimators?

Have all functions required by the user or the systems design been accounted for? Have algorithms that are intrinsic to the functional requirements been described? For real-time systems, has the frequency with which each function must be computed been specified?

For each function, can acceptance criteria be inferred?

Are all significant accuracies specified?

Is the initial system state defined, as well as any initialization operations required of the software for the satisfaction of external operations?

Have unique requirements for input validity checks been given? Have fail-safe and self-test provisions been specified? Degraded operation modes?

Is the specification capable of being comprehended by those who will implement it in the design phase?

Are the requirements overspecified? That is, will the designers be overly constrained on unimportant matters?

Have any identifiable plans for later expansion been provided?

Has the experience level of operational personnel been defined?

Does the requirements documentation include descriptions of aspects of the overall system operation the designers should know about?

Are all assumptions, limitations, and constraints identified? Are they all acceptable?

Are all planning documents required by local standards complete and feasible?

Top-level design reviews

Is the output from the design language processor complete (with respect to top-level design standards) and fault-free?

Are global constants and passed data parameterized?

Does the data base specify the structure of tables and files and — to the extent required for traceability to the requirements specification — the format, range, and scale of table entries?

Is the architecture decomposed to the point at which the next phase of design can be started? (This is a matter of project or company standards. If there are no intermediate design phases, three of four hierarchical tiers is a typical standard.) Has each identified component been completely and testably specified?

Is the modular decomposition consistent with local standards for modular strength and coupling?

Is each aspect of the requirements specification addressed?

Is the control system clearly outlined? Does it, or a separate I/O system, avoid potential lockups caused by defective external devices? Is it expansible? If applicable, is it compatible with asynchronous input?

Are there analyses to demonstrate that required throughput, response times, and accuracies will be achieved? Are they sufficiently fine-grained to be credible?

Is there a memory budget to allocate estimated storage requirements for each module, table, and file? Does it leave adequate reserve?

Have self-test, fail-safe, and degraded mode requirements been accounted for? Has an error-handling mechanism been identified?

Have file maintenance procedures been addressed?

How are processing priorities handled?

Are operator interface considerations addressed?

Are stack and queue sizes estimated? Are provisions made to guard against overflow?

Are hardware and software test resources identified? Is further action required to obtain them when needed?

Does pretest documentation (including integration plans) conform to standards?

Are any unique programming conventions, tools, or techniques anticipated that are not covered by the computer program development plan?

Are all assumptions explicit and acceptable?

Are there any limitations and constraints beyond those found in the requirements documentation?

Detailed design

Is the output from the design language processor complete and fault-free?

Does the decomposition of each applicable component, as identified in the top-level design documentation, adhere to local standards of modular strength and coupling?

Are the external specifications of each module complete and testable?

For the lowest ranking program unit (if different from a module), are the external specifications complete and testable? For these program units (whether or not the same as modules), is the description of each sufficiently detailed that each design quantum (flowchart symbol, PDL statement, or whatever) clearly indicates the scope of the code that will implement it?

Are all relevant aspects of the top-level design traceable to elements of the detailed design?

Have missing details from the system data description (tables and files) been filled in?

Have all numerical techniques (e.g., polynomial approximations) been analyzed for accuracy and range? Are they consistent with higher specifications? With processing load allocations of those specifications?

Has critical timing, if any, been analyzed? Are module or transmodule execution load estimates consistent with requirements?

Has the top-level design memory budget been expanded into further detail and updated? Are memory reserve requirements violated?

Is the design structured? Have typing capabilities of the programming language been utilized to advantage?

Have validity checks been stipulated? Can corrective action be taken by the module that traps an error? Are diagnostic messages usable?

Are corrective actions for potentially invalid conditions (e.g., dividing by zero or the "noise" remaining after the subtraction of two similar values) reasonable with regard to minimizing the effect of system or input failures? With regard to the full range of valid input?

Can the termination conditions for each loop be realized?

Are conventions for the nesting of loops and conditional branches violated?

Are queues protected against interrupts?

Are procedure linkage conventions violated?

Have operator dialogues been completely specified?

Are all local data identified?

Are all loop variables properly initialized? Indexes properly incremented?

Are all predicates correctly specified with regard to sense?

Are all data units and formats consistent with global and interface data specifications?

Have functional test specifications for each module been prepared? Have structural test criteria been specified?

Are there any limitations or constraints beyond those specified by higher-level documentation?

3.9   Walk-Throughs

Walk-throughs can take as many forms as their spelling.* The kernel of a walk-through is a review meeting devoted exclusively to technical matters, as in contrast to planning business and documentation standards. Beyond that, the usual variables are:

- Participants. Peers of the person whose work is being reviewed or a heterogeneous team as in design reviews or a combination of the two.
- Preparation. Since the reviewee will describe the work in considerable detail, the amount of pre-walk-through study is sometimes reduced to little more than orientation.
- Checklists. Sometimes used, sometimes not.
- Traceability to higher-level specifications. Sometimes explicitly sought, sometimes not.
- Attention paid to quality matters other than defects (as in Section 3.4). Some are included, others not.

Some notes on applicability: Designs are more easily walked through than are requirements specifications. Accordingly, requirements walk-

---

* Walkthrus, walk-thrus, walk thrus, walkthroughs, walk throughs.

throughs are encountered more rarely than are design walk-throughs. Even within design, the more detailed the design stage, the more popular is the walk-through as an alternative to a review.

The format of the walk-through is based on the author's stepwise exposition of the work, a sort of software show-and-tell. Interruptions occur frequently, with further explanation given or a fault noted for subsequent action. Unless the participants have prepared themselves much as for a design review, they will have to think in real time to spot problems, yet not fall behind the exposition. As fatiguing as design reviews are, this can be worse.

Where peer walk-throughs are used, the effectiveness of the review is a measure of the reviewers' willingness to set aside their own work to prepare themselves to help improve the work of another. Clearly, some are more willing to do so than others.

Walk-through follow-up is generally more informal than that of reviews, although there is no inherent reason for this.

Walk-throughs that follow the methodology of reviews (with respect to defect findings, not withstanding the restriction of scope) should produce EORs equal to those of reviews. All other types of walk-throughs will find fewer. Their redeeming quality is that they require fewer labor-hours. Even if a walk-through slanted toward reviews is used, it remains to examine planning aspects and to audit for adherence to standards. The former can be handled by a relatively brief meeting between, say, the designer's supervisor, perhaps a test group representative, the designer, and the software quality assurance representative. Auditing for standards can be left to quality assurance to perform in isolation.

In short, walk-throughs are increasingly effective as the distinction between them and reviews narrows, but matters of format aside, topics not covered in walk-throughs still need to be attended to by one means or another.

We might also note that walk-throughs tend to have the same problems concerning their duration that attend more formal reviews. Efficiency remains paramount regardless of format if all items are to be covered. Perhaps because technical matters always seem the more pressing — and are in any case the more interesting — the last business of reviews is nearly always that related to planning. This, and the principal differences between walk-throughs and reviews, suggest the following observation:

> There was a young software guru
> Who decided to hold a review.
> So much for intent;
> The time got all spent,
> And he said, " 'Twas a lovely walk-through."

3.10   Summary

1. Apart from the direct exposure of defects, of which there are many kinds to look for, the verification aspects of reviews serve as a mechanism for project control.

2. The reports generated by requirements language and design language processors yield insights useful to reviewers. These processors, however, should properly be used by the authors of the pseudocode, rather than reviewers, to uncover defects.

3. Besides clear-cut defects, reviews should not neglect other issues related to quality. These include testability, readability, the thoroughness of analyses, reliability, usability, complexity, maintainability, and the potential for reusability.

4. Of equal importance to the finding of unqualified defects are assumptions, limitations, and constraints. These should be evaluated (and uncovered if not explicit) with regard to the presumed operational conditions.

5. Prior to a review meeting, each of the participants should study the material to be reviewed and should prepare lists of issues to be raised. Checklists should be used.

6. The participants at a review should be a small but diverse group of persons all of whom have specific project responsibilities. Included among these persons are representatives of each function directly influenced by the contents of the material reviewed.

7. The reviews in a minimum set are those of requirements, top-level design, and detailed design. Large systems will require intermediate design reviews as well, and possibly more than one staged requirements review.

8. Reviews are conducted not as adversary proceedings, but as cooperative projects that, in the end, will pay off most of all to the originator of the work.

9. The first items of business at a review meeting are to update the material reviewed and to confirm fault-free output from the pseudo-language processors used.

10. A preferred format is that in which the author of the work reviewed guides the progress through the material in an expository manner interrupted by the other participants at any time.

11. Review meetings are not for the purpose of solving problems, but for identifying them. To solve all but the most obvious problems is inefficient.

12. The use of checklists by all participants, not just the chairperson, should be mandatory.

13. Before concluding a review meeting, agreement should be obtained on all action items. Moreover, the items should be prioritized to the goal of earliest complete and correct input for the next phase of work.

14. The minutes of the meeting, comprised mostly of action items, constitute an auditable log of required corrections and completions.

15. Major revisions and those critical to performance may require the convening of a second review.

16. Walk-throughs are much like design reviews of the preferred format (item 10, above), but they are directed exclusively to technical matters to the exclusion of planning issues and adherence to standards. They also may be less formal with regard to ensuring diverse participation, preparation, the use of checklists, and traceability to higher-level specifications. They may give short shrift to quality matters apart from clear-cut defects.

17. Walk-throughs are more suitable to design than to requirements and more suitable to detailed design than to top-level design.

References

1. Robert Dunn and Richard Ullman, *Quality Assurance for Computer Software,* McGraw-Hill, New York, 1981, pp. 230–231.
2. M. E. Fagan, "Design and Code Inspection to Reduce Errors in Program Development," *IBM Systems J.,* vol. 15, no. 3, 1976, pp. 182–211.
3. Gerald M. Weinberg, *The Psychology of Computer Programming,* Van Nostrand Reinhold Company, New York, 1971.

Chapter

4

Code Reviews

In the Paleolithic Era of computing, the only product of what we now call software development was computer code. If not the only product of our enlightened times, it remains the central issue of development. We encounter it here for the first, but scarcely the last, time. Most of the balance of the book is also focused on code.

The act of writing source code and entering it into a file has obvious hazard for error. But it is not only these faults that must be routed out but also those left over from the requirements and design phases. Unfortunately, they are not as obvious in code as they were in documentation. Perhaps it would be more accurate to say that they are even more disguised in code than in their native form. Were code reviews to pay the kind of attention to requirements and design defects that was the substance of the earlier reviews, they would be excessively costly. Going one step further, it can even be said that it is unlikely that they will detect any defects in the requirements definition or the top-level design. Detailed design faults may be detected, however; especially those that derive from ambiguities in the detailed design documentation.

In any case, the number of faults minted during the code production phase leaves ample opportunity for profitable defect removal. A number of examples of these follow.

4.1 Code Defects

The following set of defect types does not include any that we can reasonably expect an assembler or compiler to detect. Defects that yield to static analysis techniques are defined more fully in Chapter 5. For convenience, the set of code defects is divided into three classes: logic and control, data operations and computations, and all others. The following constituents of these classes represent those that are found in the code review records to which I have access. More imaginative programmers than I have known may have invented others.

Logic and control

Unreachable code. This results from contradictory or redundant branch conditions. Described in Section 5.2.

Improper nesting of loops and branches. This is defined in Section 5.1.

Inverted predicates. A common fault. *If* A > B *then exit* is a fault if the exit condition should be that B exceeds A.

Incomplete predicates. Actually, we should not exit until B > A *and* COUNTER > A, but the second part was forgotten.

Improper sequencing of processes. See Section 5.1.

Infinite loops. See Section 5.1.*

Instruction modification. Is this a defect or a violation of standards? Let us call it a defect, since this once common practice is the very antithesis of structured programming. In any case, there are few programming shops today that will not demand the removal of instances of dynamic instruction modification — if they are detected.

Failure to save or restore registers. One of the burdens laid on assembly language programmers is the necessity of saving the contents of whatever registers they need at the time of procedure entry and then restoring them as part of the exit process. When registers are few in number (by definition, they almost always are), this save-and-restore process may bracket loops within procedures as well, as programmers try to optimize their inner loops with efficient register operations. Register housekeeping leaves much room for programmer error.

Unauthorized recursion. See Section 5.1.

Missing labels or code. Also in Section 5.1.

Unreferenced labels. These are treated in Section 5.2.

Data operations and computations

Missing validity tests. For its own protection, any data imported by a procedure — either as program input or from another procedure — that have the potential of causing catastrophic error should be tested before being used.

---

* If Section 5.1 says to see Section 4.1, we have one.

For example, the Fortran computed *goto* [*goto* $(I_1, I_2, \ldots, I_n), K$] may, depending on the language implementation, cause a branch out of the program boundaries for $K = 0$. Another important validity test is that of a divisor that has the potential of "noise":

```
read A,B
C: = A/(A − B)
```

Before computing the ratio, a validity test should be applied to make certain that $|A − B|$ is above a computational threshold. Operating systems that provide recoverable run time error traps (they will allow processing to continue after taking predictable recovery action and outputting an error message) reduce the need for validity tests of unlikely failure conditions.

Incorrect access of array components. If a computed subscript or index can exceed the boundaries of a declared array, we have the potential for failure. If it is impossible to recode to avoid this contingency, validity checks should be incorporated as for missing validity tests.

Mismatched parameter lists. See Section 5.1.

Initialization faults. Usually this means failure to initialize, but it may imply incorrect initialization as well. For example, the header record of a file may contain the information needed to initialize the variable X, but the computation $Z = X + Y$ may erroneously be made before reading the record by using background data or the header record of the last file processed.

Anachronistic data. This is the more general case of which using the header record of the last file processed is an example. In any iterative process, the data being operated on may erroneously include a mix of the data pertinent to the current iteration and data from previous iterations.

Undefined variable. Often found as an initialization defect. See Section 5.1.

Misuse of variables, both locally and globally. Limited discussion of this omnibus defect class is found in Section 5.1.

Data fields unconstrained by natural or defined data boundaries. An example is the definition of six fields of three binary flags each, all to be referenced as a single word of a 16-bit machine. Or trying to input two Hollerith characters in one byte. Or defining a 40-byte record and then cramming it with a 41-character string.

Inefficient data transport. Poor handling of input and output operations will not cause a program to fail, but it may have a fatal effect on throughput. Programmers learning a new language frequently give least attention to input-output statements or library routines. Having learned one way of gaining access to data, a programmer may stick with it while sharpening skills in the use of more frequently required semantic and syntactical forms. In a program written in an eccentric Fortran II dialect, it was necessary to locate the last record of a sequential file. The system allowed no way to do this except by sequentially reading each record until encountering an end of file. Each of the records was read by using Fortran format conversions, even though the data went unused. As it turned out, the programmer was unaware that a high-speed binary input construction was available to be used.

All others

Calls to subprograms that do not exist. See Section 5.1.

Improper program linkages. Also in Section 5.1.

Input-output faults. These include incorrect communication protocols and external data mismatches. The former is a frequent code defect in embedded programs. The programmers must interface with a variety of equipment each of which may have a unique set of status flags, query commands, and time-outs. External data mismatches may take a number of forms: reversing the order of bits, wrong weight for the least significant bit, inverting the sense of discrete flags, and so on.

Prodigal programming. If ever there was an inclusive category, this is it; for it encompasses all constructions that are wasteful of execution time or hardware resources. The examples under the inefficient input-output category could fit here as well. Other examples include placing one-time operations within a loop instead of preceding it, recursive routines that require excessive stack storage for variables, tardiness in releasing input-output ports, manual assignment of procedure origins that leave "enough room to spare," and so forth. Although these are most frequently the products of inexperienced programmers, no one is immune from an occasional oversight.

Failure to implement the design. Most of the above defect types are absolute faults, that is, faults that are independent of the purpose of the code. Even more importantly, they may be independent of the dictates of a program design. That leaves us with verifying that the code conforms to the design for it, which is a topic in itself.

4.2 Code Reviews as a Verification Technique

At the most detailed level, it is fairly simple to verify that the code implements the design. For a given procedure, it is an easy matter to take each quantum of design (flowchart symbol, design language statement, and so on) and find its counterpart in the code. This is especially fast work if PDL statements are used to annotate the code. However, it is not a trivial job. Good design documentation, even at the detailed level, is versed more in terms of the problem — or at least the overall software design — than in the last step of solution: code. Thus, we find that a design statement FIND MOST RECENT PAYMENT may resolve in source code to

```
16   rewind, FILEA
17   LAST_DATE: = START_DATE
18   do while not EOF
19     call GET_RECORD(FILEA,RECORD,EOF)
20     call GET_DATE(RECORD,DATE)
21     if CONV(DATE) > CONV(LAST_DATE)
22       then LAST_DATE: = DATE
23     endif
24   endo
```

Thus, even with single-statement array assignment (lines 17 and 22), we have nine statements, two subroutine calls, and one function call (CONV, which converts characters to binary) to relate to a single line of pseudo-code; not difficult, but not insignificant either.

Establishing correspondence between design details and code is only part of the verification task. Although previously the detailed design has been verified with respect to the overall software structure, we want also at this time to double-check that verification. Specifically, the code should be examined for traceability to the external specifications of the design represented by the code. Depending on how detailed the detailed design gets — a matter of management policy — these external specifications are those for either individual procedures or collections of procedures identified as a single module in the overall design structure. In either case, it is both possible and profitable to attempt to determine on paper if the code will perform the role explicitly assigned to it.

There is only one systematic way to accomplish this. In much the same manner one used for choosing funtional test cases,* module or procedure entry conditions are selected. Step by step, each instruction reached by them is manually "executed." When the exit conditions are satisfied, the status of output variables and associated global data is examined and compared with the status implied by the external specifications.

Undeniably, this procedure may be painstaking; indeed, if the overall design has poor structure, it may be impractical except for a very small sample of the specification space. Given good structure, however, with

---

* The proper selection of functional test cases involves several factors, and it is discussed in Chapter 9. For the present, let us assume it is adequate to select input that is characteristic of the input space. An example (the input conditions in Figure 4.1) follows shortly.

individual elements of the program performing single or closely related functions, the external specifications are normally narrow enough in scope to permit selection of a usefully representative set of test cases. Anticipating Section 4.5, code reviews are performed on individual procedures or (more reasonably) small groups of functionally associated procedures. Also, no attempt is made to trace all path domains. Verification to procedure or module external specifications is limited to the scope of those specifications. However, housekeeping, validity checks, and the like, while not explicitly called out in the definition of performance for the software under review and thus not properly a part of the verification process, are attended to — if less rigorously — when step-by-step simulated execution is used as the medium for code reviews. As will be seen in Section 4.6, the procedure of simulated execution is the recommended format for most of the activity that goes on in a code review.

When manually stepping through a program, it is difficult to remember the state of the several variables at each point. One can scribble directly onto the listing, but one runs out of both space and pen colors after several iterations of the same loop. A helpful technique is to build a table of external parameters, local variables directly associated with performance characteristics, and applicable system tables and files. As one steps through the table, each entry is filled in to represent the response (to relevant changes of input) of significant lines of code — branches, procedure returns, loop terminations, and so on. The table, in effect, acts to display the state of the program at critical times.

Consider a program to compare two files of 80-character records. If the two corresponding records do not agree, the record number and contents of each are printed. However, to most concisely report that the two files are skewed by one record (a record deleted or added at an arbitrary location in one file but not the other), the program is to recognize that this has happened and recover from the skew. Let the following represent the code for this problem, and let Figure 4.1 represent the table used to summarize the program status:

```
     procedure COMP(FILEA,FILEB)
     boolean variables: AFLAG,BFLAG,AEOF,BEOF,SAME
     integer variables: AKNT,BKNT
     string arrays: A(80),ALAST(80),B(80),BLAST(80)
1    AKNT: = 0
2    BKNT: = 0
3    AFLAG: = TRUE
4    BFLAG: = TRUE
5    do while not AEOF and not BEOF
6      if AFLAG   --Don't read A if B is behind by 1 record
7        then
8          AKNT: = AKNT + 1
9          call BININ(FILEA,A,AEOF)    --BININ reads one record
10       else AFLAG: = TRUE   --But read the next
```

```
11  endif
12  if BFLAG    --Don't read B if A is behind by 1 record
13    then
14      BKNT: =  BKNT + 1
15      call BININ(FILEB,B,BEOF)
16    else BFLAG: =  TRUE    --But read the next
17  endif
18  call COMPRA(A,B,1,80,SAME)    --Are current records
19  if not SAME    --the same?
20    then
21      print AKNT,A,BKNT,B
22      call CMPR(ALAST,B,1,80,SAME)    --Does current B record
23      if SAME    --equal the last A record?
24        then AFLAG: =  FALSE    --Don't read next A
25        else
26          call CMPR(BLAST,A,1,80,SAME)    --Does current A record
27          if SAME    --equal the last B?
28            then BFLAG: =  FALSE    --Don't read next B
29          endif
30        endif
31      endif
32      call MOVE(A,ALAST)    --Save A and B
33      call MOVE(B,BLAST)
34    endo
35  print AKNT,BKNT
36  end COMP
```

The person best able to construct a table like that of Figure 4.1 is the programmer of the subject code. However, the programmer is not the best person to fill in the entries except when accompanied by others. If we leave completion of the table to the programmer working in isolation, we run the predictable and entirely understandable risk of the table's being filled in as the programmer *intended* the program to work, not as it was actually coded.

Programmers, in fact, often use devices similar to Figure 4.1 when desk-checking their own work prior to testing or when attempting to find the cause of a failed test. Desk-checking has a venerable position in computer programming, and it is quite possible that desk-checking by a second programmer is the progenitor of code reviews. But desk-checking and code reviews are not the same thing.

4.3   Desk-Checking

If the term "code review" has not quite the same meaning in all programming quarters, "desk-checking" does not necessarily have the same meaning to two programmers working in adjacent offices. It would seem that desk-checking (or code reading) can mean any of the following:

- Looking over the code for obvious defects (e.g., misspelled tokens)
- Checking for correct procedure interfaces

FILEA: ABLE, BRAVO, CHAS, DELTA, EASY, FOX, HOTEL, INDIA, JULIET, eof

FILEB: ABLE, CHAS, DELTA, ECHO, FOX, GOLF, HOTEL, INDIA, JULIET, eof

Line	AKNT	BKNT	A	B	ALAST	BLAST	AFLAG	BFLAG	SAME	Print Output
15	1	1	ABLE	ABLE	UND	UND	T	T		
19									T	
33					ABLE	ABLE				
15	2	2	BRAVO	CHAS						
19									F	
21										2, BRAVO, 2, CHAS
23									F	
27									F	
33					BRAVO	CHAS				
15	3	3	CHAS	DELTA						
19									F	
21										3, CHAS, 3, DELTA
23									F	
27									T	
28								F		
33					CHAS	DELTA				
9	4		DELTA							
16								T		
19								T		
33					DELTA	DELTA				
15	5	4	EASY	ECHO						
19									F	
21										5, EASY, 4, ECHO
23									F	
27									F	
33					EASY	ECHO				
15	6	5	FOX	FOX						
19									T	
33					FOX	FOX				
15	7	6	HOTEL	GOLF						
19									F	
21										7, HOTEL, 6, GOLF
23									F	
27									F	
33					HOTEL	GOLF				
15	8	7	INDIA	HOTEL						
19									F	
21										8, INDIA, 7, HOTEL
23									T	
24								F		
33					INDIA	HOTEL				
10									T	
15		8		INDIA						
19									T	
33					INDIA	INDIA				
15	9	9	JULIET	JULIET						
19									T	
35										9, 9,

Figure 4.1 Program states during a manual "test."

- Looking for any small subset of the defects listed in Section 4.1
- Reading the comments to develop a sense of what the code does and then comparing it to its external specifications
- Comparing comments to design documentation
- Stepping through with input conditions contrived to "exercise" *all* paths, including those that are not directly related to the external specifications
- Checking for compliance with programming standards (of which more in the next section)
- Any combination of the above items, but rarely more than two or three of those items.

In theory, there is no reason why desk-checking should not find as many defects as code reviews. Indeed, if the desk-checker uses a checklist, such as that of Section 4.7, and steps through the program as in Section 4.2, desk-checking is tantamount to a one-person code review, equally effective and less costly. The problem is that it takes an unusual degree of discipline for a programmer, lacking the reinforcement that team play offers, to sit down and grind through several pages of someone else's code. It is easy to lose interest after an hour or so. Any overheard conversation immediately engages one. One suddenly recalls a telephone call that should be made before the end of the month. One thinks of the report due next week and starts to mentally organize it. Anything but digesting the dreary dust-dry material sitting on the desk.

Still, there are some people who are capable of doing this. (I know of at least one who actually enjoys it and is good at it.) However, such persons are few, and rarely can it be prudent to plan on having the right persons available when needed. It is far more realistic to plan on code reviews structured with checklists and aids for manual "execution" with the author of the code present to remind the other participants of the meaning of local variables and with the involvement of each person serving to reinforce the interest of the others and to ensure that the standards for reviews are not relaxed.

Most importantly, managers should make a clear distinction between both code reviews and independent desk-checking and the desk-checking performed by the author of the code. Although the author will discover some faults, he is likely to view some constructions from the same erroneous point of reference that existed when the fault was created. Whatever causes a programmer to transpose the terms of an expression so that a binary switch is coded as FLAG:= FLAG − 1 may occur with equal likelihood when the same statement is read by the same programmer. Moreover, whatever misinterpretations of the external specifications or the design were originally made by the programmer will surely be repeated upon reading the code.

4.4 Standards Checking

Deviations from programming standards are not defects, at least not in the sense that they lead directly to failures or cause inefficient operation, but they may be detrimental to program maintenance, may result in undue complexity and the camouflage of defects, and may by detracting from readability, slow the process of failure diagnosis during active test. Code made less readable by lax attention to standards is also slower to review, which establishes a case for a one-person standards check prior to a code review.

The scope of standards differs among the thousands of programming shops, but a representative list includes:

- Annotation — banners, prologues, in-line comments
- Placement of nonexecutable statements (Fortran formats, order-of-data declarations, and so on)
- Indentation conventions (unnecessary if the software development environment includes a pretty-print tool)
- Structured control flow
- Data and statement naming conventions
- Extent to which typing capabilities must be exploited
- Aliasing restrictions
- Maximum nesting levels of branches and loops
- Prohibited use of constants as procedure call parameters
- Any standards peculiar to the semantic or syntactical forms of the programming language

None of these is unimportant (some even smack more of good programming practice than the desire to establish local conventions for improving efficiency), but failure to find every violation will not evoke a calamity, either. Thus, the manner in which compliance to standards is confirmed should weigh the cost of reviewing against the appropriate level of standards purity. A 95 percent level of compliance is a reasonable level to attain, and it can be achieved at fairly low cost. That is, depending on just how badly the raw code adheres to standards, 95 percent compliance is possible with scanning (as opposed to more careful examination). A page of code can be scanned in less than 5 minutes. Occasionally, one has to backtrack to close a loop, but the 5-minute limit holds most of the time. This means that the total time spent in checking a large system, say a 200,000-line program, will only be about two labor-months at most — not a bad price. To strive for 99 percent conformity, however, will increase the cost fourfold or more.

The most simple way to document standards discrepancies is by annotating the margins of the source listing.

To maximize total productivity, code standard compliance should be audited prior to the code review. A quality assurance representative is an obvious candidate for this job. The alternative, covering standards at the code review, is certainly feasible, but the reviewers will have to remind themselves not to overlook standards in the quest for defects more directly related to performance.

4.5   How Much Code?

The real question posed is "What is the appropriate decomposition level for a code review?," and the answer is influenced both by management needs for visibility and control and by technical matters. Superficially, it might appear that a good answer is to define the scope of a code review as the quantum of code for which there exist external specifications identified in the overall program structure. However, this may often lead to code reviews covering only single procedures. It scarcely seems worthwhile to try to accommodate the schedules of, say, four persons to convene a review meeting devoted to only one procedure.

An alternative approach is to define the scope of a code review as the group of connected procedures assigned to a single programmer as a single item in the work-breakdown structure. Such a group may often appear only as a single module of the software architecture prior to the start of detailed design and in that case the approach also satisfies the objective of the first solution offered. It also provides an excellent opportunity to detect inconsistencies among the several related procedures.

It may also be necessary to consider the influence of top-down development in it purest form. Here a module at a given hierarchical tier is designed, coded, and tested before design is even started on its subordinate modules. Assuming that code reviews should be held prior to unit test (as they should be), we really have no choice of the scope of a code review.

Most production milieus do not demand a one-to-one correspondence between the preliminary hierarchical decomposition and the program structure chart. That is, a given module defined in the top-level or intermediate stages of design is allowed to be further decomposed into individual procedures during detailed design — moreover, often by the programmer who will write the necessary code. Even when pure top-down development is the stated methodology, the actual module that is designed, coded, and tested is, generally, a collection of procedures of several structural tiers.

In any case, it seems most attractive to define the scope of a code review in terms of the elements of the system visible on a management-level family tree of modules. Those elements lend themselves quite tidily to single tasks in the work-breakdown structure as it applies to the detailed design, code, and (possibly) unit-level defect removal procedures. Moreover, such elements of the family tree will have documented performance specifications assigned to them against which the code can be verified.

4.6 The Review Process

As with requirements and design reviews, we have three phases to consider: preparation, the review meeting, and follow-up. As we shall see, there is much similarity between code reviews and the earlier reviews, but there are notable differences as well.

Preparation. There is little disagreement that the proper time to conduct a code review is after the subject code has been written and before it has been exposed to active test. (This notwithstanding the common knowledge that some programmers will want to perform some informal testing on the sly, as it were, before making their code public information.) However, other events also occur in this interval: compilation or assembly, audit to code standards, and static analysis. We then have four events, and it is possible that all 24 chronological permutations of them have been advocated at one time or another. In my view, there is only one correct sequence.

Scheduling the review. For maximum productivity, the sequence should be

Compilation or assembly

Static analysis

Standards audit

Review

Although it has been recommended that compilation follow review, this order seems almost totally lacking in merit. Compilation for the amount of code that can be handled by a single review will take a minute of computer time and 15 minutes (not including the search for elusive defects hinted at by obscure compiler diagnostics) of programmer time for each iteration of the compilation process. A code review will involve, say, four persons for 2 hours or so. Why use their expensive time to accomplish the work of a machine? The only mitigating circumstance is that caused by recondite compiler diagnostics.

```
LINE 85: ILLEGAL OPERATION
```

The programmer looks at line 85 and reads

```
HYP(I):= SQRT(S(J) ** 2 + S(K) ** 2)
```

There is nothing patently illegal about this. Parentheses match; SQRT must be in the library (would the compiler know if it were not?) since it was used 10 lines earlier; and nothing else looks amiss. Only after 10 minutes of study does the programmer think to check the array declarations. There the problem is found: HYP is declared as a two-dimensional array. Now admittedly, keen-eyed reviewers might have spotted this and saved an additional 10 minutes of programmer time — but then again they might not have. Of course, programming managers who have the luxury of compilers that really care to output their very best will not give the issue a second thought.

Static analysis is a powerful enough defect detection mechanism to be discussed in a separate chapter, and it is — the next. No two static analysis systems provide the same defect detection capabilities or the same synopses of the code processed, but to the extent that they can find faults, such faults may be ignored by the code review team. As we saw with the use of pseudolanguage processors in Chapter 3, the reports summarizing code structure are useful for reducing the code review effort. In particular, the most useful are

- Cross-references of where variables and constants are used
- Use of symbols (as string, integer, and so on)
- Hierarchy of procedure calls

These are discussed in Section 5.4. Their use is analogous to the summary reports produced by pseudolanguage processors. Accordingly, we have yet another reason to delay code reviews until the use of static analysis has been completed.

Static analysis systems may include capabilities for identifying violations of coding standards. If so, we should want to delay the standards audit until the static analyzer has had a chance to do its thing, again for the obvious reason of not wanting to use a person to do the work of a machine.

For the reason given earlier, improving readability, the code standards audit should precede the code review. Thus, the review brings up the rear of these four related activities.

Before launching further into the business of review preparation, we digress to consider other issues related to the order of passive defect removal. Assuming one is of the small minority having access to the necessary tools, when should symbolic testing (or symbolic execution, if you will) and formal correctness proofs* be applied? Since both are labor-intensive, it seems most productive to delay their use until after active unit test. Indeed, since changes to the code of modules are not unlikely during integration testing, it may be advisable to delay symbolic testing and proof of correctness until after the module in question has had all of its directly subordinate modules integrated (assuming that there are subordinate modules). On the other hand, incorrect results obtained by symbolic testing require much less diagnosis to find the embedded defect than do the results of active test. Thus, a good case can be made for using symbolic testing prior to unit testing. At the risk of equivocating, I suspect that the order of testing should depend mostly on the type of code. For procedures that are concerned mostly with mathematical or logical operations, as opposed to data pushing or input-output handling, symbolic execution should probably come first. Others should be dynamically tested first. (In either case, formal proofs should await the completion of dynamic testing.)

Finally, let us note the argument that since code reviews are also labor-intensive, perhaps symbolic testing and correctness proofs could equally well precede code reviews. This contention may be rejected if we consider that the time duration of a code review is less a function of the number of resident defects than it is of other factors.

Participation. Fewer people are required for a code review than are usually needed for a requirements or design review. A typical cast includes the programmer, someone from the design team, a quality assurance representative, and a member of the software test group. The test people will have to know the code fairly well if they are to be able to devise structural tests across module boundaries and diagnose problems, so for them reviews serve as a learning experience as well.

Some explanation is required to define the design group that is represented. This is the lowest-level design group not tasked with writing code. For example, if we have but two design groups, as in Table 3.1, one concerned only with top-level design and the other with both detailed design and coding, the design representative at the review is one of the senior designers responsible for the overall design.

The quality assurance representative serves two purposes: This person

---

* If not generated concurrently with code, of which more in Chapter 6.

increases the team to a size big enough to provide confidence that there will be some mutual stimulation (three is just too few) and further acts as the cop on the beat to ensure that the standards for the review are adhered to.

It must, of course, be remembered that everyone at the review must be fluent in the language of the source code.

Activities before the review.   For the reasons given in Section 3.7, the ideal person to call for the review is the author of the code. Alternatives include the author's supervisor and quality assurance.

Oddly, the most important material to be distributed to the participants before the review is not the code but the relevant design documentation. To trace the code back to its design and its external specifications, one must know what they are. The reviewers should be sufficiently familiar with them that, in the course of the review meeting, they will know where to find senior referents for the code. The documents are all that really need to be studied ahead of time. Compilation and assembly listings may be studied in isolation by each participant if the spirit so moves, but the code will be examined in detail at the meeting anyway. As a practical matter, to expedite the production process the meeting will very likely be called before a clean compilation or assembly is available, so a study may be a moot business.

It is possible that the results of static analysis will be available before the meeting. If so, copies of the analyzer system output may be distributed to help the participants orient themselves to the detailed code structure.

The review meeting.   If the review team can be held to as few as four persons, it is doubtful that a chairperson is required. However, there are those who hold that no meeting can be productive unless a specific person has been designated to be responsible for its success. If a chairperson is necessary, the quality assurance representative is the first choice for the same reasons as given in Section 3.7. The second choice is the design team member. In a sense, the designers whose work is implemented by the subject code are the customers of the code. Why not let them preside over this form of preliminary acceptance auditing? Whether or not there is a chairperson, someone must be responsible for keeping track of the items requiring correction. In the absence of a chairperson, I would go with software QA as my first choice and either the design team or test group delegate as my second choice.

The first item of business is to make certain that everyone agrees that the code is in response to the correct design information. It is quite possible that, in the interval since the programmer started code generation, design changes had been made. Now, if the programmer also authored the detailed design that is implemented by the reviewed code, there should be no question that the code agrees with that design. However, any changes made to the (previously reviewed) detailed design should be referred to the appropriate change control board. In the event others were responsible for the detailed design, it is necessary that the version or revision identification in the source file agree with that on the design documentation. Whether or not the programmer is the detailed designer, we have also to check that the next higher level design has not changed without the programmer's knowledge (or implementation of that knowledge).

To this end, more times than not, the design representative or the programmer or the two talking in unison will draw attention to at least one undocumented change to a higher-level design document. Given this, the minutes for the meeting will show an action item for a change request to be considered, a request that will ultimately touch other project functions possibly all the way back to the system analysts.

Directly the configuration traceability issue has been dispensed with, the reports generated by static analysis and the code standards auditor are examined. In looking over the static analysis results, the review team must assure itself that all of the defect detection faculties of the analyzer have been used. The potential scope of the review will have been reduced by the checks falling within the capabilities of the analysis system, so it must be established that they were used. Analogously to the use of pseudocode processor defect detection reports (Section 3.7), any faults remaining in the static analysis reports should be explained by the programmer or by the person, if other than the programmer, who ran the static analyzer. The code should also be checked to confirm the resolution of discrepancies reported by the standards auditor (presumably, a member of the review team).

Now it is time to get to the meat of the review, the quest for those faults beyond the ken of both the compiler and the static analysis system. Assuming the reviewers did not individually attempt to find bugs prior to the meeting, the only feasible formats are those of a step-by-step audible reading of the code or a walk-through. In no other way can everyone focus on the same area of code. If one is always to make sense out of code segments, linear step-by-step reading (that is, not deviating from the sequential progression of statements) can work only with structured code.

In any case, the walk-through format seems the more advantageous.* However, a walk-through format does not guarantee an efficiently orga-

---

* Some people consider a code review using a walk-through process to be a code walk-through in contradistinction to a code review (or inspection). For example, "Walk-throughs differ from inspections in that the programmer does not narrate a reading of the product by the team."[1] I think that the differences lie elsewhere (see Section 4.8) and that the precepts of a code review can be embraced by either format. In any case, nomenclature is less material to defect removal than is process.

nized perusal of the code. A fairly reliable way of avoiding uncorrelated random excursions through the code is to use test cases, as described in Section 4.2. (Many software engineers regard the use of test cases as an intrinsic part of the walk-through process. To them without test cases you may call the meeting anything you like, but not a "walk-through.") Finally, let us note that the use of test cases will further satisfy the goal of verification; assuming, of course, that the reviewers can be assured that the test cases are sufficient in scope for that purpose.

As the author steps the test data and their transformation products through the program, the reviewers will continually refer to their checklists for evaluation criteria. The synopses generated by the static analysis system will be used extensively as reference material. Someone — perhaps the programmer — will mark one of the listings to show the first "execution" of each decision-to-decision path. It may be instructive not only to note that a decision-to-decision path has been traversed but also to mark each time it happens. The count of path executions can lead to unexpected insights into the structure of the program. Among possible results is the identification of inner loops that are candidates for further study aimed at improving efficiency.

Also, as each element of the design has been found to be correctly implemented, the design documentation should be so marked. This is not necessary, however, if the detailed design was documented in program design language and was reused as the annotation of the source code.

It would be useful to synopsize the actual review process by a dialogue, such as one finds in various training and promotional films.* This is, of course, made impossible by the number of variables involved. However, for those who have never seen one, perhaps the low key of a code review can be conveyed through the following short scenario:

> NARRATOR (PROGRAMMER): So with the two pointers now equal, we escape the loop at this point.
> FIRST VOICE: Do we know they'll always end up equal?
> SECOND VOICE: Eventually they have to be.
> 1V: Unless, of course, *Demob* made an irregular exit.
> N: Yeah, that's why I check the entry pointer first thing.
> 1V: Right.
> 2V: Okay, we're out of the loop now, but before we go on, can you summarize the status of the data at this point?
> 1V: Hold it a moment. Can the ascending pointer, *Upside,* skip over one

---

* You've seen them: the group assembled around a conference table laying plans for the Combined Charities Fund Drive; the quality circle in earnest deliberation; etc.

location if there's an interrupt and another routine grabs hold of it? I'm a little nervous about global pointers, anyhow.

N: I don't know. I'm not sure who else uses *Upside.* I don't know the whole system that well.

2V: At least two other procedures that I can think of can set the pointer, but I'd have to think on that a while to know whether they might increment while this routine has been interrupted.

N: Suppose I just change the test to greater or equal.

1V: Sounds safer.

2V: Good idea.

Occasionally, a code review results in a recommendation to revise both code and design. Design details that looked like a good idea at the time sometimes result in extremely inefficient code. Many times, while in the process of writing code, the programmer will recognize this, but not always. Nor, given that it has been observed, will the programmer necessarily do something about it. I recall a code review in which it was apparent that certain global data structures led to an untoward amount of reformatting and housekeeping processing steps. The programmer had not previously drawn this to anyone's attention because she regarded anything global as sacrosanct. It was not. The development status of the module under review was well ahead of that of any other modules dealing with the data, and it was not too late to revise the data structure without jeopardizing the schedule.

As was the case with requirements and design reviews, it must be remembered that the object of code reviews is finding problems, not fixing them. (Except, of course, when the fix is obvious or, as in our dialogue, when it obviates the need for further analysis.) This can, from time to time, create minor problems. The fix of a code defect may affect more code than is immediately apparent. Consider this example of unreachable code:

```
integer A,B,X
if A ≥ B
  then exit
  else if A > X ** 2 and B < X
    then call ANYPROC(A,B)
```

It may be that either of the two predicates is miscoded. If not, the seemingly well-bounded defect must be the result of faulty reasoning that extends at least several statements outside these four lines. In that case, completion of the code review will be delayed until the full depth of the problem that prevents ANYPROC from being invoked is unscrambled. Until then, there is no assurance that the defect in our example is not masking other faults.

If solutions are admitted to the scope of reviews, the reviews are vulnerable to being dominated by problem solving, regardless of whether recoding by committee can be justified. A way around this awkward situation is to refrain from fixing any bugs, but to note the problem solutions that will have to be reviewed when they are available.

As with requirements and design reviews, the code review should result in a list of action items to which all hands agree. To simplify matters — certainly to reduce the amount of writing — the action items assigned to the code's author can be documented in the form of comments written directly on the listing, as in Figure 4.2. (One must not forget to append copies of such listing to the minutes of the review.) Any other action items

```
      SUBROUTINE PAINV(X1,Y1,X3,Y3,LA,IER)
C PAINV PAINTS VERTICALLY ORIENTED RECTANGLES
C LA IS LAST APERTURE USED, IFS IS FILE SLOT
C IST FLAGS END OF RECTANGLE LAST DRAWN,= TOP
C        AFTER FIRST PASS
C LAST=LAST POSITION IN X OF CENTER OF SLIT
C YMAX IS TOP POSITION OF SLIT, YMIN IS BOTTOM
      INTEGER SLITS(14,2),WIDTH,WHALF,X,Y,X1,Y1,X3,Y3
      COMMON SLITS
      COMMON/P/ISUBF,IBL,IPOWN,LINTYP,IPUP,WHALF,IFS
      IST=1
      CALL PENSEL(X3,X1,LA,SLITS(2,1),SLITS(2,2),LNGTH,$10)
      LHALF=LNGTH/2
      X=X1+LHALF
      YMAX=FLOAT(Y3-WHALF)/1000.
      YMIN=FLOAT(Y1+WHALF)/1000.
      WY=YMIN
      EX=X/1000.
      WRITE BINARY(IFS) IPUP,ISUBF,IBL,LINTYP,LA,EX,WY
      WY=YMAX
      WRITE BINARY(IFS) IPDWN,ISUBF,IBL,LINTYP,LA,EX,WY
      LAST=X
C START OF SHUTTLE LOOP
    5 IF((LAST+LHALF).GE.X3) RETURN
      X=LAST+LNGTH-2
      IF((X+LHALF).GT.X3) X=X3-LHALF
      EX=X/1000.
      WRITE BINARY(IFS) IPDWN,ISUBF,IBL,LINTYP,LA,EX,WY
C SLIT NOW MOVED TO POSITION FOR NEXT PASS
      LAST=X
      WY=YMAX
      IF(IST.EQ.1) WY=YMIN
      WRITE BINARY(IFS) IPDWN,ISUBF,IBL,LINTYP,LA,EX,WY
      IST=1-IST
      GO TO 5
   10 RETURN IER
      END
```

Handwritten annotations: SLITS(1,2) [pointing to SLITS(2,1)]; No compensation for offset [pointing to X=X3-LHALF]; On a PENSEL error return, PAINV should output a diagnostic message, including the PENSEL calling parameters, before returning. [pointing to line 10 RETURN IER]

Figure 4.2   One way to log required code corrections.

will most likely apply to designs, whether previously prepared by the programmer or by others. Since there will be fewer of these items, it is simpler to describe the requirements for design corrections in the text of the minutes.

Unlike requirements and design reviews, there is no need to assign priorities to corrections. At the level of code, either a defect is easily corrected once detected or — if the correction is not fairly obvious — is of sufficient gravity and scope that it must in any event be corrected before testing starts.

Follow-up. The format for the minutes is not important. The content of the minutes is: library control identifier of the code, date of the review meeting, names and functions of the attendees, and each item requiring correction. In Figure 4.2 we saw the source code listing itself used as the vehicle for logging code defects. For the correction items noted in the text, the person or function to whom or to which they are assigned also is recorded.

As in Section 3.7, a quality assurance person is an obvious candidate for confirming the closeout of deficiences, although the person charged with this responsibility may have to confer with others on the items for which the correction does not have an evident correlation with the description of the defect. As was previously noted, an iteration of the code review is called for if a required correction extends significantly out of the space of the observed fault.

Finally, after all corrections have been made, the code should once again be statically analyzed, by whatever tools are available, as a precaution against the introduction of new defects.

4.7   Checklists

Code review checklists take the form of evaluation criteria applied to statements and constructions. To keep the reviews cost-effective, checklists are usually restricted to defects that historically have occurred with the greater frequencies. Exactly which defect classes are included is a function of the type of programs produced, the language of the source code, the capabilities of the compiler and static analyzer, and the standards in use. The checklist that follows can only be considered as an example, and not a very good one at that, since its attempt to be globally comprehensive makes it 50 to 200 percent longer than a typical contextually relevant checklist.

Is the compilation (or assembly) listing free of fault messages?

Have the deficiences noted in the standards audit been corrected?

Do data definitions exploit typing capabilities to advantage?

Are mixed-mode expressions in violation of project standards?

Do all pointers and indexes adhere to binding conventions?

Except for appropriate delimiters (for example, those in *for* N *in* 1..10), are constants expressed as parameters?

For assemply language programs, have registers been saved on entry and restored on exit? Have stacks been properly initialized?

For assembly language programs, have project standards for register use been observed?

For branch points that correspond to the detailed design documentation, are the conditions sufficient? (That is, if n conditions are required for a decision, are all n present and properly accounted for?)

Are all conditions expressed in the correct sense (for example, $A > B$ versus $B > A$)?

Do control constructs conform to structured programming standards?

Are standards that restrict the depth to which loops and branches may be nested adhered to? Are loops and branches properly nested?

Are indexes or subscripts properly initialized?

Are loop termination conditions invariably achievable?

Are any branch conditions mutually exclusive (such that they can lead to unreachable code)?

For assembly language programs, are the expected contents of memory used in lieu of their addresses?

Do processes occur in the correct sequence?

Where applicable, are divisors tested for zero or noise?

Where applicable, are indexes, pointers, and subscripts tested against array, record, or file bounds?

Are imported data tested for validity? Are they ever reassigned except when they were transmitted for the express purpose of updating?

Do actual and formal interface parameter lists match?

Do data declarations observe data boundaries implied by machine architecture, language, or user-defined declarations?

Are all variables used? Are all output variables assigned?

Can any statements that are enclosed within loops be placed outside the loops without computational effect?

Is a more efficient mechanism for an input or output operation possible?

Are the correct data being operated on at each statement?

Are any labels unreferenced (a warning that something else may be amiss)?

Are equations properly formed [e.g., if both A and B are to be divided, $(A + B)/C$ and not $A + B/C$]?

Can a connection to an external device result in an interminable wait?

If there are requirements on execution time, will they be met?

Does the code fit within its allocated storage? Local data?

Have all the elements of the design been implemented as they were specified?

Has each function of the external specification for this code been correctly complied with?

4.8 Walk-Throughs

Walk-throughs differ little from reviews as Section 4.6 defined reviews. The essential differences follow:

- Participants. Usually, fellow programmers rather than representatives of other functions. The absence of expert knowledge of higher-level specifications is particularly noticeable.
- Preparation. Frequently none.
- Scope. Standards are usually ignored. Successful static analysis results generally are not confirmed.
- Checklists. Rarely used.
- Follow-up. Often ignored.

Their inherently more informal demeanor, as contrasted with reviews, somehow makes walk-throughs less intimidating to the more timorous programmers. This may be the only unqualified advantage that attaches to the walk-through, but it is not much of one. Even the neophyte programmer should learn from the first couple of (properly conducted) code reviews that code reviews offer no real ground for fear.

In general, the remark of Section 3.9 bears restating: walk-throughs are increasingly effective as the distinction between them and reviews narrows. In any case, it should be noted that separate audits can be used to supplement walk-throughs. Three areas that immediately come to mind — standards, confirmation of successful static analysis, and follow-up — can to little disadvantage be dealt with by quality assurance.

Finally, for either walk-throughs or reviews using a walk-through format, we should note a problem that can arise in the presence of well-annotated listings: the temptation to read carefully the comments that state what the code that follows is supposed to do and then skim the code itself. This temptation is especially easy to succumb to when the narrator-programmer is going through the code at a rapid rate. However, at least one walk-through team remained unseduced by good annotation:

> There's a listing that took it real rough,
> Though they do say it reads well enough.
> That's the comments they mean;
> Not the lines in between,
> 'Cause the code don't do none of that stuff.

4.9   Summary

1. Manual verification of code entails stepwise evaluation of the code's response to test cases representative of the external specifications for the design implemented by the code.

2. Desk-checking, although it means different things to different people, may be thought of as a progenitor of code reviews performed by a single code reader.

3. Auditing for deviations from code standards can best be done by a single person prior to the code review.

4. Although rigid criteria need not be applied to the determination of the amount of code a single review should cover, one can do worse than base each review on the code representing each applicable element of the detailed design and code work-breakdown structure.

5. The optimum sequence of events between the completion of code writing and the start of active test is (a) compilation or assembly, (b) static analysis, (c) standards audit, and (d) code review followed by a repetition of steps a and b.

6. A typical cast for a review is comprised of the programmer of the code and one representative each of the design team, quality assurance, and the software test group.

7. Prior to the review meeting, the participants should expend the effort to become familiar with the design implemented by the code.

8. Of the two review formats in use — linear step-by-step examination and a walk through the code with test input — the latter offers the advantages of achieving verification objectives and providing functional coherence to the proceedings.

9. Code defects often mask other bugs. Extensive recoding after a review calls for a second review.

10. The log of correction items can, for the most part, take the form of a marked-up code listing.

11. Completion of corrections (followed by a new compilation and a repeat of static analysis) should be confirmed prior to active test.

12. To keep checklists to a cost-effective size, they should only include items related to types of defects that have been historically significant. They should not repeat the capabilities of the static analysis system in use.

13. Walk-throughs are very much like reviews of the preferred format, but they are more informal and of less predictable effectiveness.

References

1. W. Richards Adrion et al., "Validation, Verification, and Testing of Computer Software," *ACM Computing Surveys,* vol. 14, no. 2, June 1982, pp. 159–192.

Chapter

5

Static Analysis

There is a lack of agreement on the position that static analysis occupies in the overall scheme of defect removal. Since static analysis is performed by software tools, it is attractive to view it as an automated code review, but the sets of defect types that yield to the two methods are not quite congruent. To many software engineers, static analysis is the preprocessing that sets the stage for dynamic analysis, to which we shall turn in Chapter 8. This restriction ignores the fact that there are software faults directly susceptible to static analysis. Even among those who recognize that static analysis is itself a defect removal process, we find the common misconception that it can be fully performed by compilers and link editors. It is true that some of the faults that will be found through static analysis can also be picked up by those production tools, but most will not be. And certainly, if a static analysis system includes symbolic execution, there is no way that this feature should be confused with the diagnostics output by compilers and link editors.

Perhaps the hazy perception of static analysis accounts for its frequent neglect. This is unfortunate. Static analysis can play a major independent role in defect removal. It will expose faults that will escape other static techniques, and it will do it economically. Moreover, unlike any of the forms of active, or dynamic testing, it does not produce failures that have to be traced to latent faults; it is faults themselves that are revealed by static analysis. (This is somewhat arguable in the case of symbolic execution, but even then the "failures" may be expressed in terms of program symbols, not numbers or strings of uncertain relation to input data.) Further, static analysis can warn of potential problems and can also provide information to yield further insight into the structure of the software. If there is a major drawback to static analysis, it is that it is inherently language-dependent. An analysis system for Cobol is useless when applied to PL/1 source code files.

To provide an overview of static analysis, the capabilities of analysis tools are tabulated below. The taxonomy implied by the tabulation format, although artificial in the sense that it does not reflect the structure of analysis systems, is an attempt to classify the capabilities as the user might see their application. As, later, each category is examined separately, we shall see that there is more subjectivity to this organization than first meets the eye.

Defects likely to be exposed

Misuse of variables, both locally and globally

Mismatched parameter lists

Improper nesting of loops and branches

Improper sequencing of processes

Undefined variables

Infinite loops

Unauthorized recursion

Calls to nonexistent subprograms

Missing labels or code

Improper linkages

Potential sources of problems

Unused variables

Unreachable code

Unreferenced labels

Suspicious computations

Potentially infinite loops

Symbolic testing (symbolic execution)

Outputs not directly related to defects

Number of occurrences of each source statement form

Cross-reference of where variables and constants are used

Manner of use of identifiers

Procedures-calling hierarchy

Violations of coding standards

Preprocessing for further defect removal

Selection of test cases

It is important to understand that not all static analysis tools have the capability of producing each item of the above output. For example, we should not expect an analysis system designed to operate on Ada source statements to trap unauthorized recursive calls, since these are a feature of the language. More significantly, many of the analyses (e.g., symbolic testing) require an order of complexity beyond the ambitions of more modest systems. Rather, what we have is an enumeration of the types of analysis results that may be classified under the umbrella term "static analysis." Recalling the first paragraph of this chapter, in the ambiguity that seems to attend most software semantics, the term "static analysis" is sometimes used to describe the generation of semantic and structural reports only, sometimes to refer to symbolic testing or data flow analysis exclusively, and occasionally to allude to nothing more than the preprocessing for dynamic analysis. Also, any two of the above. Also, all of the above. It is tempting to avoid this confusion by coining a new term — perhaps, "source code static processing" — but the last thing we need is more fat in the stew of software nomenclature. In any case, if one examines the manner in which analysis systems are built, there are strong interrelations among the various aspects of static analysis. For example, a system capable of symbolic testing is inherently able to detect unreachable code. Accordingly, "static analysis" will be used inclusively; and with that understanding, let us look beyond the simple naming of capabilities and see how static analysis can improve productivity and quality.

5.1 Exposure of Defects

The capability of static analysis to expose defects is our primary interest, at least for defect removal processes that do not include symbolic execution or static preprocessing for dynamic analysis. Each defect that is directly exposed is one that will not have to be made visible through the process of dynamic testing or, worse, remain latent through all of testing only to manifest itself during the operational life of the software.

Misuse of variables. With strongly typed languages, we should expect the compiler to detect most variable misuse. However, strong data typing capabilities do not necessarily mean that all programmers will make use of the redundancy inherent in typing. Many an Ada programmer will decide that derived types, anonymous types, and subtypes are a bother; that he can accomplish his end quite happily with Ada's generous supply of predefined types. With regard to more widely used languages, the classic case of this is the friendly Fortran compiler that allows mixed-mode arithmetic. Given this, there is no way that a statement such as

```
V  =  SOMEREAL  +  SOMEINTEGER
```

will be flagged as a compiler error. However, the statement, if a violation of local programming standards, will not make it past the static analyzer.

Globally, other forms of misuse can be caught. A typical and troublesome inconsistency that transcends module boundaries takes the following forms. As a calling program:

```
integer declaration A,B(10)
        .
        .
call ANYPROC(A,B)
```

And as a called program:

```
procedure ANYPROC(A,B)
integer declaration B(20)
real declaration A
        .
        .
```

As the use of more strongly typed languages increases, the capability of static analysis to buttress the advantages of typing will make use of the tool even more attractive.

Mismatched parameter lists and improper linkages. The most common fault of the mismatched parameter list and improper linkage kind is found in procedure calls where the parameter or argument list of the calling program differs in number or type from that of the called program unit. This can not be known at compile time (unless the compiler has access to the entire program), nor is it usually a matter of concern to a link editor. However, a static analyzer with access to both parts of the system will find the defect.

Multitask systems can exhibit an analogous mismatch when the parameter requirements of the task being scheduled differ from those encoded in the invoking command. This, too, is visible to static analysis.

It is surprising how often function subprograms are invoked with procedure calls and vice versa. For example, S = FIRSTBLANK(STRING) instead of CALL FIRSTBLANK(STRING,S). Usually, the first time one learns of this is after an arcane run time diagnostic is output. This, too, can be tedious to run down. Mercifully, flushing such defects to the surface is a small matter to an analysis system.

Another type of incorrect linkage occurs when a function subprogram of one data type has been declared to be another data type by the calling program. To use a Fortran illustration, if

```
integer function ANYFUN
```

is called by a program that does not explicitly declare ANYFUN to be an integer (in Fortran, a variable starting with the letter A is implicitly a real), a subtle run time error will ensue.

Improper nesting of loops and branches. Compilers will generally catch instances of improper nesting that violate the rules attending standard constructs: *do, for, if-then-else,* and so on. However, a compiler will be as bewildered as any of us by a page of code that boils down to

```
LABEL A  I: = I - 1
         call PROCA(I)
         if (I + 10) < 0 goto LABEL C
LABEL B  call PROCB(I)
LABEL C  if I < 0 goto LABEL A
            .
            .
            .
         I: = I - 1
         goto LABEL B
```

The analysis of loops and branches is not made directly from the source code; instead it is made from an abstraction of the code called a program graph. In the most abstract form of the graph, sequential operations are represented by processing nodes, and the nodes are interconnected by decision-to-decision paths. As we shall see, the construction of the program graph is useful for other static analyses as well.

Improper sequencing of processes. This category of defects includes attempts to read or write a file before it is opened, initialization of system resources at some point after the first use, and anachronism in the scheduling of other tasks within a multitasking system. Generally, such faults will be trapped by the operating system, but the clear identification of the problem by a static analyzer is much preferred to the sleuthing that must follow a cryptic run time diagnostic.

Infinite loops. It may be asking too much of a software tool to provide a general solution to the halting problem, but constructions such as the following, in which the wrong variable is incremented, can be caught:

```
while I < J loop
   call CONCAT (STRING,CHAR(I))
   J: = J + 1
end loop
```

Infinite loops come in an infinite variety, but the example is one I remember well, having authored it. The loop was not truly infinite, since the 2s complement machine I was using overflowed positive integers into negative integers, but the number of hours spent trying to debug the execution failure seemed at the time to be infinite.

Unauthorized recursion. The fact that a language or its implementation does not support recursion does not always stop a programmer from writing the following:

```
function ANYFUN(N]
       .
       .
       .
ANYFUN: =  ANYFUN(N  —  1)
```

This problem may also crop up when a software system, initially installed on a computer with stack architecture, is transported to one without.

Calls to nonexistent subprograms. If, indeed, a subprogram is not yet in the system — neither in a library nor as an independent relocatable module — we can assume the link editor will catch the problem. This link error is frequently encountered in top-down integration when the integration people fail to notice the requirement for a stub or simply forgot to enter it into the system.

A link diagnostic may, however, be misleading. Consider the following:

```
real declaration ERRAY(1000)
       .
       .
       .
A: =  ERRAY(I)  +  ORRAY(I)
```

With no declaration of ORRAY as an array, the compiler declares it as an external to be resolved by the link editor. The link editor finds no entry point ORRAY among the entry points to which it has access, and so it aborts the linking process. Now, if the author of the program is its tester, he will, upon reading the unwelcome diagnostic, immediately recognize the name ORRAY as that which he had given to an array. However, if a person unfamiliar with the code is the first to encounter the problem, as might happen in a production milieu employing the purest form of top-down integration (no previous module test *in situ*) and an independent test team, uncovering the defect will be a less trivial task.

Missing labels or code. We can depend on a compiler to flag a referenced but uncoded statement label, since it cannot complete the compilation. Nevertheless, for those who would prefer to perform static analysis prior to compilation, the feature is helpful. Unfortunately, our confidence that missing labels will result in compile-time diagnostics cannot be extended to missing code. For example, in a block-oriented language, there is nothing uncompilable about the following:

```
begin
*COMMENT: WAIT FOR MELVIN TO SUPPLY ERROR HANDLING DETAILS
end
```

Such constructions have been known to survive the stages of code review, development testing, and even qualification testing, thereby providing a rationale for the use of static analysis after, as well as before, active testing.

5.2   Exposure of Potential Defects

Semantic and structural anomalies detected by static analysis may indeed be defects. Alternatively, they may be harmless in the sense that they may not, presumptively, be identified with future failure. They are classified here as "potential defects" because to do otherwise implies the capability of a software tool to know and comprehend the history of the code it operates on or the data environment to which the code will be subjected.

Unused variables and unreachable code.   Unused variables and code to which there is no feasible path may be symptoms of faulty structure, a true defect often detected by the compiler, but more often they are the vestigial remains of code segments long since abandoned. After the analyzer has reported the anomaly, examination of the code will answer the question.

Even if examination of the code finds that proper operation is not jeopardized, the matter should not be ignored. Nothing seems as easy to change as source code. Whatever the reason — changes to the external specifications or rewrites to remove defects — code modifications are liable to leave once-useful source statements as monuments to the changes that were made. Although they seem harmless, they are a source of confusion to programmers who, some months or years hence, will be charged with making unrelated changes to the program. Worse, code currently dead may fortuitously become viable as the by-product of a future modification. Unused variables and unreachable code left in the program in this manner should be purged.

Unreachable code is generally detected from analysis of the program graph. The amount of processing required to interpret the graph increases as the square of the number of nodes. Thus, program graphs tend to be restricted to individual procedures, which rules out detection of code that is unreachable over the span of two or more modules. Consider the following:

```
if POINTER < 1 or POINTER > MAX
  then call ERROR(POINTER)
  else call SOMEPROC(ERRAY,POINTER,ITEM,MAX)
                .
                .
                .
```

Let us now look at SOMEPROC, the first executable statements of which are

```
if POINTER < 1 or POINTER > MAX
  then call ERROR(POINTER)
  else call UNPACK(ERRAY,POINTER,STRING)
                .
                .
                .
```

Here the thoughtful programmer of SOMEPROC had taken the trouble to protect his procedure against an invalid parameter set. However, the equally thoughtful programmer of the calling procedure had made certain that an invalid parameter set would not be passed. Of course, by any standard this is a wholly harmless example of unreachable code; gold stars for the programmers would be more appropriate than discrepancy reports. In any case, with static analyzers generally restricted to the processing of program graphs that encompass only single procedures, we should not expect it to be found.

Unreferenced labels. As are unused variables and unreachable code, unreferenced labels too may be symptoms of missing code, specifically that which was to have referenced the labels. Again, they may also be left over from earlier versions of the program. If so, despite the potential value to software archeologists, they should be removed lest they confuse maintenance programmers.

Suspicious computations. Of the defects classified as potential, suspicious computations quite possibly are the ones most likely to result in failure. For example, any conversion of a real to an integer for subsequent use as an array index or loop range parameter is cause for concern. However, if the integer is tested against limits prior to use, there may be no problem at all. What static analysis does in this case is alert one to the potential danger: the astute programmer then looks to see if precautions (e.g., a range test) have been taken. Unfortunately, not all questionable practices can be protected by built-in armor. What can be done with the use of a constant in the parameter list of a procedure call?

Another common offense that should be detected is a branch condition determined by the difference of reals:

```
if REALA = REALB then return
```

If this is the only way to get out of an iterative mathematical procedure, we may have a potentially infinite loop. Of course, the preferred form is

```
if ABS(REALA — REALB) ≤ EPSILON then return
```

Perhaps the most frequently encountered suspicious computation arises from the use of an integer variable as an index to an array. This is scarcely to suggest outlawing the practice; for to do so would make most programming tasks impossible, or at least impracticable. However, there are occasions when the operations performed on integers prior to their use as subscripts may be failure-prone. For example,

```
N: = INDEX/2
A: = ERRAY(N) * 5
```

If INDEX were equal to 1, this would produce a failure. Static analysis systems may specifically be designed to look for such situations and present warnings of any questionable computations that are found. Much more ambitious static analyzers can symbolically evaluate subscripts and output an expression of the relevant input parameters that will cause an array declaration bound to be exceeded. When a loop parameter is used as an array index, such an analyzer can produce an expression for the loop terminator that will cause the array bound to be violated, or, in the case of a constant loop terminator, simply compare the terminating number with the declared bound.

```
procedure ANY(BUNCH,LOTS,N,M)
real array BUNCH(100),LOTS(100)
integer variable I,QUIT,N,M
begin
  QUIT: = ABS(N — M)
  if QUIT = 0
    then return
    else begin
      for I from 1 to QUIT loop
        BUNCH(I): = LOTS(I) ** 2
      end loop
    end
  end if
  return
end
```

Given this construction, a static analyzer so designed would output:

```
BUNCH ARRAY BOUND OVERFLOW CONDITIONS:  N - M > 100
                                        M - N > 100
 LOTS ARRAY BOUND OVERFLOW CONDITIONS:  N - M > 100
                                        M - N > 100
```

Potentially infinite loops. The distinction between an infinite loop and a loop that is potentially infinite may be more semantic than substantive. That is, a loop that one programmer views as potentially infinite may be regarded by a less tolerant person as truly infinite, even if there is no certainty that it will ever be faced with a data set that will cause it to loop forever.

```
for I from 2 to 1000 loop
  call RETRIEVE(TABLE,I,LOCATION)
  if LOCATION = 0
    then I:= I - 1
      call MODIFY(TABLE,I)
    else call SOMEPROC (MESA,LOCATION)
  end if
end loop
```

What we have is a program that searches an array TABLE for a pointer to an entry in another array, MESA. However, finding a pointer of zero, which implies that there is no corresponding entry in MESA, seems to require that the contents of the previous entry of TABLE be modified. Quite obviously, good programming practice would have called for a new variable to be set to $I - 1$. As written, the program will surely loop endlessly if ever a zero pointer is encountered in TABLE. Since we cannot presumptively say that a zero pointer will someday be found, it seems somewhat inaccurate to call this an infinite loop rather than one with the potential for immortality. Does the distinction really matter? It is difficult to imagine that this construction, cited by a static analyzer as a potentially infinite loop, would not be quickly corrected once it was brought to the programmer's attention.

One can go overboard in the design of a static analyzer by labeling too many constructions as potentially infinite loops. Any loop of the form

```
for I from 1 to MAX loop
```

can, theoretically and apart from the consequence of integer overflow, be called potentially infinite. However, to so designate every loop having a variable for the terminating condition would be to cry wolf,* with the result

---

* Or, if you will, to cry *lupus*.

that all warnings of infinite loops would soon be ignored. One can get into gray areas here. Some may regard it as valid to raise a warning for any loop having a variable terminator on the left side of an assignment statement or in a procedure call within the loop. Style and local programming standards, as much as any other considerations, seem to govern in this matter.

5.3   Symbolic Testing

Users of static analysis systems are likely to consider symbolic testing as a feature apart from the other categories of this chapter's taxonomy, notwithstanding the fact that many of the other analysis outputs may be formed as by-products of the processing necessary for symbolic testing. The unique quality of symbolic testing, often referred to as symbolic execution, is that it provides synoptic expressions of what the code under test will do, whether correct or incorrect. This output may then be compared with the external specifications for the subject procedure. Any differences imply the presence of one or more defects. Symbolic testing can reveal defects to the extent that the specifications have been expressed with equal mathematical rigor. Indeed, if it can be assumed that all paths through a procedure have been symbolically executed and if the results — combined or rearranged to be congruent with the specification for the procedure — are identical with those specified, it is reasonable to say that the procedure has been demonstrated to be correct with respect to its external specification.

Symbols, rather than numbers, are the input for symbolic testing. For

```
function ROOTNR(A,PREC,GUESS)
```

the input might be the symbols A, PREC, and GUESS. Each assignment statement in the routine is "executed" in terms of these and any locally used constants. Execution of branches requires evaluation of the conditions (predicates) that determine the next instruction to be executed. A complete path consists of a set of these symbolic predicates and their intervening assignment evaluations.

Consider a function for computing square roots by Newton-Raphson iteration. The formula for finding the square root of A is

$$X_{i+1} = \frac{1}{2}(X_i + \frac{A}{X_i})$$

We might program the routine in the following manner:

```
function ROOTNR(A,PREC,GUESS)
* ALL VARIABLES REAL
* FORM SQUARE ROOT OF A TO CONVERGENCE PRECISION OF PREC
```

```
* GUESS IS INPUT FOR ZEROTH ITERATION
XLAST:= 0
XNEXT:= GUESS
while ABS(XNEXT — XLAST) > PREC loop
  XLAST:= XNEXT
  XNEXT:= (XLAST + A/XLAST)/2.
end loop
ROOTNR:= XNEXT
return
```

After the first iteration, we would have a static symbolic output for the variable XNEXT of

```
(GUESS + A/GUESS)/2.
```

And after the second iteration,

```
((GUESS + A/GUESS)/2. + A/(GUESS + A/GUESS)/2.)/2.
```

Also after the second iteration, the symbolic predicate would be

```
ABS(((GUESS + A/GUESS)/2. + A/(GUESS + A/GUESS)/2.)/2. —
                        (GUESS + A/GUESS)/2.) > PREC.
```

Unless the analysis system is also endowed with algebraic simplification properties, it is clear that interpretation of the results is no casual affair. Even if simplified, things can get messy. The best that can be done with the symbolic predicate is

```
ABS( — (GUESS + A)/2. + A/(GUESS + A/GUESS)) > PREC.
```

It might have helped a bit had GUESS been replaced with a single character, but not much. To simplify things, symbolic testing programs can be given the capability of introducing numeric values for certain of the input parameters.

For a more complex program, it may be too unwieldy to attempt to execute all the possible paths symbolically. A valuable feature is one that permits the user to select the paths that are to be evaluated, although, if any numeric parameters are to be used, the user may then be confronted with the problem of determining a priori the numeric data that will cause a given statement to be executed. We shall see this problem again in Chapter 8 when we examine the issues attending active branch testing.

Another problem concomitant to symbolic testing is ambiguity in the determination of which element of an array is referenced in a symbolic assignment value or branch predicate evaluation. A subscript appearing in the results may have been assigned not during the iteration being reported, but during an earlier one. One could, of course, list, for each such ambiguous output, all the preceding assignment statements bearing on the sub-script and condense them in some succinct manner. William Howden, whose DISSECT[1] system takes both string and numeric input, suggests that a satisfactory solution is for the user to assign numeric values to any input that can occur as an index variable. This thought may be extended to the assignment of actual values to any input from which a subscript may be derived. It should also be noted that reference to external procedures and functions introduces some uncertainty in the evaluation, at least to the correctness of the responses forced for the calls.

It is evident that the use of symbolic execution is not a casual matter. Care must be taken in the selection of test cases, although no more than is required for dynamic analysis;* comparison of the symbolic results with the external specifications may be algebraically messy; and then there are the problems of indexing array elements and the use of external code, each of which may demand considerable thought. But those who have at-tempted to integrate a large program comprised of a great number of buggy modules will easily appreciate the merit in taking extra pains to purify each procedure before active testing starts.

5.4   Ancillary Static Analysis Output

One might infer from the adjective "ancillary" that the results in the ancillary static analysis output category are relatively unimportant. This conclusion is correct only to the extent that, within the context of this book, the principal subject of this chapter is the direct detection of defects by static analysis. However, as a class, the other forms of output are of considerable value. Indeed, those related to the implantation of probes and assertions are possibly the most significant.

Number of occurrences of each source statement form.   This form is a substan-tial time saver for various statistical analyses of program contents. An example of the use to which one may put such an enumeration is the application of Halstead's software science measures.† Another is an evalu-ation of complexity or prediction of reliability based on multiple-regres-sion models that relate complexity or reliability to statement-type fre-quencies. There may also be some merit in knowing which members of the programming team use the highest percentage of *goto* statements.

---

* A good case can be made for including symbolic execution under the category dynamic analysis. After all, in a sense one is given the opportunity to observe program performance under the conditions of stepwise changes of state. As used here, however, "dynamic analysis" refers to observations made while the program is running in its native (whether instrumented or not) execution mode.

† See Chapter 7.

If one is maintaining statistics of defect counts or productivity rates versus some classification of module types (e.g., mathematical, transaction handling, string processing), these enumerations — especially if extended to include library routines directly related to the types of interest — may help in deciding in which categories questionable modules belong.

Perhaps one of the reasons why software people have been reluctant to undertake various measurements and predictions is the time spent in gathering and classifying data. Semantic synopses obtained through static analyses can ease the burden.

Cross-reference of where variables and constants are used.   There are various reports that can fall in this category. As diagnostic aids, they are of great value in determining the cause of test failures. In their attempt to understand software structure, maintenance programmers will also find them useful. More immediately, it is even possible to deduce the presence of certain faults from them, an indirect form of static analysis defect removal. For example, many software people recall the early space-tracking program that used five different values for the radius of the earth. An astute reader of the cross-reference report, had one been available, might have noticed something peculiar about

```
EARTHRAD        1390700 (DEC)          SUBA
ERADIUS         1390500 (DEC)          SUBB
    .               .                   .

    .               .                   .
RADIUSOFE       1390650(DEC)           SUBE
```

To avoid cluttering up a report of the constants used throughout the program, it is best to ignore the constants not equated to a symbol prior to the first executable statement of each procedure. Else, most of the report will be devoted to the less than fascinating information that in SUBA, INDEX equals 1. Alternatively, one could design a static analyzer to allow the reporting of symbols set to constants anywhere in the code but to include (in addition to those found in data declarations) only the symbols appearing but once on the left side of an assignment statement.

Many compilers routinely list each constant used. Typically, however, such reports do not relate each constant to the name of a datum; the compilers being content to simply list the constant (for example, 3.14159) and, possibly, its relative address. Nor can compilers list in one place all the constants used in a system.

Some languages allow individual modules to rename global data. For example, in Fortran, we may have in one module

```
COMMON/A/EARTHRAD,PI,TARGET(20,3),NEXT
```

and in a second module

```
COMMON/A/ERAD,PI,POSITION(20,3),START
```

Having these names correlated and knowing where data are used is a great help to persons attempting to understand the structure of the software or where data come from or where they go. This information can also be used as an input to a checklist for studying the possible effects of a planned change. Going a step further, it is helpful to have a cross-reference of names that take into account equivalence declarations as well. Moreover, a static analyzer can be designed to also note which modules set or use or set and use each symbol. The reports are further increased in value if they also indicate whether symbols are global, are local, or are intermodule parameters.

Symbol use. We run into difficulties, both globally and locally, when data are asked to assume inconsistent roles. The use of a character representation as a table index is archetypically "clever" programming: an invitation to a future failure or a botched enhancement. Similarly, we have arithmetic operations on strings, boolean variables used as loop parameters, pointers used as exponents, and the like. Within a given procedure, many of these will be caught by the compiler, at least if they are in clear violation of the language standard. However, all will not be, and certainly not those that are inconsistent only across module boundaries. A listing of how symbols are used is a most useful report.

Admittedly, even a static analyzer may have trouble finding some of these examples of symbol misuse. If, for example, a string is input under format conversion (as in the Fortran Hollerith specification) or formed in a literal assignment or declaration, the analysis system can recognize it as alphanumeric data. If input as raw binary data, however, it is only in the programmer's mind that the symbol to which the data are assigned is a string. Still, any number of unambiguous evaluations of the identifier type can be made, and if they are reported in an easily scanned format, they can alert the reader to possible deviations from good programming practice, whether deliberate or accidental. To provide clues to global inconsistencies, the static analysis system must also unscramble the renaming of common data, equivalences, and parameter strings; but these functions will have been performed for the previously described cross-reference report if that report is included in the system's capabilities.

Superficially, it would appear that the more strongly typed the language is, the more valuable the symbol use report will be. However, at least locally, the compilers for these languages can be depended upon to find deviations of type usage. To provide data from which global inconsistencies can be detected, it is helpful, if the language permits programmer definitions of unique types, to impose conventions for the naming of such types so that usage from one module to another can be correlated.

Even if a static analysis system can automatically detect some forms of inconsistent usage, as we saw in the earlier discussion of variable misuse reports, the usage report remains a valuable document with application to both maintenance and the diagnosis of failure. If inconsistencies are automatically reported, it should not be at the expense of foregoing the complete report.

Hierarchy of procedure calls. This report of where procedures are called from and which procedures they in turn invoke constitutes an as-built account of the software architecture. It is useful for the purposes of maintenance programmers, and it can also serve to check configuration control records.

Violations of coding standards. This subject has been touched upon several times. Beyond the violations previously noted, there are dozens of others that one can conceive of, depending on how rigorous local standards strive to be. As we saw in Chapter 4, standards may extend much further than stipulations on constructions to include those applying to the placement of nonexecutable statements, to rules for naming labels and data symbols, and the like. While deviations from these are a simple enough matter to detect during code audits, reviews, or walk-throughs, the program that has survived static analysis defect exposure and the several phases of active test will most likely have metamorphosed sufficiently to allow considerable departure from the approved standards. The cost of running the code through a static analysis system standards analyzer is low enough that no impediment is presented to the performance of periodic checks for adherence to standards.

The static analyzer as a preprocessor. In Chapter 8 we shall encounter a valuable adjunct to branch testing: the execution coverage monitor. In its most primitive form, the monitor will report, at the conclusion of each dynamic test, the decision-to-decision paths that have been exercised. In a slightly more elaborate form, the monitor will report the number of times each such path has been traversed. (There are variants that provide additional data, but we'll leave those for Chapter 8.)

With the identification of all decision-to-decision paths that attended the construction of the program graph, it is but a step further for a static analysis system to automatically instrument the source code with probes for the gathering of branch execution statistics. The probe may be in the form of a simple in-line counter, as in

```
DDCOUNT(I):= DDCOUNT(I) + 1
```

where DDCOUNT is a vector declared (and inserted) by the analysis system and I is the ith decision-to-decision path. Alternatively, the probe may take the form of an implanted procedure call with I encoded as a parameter.

A report related to this preprocessing capability is that which, in essence, outputs the program graph. This may assume several forms, but as an illustration consider a listing of the source code annotated with unique identifiers associated with each decision-to-decision path. Accompanying this is a report listing all the decision-to-decision paths (identified by terminal nodes) that constitute each unique entry-to-exit path of the procedure.

```
PROCEDURE USELESS (KODE,STRING)                    DD PATH
HOLLERITH ARRAY STRING(80)
CODE:= KODE                                           1
IF CODE = 'A'
  THEN CALL PROC1(STRING)                             2
  ELSE IF (CODE = 'B') AND (STRING(1) = 'B')          3
    THEN CALL PROC2(STRING)                           4
    ELSE CALL ERROR(CODE)                             5
  END IF
END IF
RETURN                                                6
PATH 1 CONSISTS OF DD 1,2,6
PATH 2 CONSISTS OF DD 1,3,4,6
PATH 3 CONSISTS OF DD 1,3,5,6
```

Note that decision-to-decision paths 1 and 6 represent no more than the procedure entry and exit paths.

As an alternative to automatic insertion of execution coverage probes, one may use the program graph* as an aid to the discretionary manual insertion of probes. Further, the graph is helpful for determining the placement of assertion statements, to which we shall return in the next chapter.

Selection of test cases. The path predicates calculated for symbolic testing may be used to reduce the total amount of test activity required to provide some given test coverage objective. Specifically, it is possible, upon dynamic execution of one path, to determine an alternative branch condition or set of conditions that will cause execution of an adjacent path. There are several ways in which this procedure may be utilized to select the test cases that will provide maximum coverage for any given, predetermined, total number of test cases. For example, if a history of previous execution paths is maintained, one may, through symbolic execution, deduce the perturba-

---

* A program graph depicts the possible program flow sequences of source statements. See Figure 7.1 for the program flow for the procedure COMP of Chapter 6.

tion of input conditions that will result in a set of predicate evaluations differing in at least one instance from any previous set. The profit here is twofold: The test based on the revised input will be certain to excite a previously untrod path, thereby avoiding redundancy of effort, and the path itself will be known. Knowing which paths have been tested is a necessity if one is to try to evaluate the thoroughness with which defect removal has been carried out.

At the loss of some effectiveness, one may directly operate on the program graph to determine the set of paths inherent to the structure. Test cases may then be selected from the set. Although this is simpler to implement, the approach lends itself to the output not only of paths that can be traversed but of those that are infeasible as well. Feasibility can be determined only by evaluation of path predicates. In the following example, a procedure reads sequential fixed-length records from a file until it has found two records that begin with asterisks. It then returns the count of records it has used.

```
procedure COUNTER(COUNT,FILESIZE)
string STAR is '*'
string array RCRD is length 40
integer STOPCOUNT, COUNT, FILESIZE
STOPCOUNT: = 0
COUNT: = 0
while COUNT ≤ FILESIZE loop
  call READFILE(10,RCRD)
  if STOPCOUNT = 2 then return
  if RCRD(1) = STAR then STOPCOUNT: = STOPCOUNT + 1
  COUNT: = COUNT + 1
end loop
```

From the program graph, a path exists directly from the procedure entry point to the return. In fact, it cannot be executed, since a minimum of two iterations is required before the condition on STOPCOUNT will permit the path to the return statement to be taken.

5.5 Implementation

Depending on which capabilities one wants, a static analysis system may range from a relatively simple affair to one involving considerable complexity. Exposure of defects involving data usage, mismatched parameters, sequences of processes, unauthorized recursion, calls to nonexistent procedures, and missing labels and code are at the easy end of the range of projects. In this category, we might also include detection of unused variables, unreferenced labels, certain suspicious computations, statement occurrences, cross-reference of variables and constants, symbol use reports, hierarchy of procedure calls, and violations of local programming standards.

For the most part, these reports can approach the problem purely semantically. For probe insertion and test case selection and for the detection of some unreachable code, infinite loop constructions, and the improper nesting of loops and branches, considerably more structural analysis is required, including the construction of a program graph. Algorithms for detecting data flow anomalies have been developed along the lines used for global program optimization.[2,3]

To perform symbolic execution and to detect many instances of unreachable code, it is also necessary for the system to be able to calculate path predicates. This is another major increment of complexity.

Whatever the investment that must be made, it is clear that the profit from it will be compromised in the absence of language standardization. The software group that must maintain a tool set for Fortran, Cobol, and a couple of favored customer languages as well is in a much weaker position to gain a decent return on investment than is the shop that can standardize on a single language. The majority of software development enterprises or departments of multifunction companies or colleges do use a single language for nearly all of their work, but then we have defense electronics contractors for whom the choice of language for a given project may be made by their customers: Jovial, CMS-2, Fortran, or whatever. Until the implementation of Ada becomes both a supportable and a contractual reality, their prospects for the acquisition or development of language-dependent tools frequently will remain dimmed by economic obstacles.

It should be observed that compiler error traps may extend beyond those implied by the language specification. If it is impractical to develop or acquire independent analysis tools, one could do worse than to choose a programming language supported by an installable compiler endowed with some of the analysis capabilities described in this chapter. The search for such a language-compiler combination need not be restricted to the manufacturers of computer hardware; it should encompass independent software houses as well. Recall, also, that the stronger the language is in data typing, the easier it is for a compiler to find violations in data usage. To one extent or another, there exist a variety of compilers, especially for block-structured languages, that offer static analysis checks at the level of individual procedures. Further, some compilation-linkage systems are capable of operating on the source code for an entire software system, and not simply one module at a time.* Although it is not necessarily exploited, such compilers have the potential for finding defects that transcend module boundaries.

---

* Unhappily, included in this group are those that can *only* process source code in this way; scarcely a way to improve efficiency.

A survey of the literature demonstrates that static analysis systems have been developed for several languages. Fortran has been the most popular target, being supported by DISSECT,[1] DAVE,[2] SADAT,[4] FACES,[5] IN-STRU,[6] and a proprietary tool,[7] RXVP80™. It is not clear why Fortran has been so favored. Perhaps its wide use in academe accounts for it, since most of these tools were developed by university research units. A relatively obscure language used by the U.S. Army, Centran (essentially a superset of Fortran) has been supported by a system called ACES.[8] SE-LECT[9] serves LISP code; code in a language styled after PL/1 has been analyzed by EFFIGY;[10] and a language, EL1, developed at Harvard University, is the target of yet another system.[11] Looking to the future, we may expect that the Ada Programming Support Environment (APSE) will have certain of the previously described analysis capabilities.

None of these systems provide all of the analyses that have been discussed. However, most perform either data flow analysis or symbolic execution in one variant or another. That over half were initially made operable in 1976 or earlier suggests that static analysis can no longer be considered an experimental technique.

5.6 Application

The programming staff fortunate enough to have a static analysis system at its disposal will find that it will want to use the tool at several discrete times while the code remains under its control. Recalling Section 4.6, for a newly minted module, one might as well let the compiler find its share of bugs first. The code is then subjected to the full repertoire of module-level analyses available. To the extent that the available system can uncover defects also susceptible to code review, there is no reason not to eliminate applicable items from the code review checklist. The redundant items are left for the less labor-intensive tool to find. However, to satisfy the objective of independent controls on defect removal, the hard copy output of the analyzer should be examined by someone other than the programmer — say, a software quality assurance representative — for the logging of any open matters related to defects or potential problems.

The application of symbolic execution should be considered apart from the other static analysis capabilities, since it requires considerable programmer labor for selecting test cases and interpreting the results. Repeating a remark made in Section 4.6, it would seem most productive to schedule the use of symbolic execution on the basis of the type of code operated on. For procedures that are concerned mostly with mathematical or logical operations, symbolic execution may be most appropriate prior to dynamic analysis. For code primarily involved in data pushing or input and output handling, it is probably more effective to delay the use of symbolic execution of applicable paths until after unit test or even until the modules subordinate to the subject code have been integrated with it.

For all static analyses, it would seem most efficient to have the programmer of the module be the first to use the analyzer on his code. Thus, in most cases, the hard copy given to the independent control authority when the programmer has finished his debugging will speak of no clear-cut defect, although there may be some potential ones shown. Until these are investigated, they remain open items.

In most production milieus, the full set of modules constituting the system under development will not be fed to the fire of dynamic test all at one time. Thus, the module that has just emerged from static analysis will most likely proceed directly to dynamic testing while other modules remain in the code or design stage. We may expect, then, that global analysis reports will build incrementally as the system does. In the early stages of integration of a new module, it will be possible to statically verify its procedure linkages, use of global data, and so on, only to the extent that they need to be specified elsewhere for the specific integration activity. The bookkeeping associated with recording which static analyses have been performed with respect to which groups of modules can easily get out of hand in the absence of adequate independent test control. Given the power of static analysis, one would hardly like to see the potential wasted for want of current record keeping.

In the same vein, it is advisable to repeat previous analyses at appropriate points during the dynamic test period. It would be inefficient to so exercise the entire system — or the part of it that has been coded — each time a bug has been fixed. Discrete milestones seem more reasonable: In bottom-up integration, reanalyze each time a module or group of modules has been added to other program elements of like hierarchical rank; in top-down integration, reanalyze each time a new hierarchical tier has been reached. For analyses restricted to single procedures, there is no purpose in repeating a test if the procedure in question has not been revised since the last such test.

One may question to what purpose static analysis iterations can be put after a module has gone through dynamic testing. The answer is found in the difference between the approaches of the two to defect exposure. Static analysis finds intrinsic semantic and structural defects. Dynamic testing finds defects that are extrinsic in the sense that externally applied stimuli must be used to force externally observed failures. Since the number of unique test data sets is severely limited, there is no assurance that dynamic testing will push to the point of failure questionable constructions or potentially infinite loops introduced during dynamic testing as a by-product of defect removal.

Once the elements of a software system have been integrated into a working program or task, more testing remains: There may be integration with other programs or tasks, integration with on-line instrumentation or control or display equipment, qualification tests, or installation tests. Good use may be made of one's static analysis tools periodically during these activities, with the frequency determined by the amount of revision that is required. At the conclusion of all tests, prior to the victory party, a final run through the structural reports will provide valuable as-built archival information for subsequent maintenance and modifications.

This brings up the matter of static analysis during the operational period of software. Clearly, static analysis is advisable after each revision to the source code.

In most instances, it may be expected that static analysis at any level will be immediately followed by dynamic testing. However, there is an opportunity for further defect removal at the procedure level that may be appropriate for some applications. The following chapter deals with the formal proof of program correctness, where we shall see symbolic execution called upon again; this time as a means of achieving the goals of this process.

A final bit of hype on the value of structural examination of programs:

Tis frugal to test economically,
Thus feudal to test just dynamically.
Cure debug paralysis
With static analysis,
And expurgate bugs anatomically.

5.7 Summary

1. Static analysis is the name used to denote the performance of software systems that operate on source code to:
   - Detect defects and questionable constructions
   - Produce various semantic and structural synopses
   - Symbolically execute code
   - Instrument code for dynamic analysis

   No two static analysis systems provide the same set of capabilities. The last two of the above items are provided by relatively few systems.

2. A static analysis system is specific to a single programming language. Compilers provide static analysis capabilities to one extent or another, but they are normally quite limited in this respect.

3. Faults that can be trapped by a static analyzer may be ignored during manual code reviews. Similarly, static analysis can partially automate code standard audits.

4. Symbolic testing (or symbolic execution) evaluates the response of source code to symbolic, rather than numeric, data. The code so exer-

cised is, in effect, evaluated in terms of its performance with respect to classes of data in contrast to the single datum represented by each test case.

5. Comparison of the algebraically couched results of symbolic testing with external specifications given in similar terms constitutes an exact verification process.

6. The various synoptic reports produced by static analysis are useful for measuring semantic properties, aiding code reviewers, reducing the effort required for diagnosing failures during active test, and giving maintenance programmers insight into the as-built structure of programs.

7. As preprocessors, static analysis systems instrument code for the collection of performance and test coverage statistics during active test. A few static analysis systems can also produce program graphs that are valuable for determining where assertion statements should be placed.

8. Static analysis can be used to select an efficient set of cases for achieving a given test coverage objective.

9. Many of the capabilities of static analyzers are achieved solely by analysis of the semantic properties of the code. Other capabilities require varying degrees of structural analysis, and some also require the evaluation of path predicates. The implementation of static analysis functions is largely an extension of compiler design techniques.

10. Static analysis is useful not only during the earliest stages of removing defects from code but also during integration, after all dynamic testing is completed, and after modifications of operational code.

References

1. W. E. Howden, "Symbolic Testing and the DISSECT Symbolic Evaluation System," *IEEE Trans. Software Eng.,* vol. SE-3, no. 4, July 1977, pp. 266–278.
2. L. D. Fosdick and L. J. Osterweil, "Data Flow Analysis in Software Reliability," *ACM Computing Surveys,* vol. 8, no. 3, September 1976, pp. 305–330.
3. R. N. Taylor and L. J. Osterweil, "Anomaly Detection in Concurrent Software by Static Data Flow Analysis," *IEEE Trans. Software Eng.,* vol. SE-6, no. 3, May 1980, pp. 265–278.
4. U. Voges et al., "SADAT – An Automated Testing Tool," *IEEE Trans. Software Eng.,* vol. SE-6, no. 3, May 1980, pp. 286–290.
5. C. V. Ramamoorthy and S. F. Ho, "Testing Large Software with Automated Software Evaluation Systems," *IEEE Trans. Software Eng.,* vol. SE-1, no. 1, January 1975, pp. 46–58.
6. J. C. Huang, "Experience with Use of Instrumentation Techniques in Software Testing," *Proc. NSIA Natl Conf. Software Tech. and Mgmt.,* October 1981, pp. D1–D10.
7. W. Dehaan, *RXVP80™ A Software Documentation, Analysis and Test System,* General Research Corporation, Santa Barbara, Calif.
8. C. V. Ramamoorthy et al., "Design and Construction of an Automated Software Evalua-

tion System," *Record, 1973 IEEE Symp. Computer Software Reliability,* IEEE Cat. No. 73CH0741-9CSR, pp. 28–37.

9. R. Boyer et al., "SELECT — A Formal System for Testing and Debugging Programs by Symbolic Execution," *Proc. Internatl Conf. Reliable Software,* IEEE Cat. No. 75CH0940-7CSR, 1975, pp. 234–245.

10. James King, "Symbolic Execution and Program Testing," *CACM,* vol. 19, no. 7, July 1976, pp. 385–394.

11. T. Cheatham, Jr., et al., "Symbolic Evaluation and the Analysis of Programs," *IEEE Transa. Software Eng.,* vol. SE-5, no. 4, July 1979, pp. 402–417.

Chapter

6

Proof of Correctness

Proof of correctness is precisely what the name says: proving that programs are correct as opposed to proving that they are incorrect (and harboring a defect that must be removed). Although this seems to imply a sunny, positive outlook that — if one believes in the power of self-fulfilling prophecies — militates against finding bugs, proof-of-correctness methods will reliably warn of the presence of defects simply because their mathematical conclusiveness mitigates the effect of the user's bias.

Or, at least, proofs would so warn if with equal or greater likelihood they did not fail because the proof, not the program, was at fault. More on this in Section 6.5. This is only one of the problems with program proofs. We shall deal at length with others as well. In fact, program proofs are worth learning about more because they provide insights to the mathematical properties of programs than because they can play a conspicuous role in a comprehensive defect removal program. It is not that, thoroughly consummated, they are ineffective at finding defects, but that their usefulness is limited by currently available theory and tools.

Proofs are most valuable during program construction, because they permit the programmer to fashion code with confidence that the code is correct. When proof techniques are introduced to symbolic execution (see Section 5.3), a stronger case can be made for the current application of program proving to completed code.

Despite the present limitations of program proving, a great deal of research has gone into the subject, and any number of subsidiary issues have been spawned. As a result, the landscape of proof of correctness is so broad that only a cursory treatment will be given here, one concentrating on the concepts while providing direction for deeper exploration into the intriguing specifics.

After the notion of correctness is introduced by way of an informal example, the axiomatic inductive assertion model (Floyd-Hoare) is described. In this method, the program is represented by a theorem to be proved in the first-order predicate calculus. Axiomatic program proving will be used as the point of departure to survey other very similar methods and the means by which proofs can be partially mechanized.

6.1   Informal Proofs

We start with a proof that we can perform algebraically. Although this informal technique lacks the authority provided by a formal system of logic, thereby making it vulnerable to human oversight, it will serve to introduce the use of assertions in program proving. Moreover, although it does not occupy a central position in the field of proof of correctness, it is a useful method in its own right. The program to be proved is Wensley's iterative algorithm for forming the quotient of two nonnegative numbers, NUM and DEN, where NUM is less than DEN. (That is, the quotient will be less than 1.) The algorithm, which uses only addition, subtraction, and division by 2, computes an additional significant bit in the result of each iteration.

The proof that will be used is after that of Elspas, Levitt, Waldinger, and Waksman[1] with the principal difference that the algorithm is shown in the form of program text, rather than flowchart form, to introduce the notion that assertions can be program statements. First, the algorithm:

```
procedure DIVIDE(NUM,DEN,E,Q)
*E is the accuracy required. E ≥ 0. Q is both the result at exit*
*and at any interim stage. A, B and W are the other elements of *
*the program vector.                                            *
  Q: = 0
  A: = 0
  B: = DEN/2
  W: = 1
  until W < E loop
    if (NUM − A − B) ≥ 0
      then
        Q: = Q + W/2
        A: = A + B
    endif
    B: = B/2
    W: = W/2
  endloop
end
```

We may observe that the variable B, derived from the denominator, is halved at each iteration, as is W, the weight of the added bit. Further, the variable A will approach the numerator as the number of iterations increases. These casual observations may be stated in the form of four assertions of what we know must be true at the beginning of each iteration:

1. $W = 2^{-k}$ for $k \geq 0$ (k is the count of previous iterations)
2. $A = DEN * Q$
3. $B = DEN * W/2$
4. $NUM/DEN - W < Q \leq NUM/DEN$

We may also note that the only way out of the loop is for the relation $W < E$ to hold and, moreover, that the result Q will always approach the real quotient from below. This yields the output assertion

$$NUM/DEN - E < Q \leq NUM/DEN$$

which, of course, looks much like assertion 4 above.

Let us now assume that our language processor can handle statements of the form *assert* (expression), and let us state these assertions in the text of the program:

```
procedure DIVIDE(NUM,DEN,E,Q)
*E is the required accuracy. E > 0. Q is both the result at exit*
*and at any interim stage. A, B, and W are the other elements of *
*the program vector.                                              *
  Q: = 0
  A: = 0
  B: = DEN/2
  W: = 1
  K: = 0
  until K < E loop
    assert W = 1/2 ** K
    assert A = DEN * Q
    assert B = DEN * W/2
    assert NUM/DEN - W < Q and Q ≤ NUM/DEN
    if (NUM - A - B) ≥ 0
      then
        Q: = Q + W/2
        A: = A + B
    endif
    B: = B/2
    W: = W/2
    K: = K + 1
  endloop
  assert NUM/DEN - E < Q and Q ≤ NUM/DEN
end
```

The addition of the new variable K is required only for the evaluation of the first assertion.

Now let us first attempt to verify the assertions within the loop directly after initialization:

1. Since $K = 0$, $W = 2^{-K} = 1$, the initial value.
2. Since $Q = 0$, $A = DEN * Q = 0$, the initial value.
3. Substituting W in $DEN * W/2$, we have $B = DEN/2$, the initial value.

4. Recalling the input assertion (only we did not call it that at the time), $0 \leqslant \text{NUM} < \text{DEN}$. NUM/DEN $- 1$ (the value of W) must be less than zero and consequently less than Q (which *is* zero). Also, NUM/DEN must be greater than Q, since both NUM and DEN are positive and Q is zero.

So much for the initial satisfaction of the assertions. All are true. If on successive iterations the assertions can be proved true, we shall have to prove them true regardless of the path taken in the *if-then* construction. Let us first consider that, on the initial test, $\text{NUM} - \text{A} - \text{B} \geqslant 0$ is false; that is, the test fails. Then, giving the new values of the program vector the symbols (A', B', W', Q', and K'), we have $\text{A}' = \text{A}$, $\text{B}' = \text{B}/2$, $\text{W}' = \text{W}/2$, $\text{Q}' = \text{Q}$, and $\text{K}' = \text{K} + 1$. Retesting the four assertions.

1. $\text{W}' = \text{W}/2 = 1/2 \, ** \, \text{K}'$

2. $\text{A}' = \text{A} = \text{DEN} * \text{Q} = \text{DEN} * \text{Q}'$

3. $\text{B}' = \text{B}/2 = \text{DEN} * \text{W}/4 = \text{DEN} * \text{W}'/2$

4. Substituting in $(\text{NUM} - \text{A} - \text{B} < 0)$, $\text{NUM} - \text{DEN} * \text{Q} - \text{DEN} * \text{W}/2 < 0$. Dividing through by DEN and adding Q to both sides of the relation, NUM/DEN $- \text{W}/2 < \text{Q}$. Since $\text{Q}' = \text{Q}$ and $\text{W}' = \text{W}/2$, we have NUM/DEN $- \text{W}' < \text{Q}'$. And $\text{Q}' \leqslant$ NUM/DEN.

It remains to test the four assertions if the *if-then* test holds. Using (A″, B″, W″, Q″, and K″) as the new program vector, we have

1. $\text{W}'' = \text{W}/2 = 1/2 \, ** \, \text{K}''$

2. $\text{A}'' = \text{DEN} * \text{Q} + \text{DEN} * \text{W}/2 = \text{DEN} * (\text{Q} + \text{W}/2) = \text{DEN} * \text{Q}''$

3. $\text{B}'' = \text{B}/2 = \text{DEN} * \text{W}/4 = \text{DEN} * \text{W}''/2$

4. Since the test at the head of the loop failed, $\text{NUM} - \text{A} - \text{B} \geqslant 0$. Substituting and rearranging as before, NUM/DEN $- \text{W}''/2 < \text{Q}'' + \text{W}''/2$ or NUM/DEN $- \text{W}'' < \text{Q}''$. And $\text{Q}'' \leqslant$ NUM/DEN.

Summarizing, regardless of the path taken, the four assertions are proved true at the start of each new iteration. We have less to consider for the output assertion. Since we know that assertion 4 holds, and since $\text{W} < \text{E}$, it must be true that NUM/DEN $- \text{E} < \text{Q}$ *and* $\text{Q} \leqslant$ NUM/DEN, and that takes care of the output assertion.

We can also use one of our assertions to prove that the program will terminate. Assertion 1 implies that W is monotone decreasing with a limit, as $\text{K} \longrightarrow \infty$, of zero. Ultimately it must reduce to a value less than E as long as E is greater than zero — another input assertion this time found as the first comment in the code. Thus, the termination predicate $\text{W} < \text{E}$ must in time be true.

This is the last we shall see in this chapter of algebraic proofs. However, assertions and the inductive arguments of assertions over the iterations of a loop (attributed to R. W. Floyd[2]) will be used in the following section also.

6.2   The Axiomatic Model

In contrast to the proof of Wensley's algorithm, formal proofs reduce the program text to mathematical forms, determine the mathematical (verification) conditions for correctness, and prove in a *formal system of logic* that the verification conditions are logical theorems. Let us first look at theorems and proofs.

In a formal system of mathematics, a *theorem* is an assertion that can be argued to be true. That argument is called a *proof,* and usually it takes the form of a sequence of assertions each of which can be inferred from a previously proved assertion or from self-evident assertions called *axioms.* Such systems are the mechanisms of mathematical reasoning that underlie the *formal verification* of programs. We now construct a formal logical system.

We shall start with *rules of inference* as the basis for linking statements about propositions in a sequence that forms a proof. Using the notation of Stanat and McAllister,[3] several of those useful for inferring assertions are given in Table 6.1 in their tautological form (that is, the propositional form that evaluates true for all possible values of its variables).

To construct a mathematical model of a computer program, we may define a program in terms of a theorem comprising the program text Q and assertions of the state of the program vector (loosely, the variables of the program) prior to and directly after its execution. Using Hoare's notation,[4] we write the theorem in the form

P{Q}R

This fundamental theorem can be applied for representing Q as either a program or a program segment. The interpretation is that if the assertion P is true before execution of Q, the assertion R will be true following Q's execution. This may also be read backwards: If R is assumed true after execution of Q, P was true before that execution.

By restating programs as theorems, correctness is reduced to the proof that the input,* output,* and intermediate assertions are valid theorems. This proof is accomplished in the first-order predicate calculus.

We must now define some rules of inference specific to computer pro-

---

* Depending on whether one works the proof forward or backwards, one of these is assumed true at the start.

Table 6.1   Rules of Inference

Name	Form	Informal interpretation
Addition	$P \Rightarrow (P \vee Q)$	Proposition P implies proposition P or Q.*
Simplification	$(P \wedge Q) \Rightarrow P$	P and Q (that is, P and the conjunction of Q) imply P.
Modus ponens	$[P \wedge (P \Rightarrow Q)] \Rightarrow Q$	If P implies Q and P is true, Q is implied.
Modus tollens	$[\neg Q \wedge (P \Rightarrow Q)] \Rightarrow \neg P$	If P implies Q and Q is false, P is false.
Disjunctive syllogism	$[(P \vee Q) \wedge \neg P] \Rightarrow Q$	If P or Q is true and P is not true, Q is true.
Hypothetical syllogism	$[(P \Rightarrow Q) \wedge (Q \Rightarrow R)] \Rightarrow (P \Rightarrow R)$	If P implies Q and Q implies R, then P implies R.

* That is, the *truth* of proposition P implies the *truth* of proposition P or the *truth* of proposition Q.

grams. The first is the rule by which we can segment. Called the *rule of composition*, we can write it in a form similar to the tautologies of Table 6.1:

if $P\{Q_1\}$ R $\wedge$ R$\{Q_2\}$S *then* $P\{Q_1; Q_2\}$S

What this is saying is that a program Q may be divided into two segments, Q_1 and Q_2, sharing the intermediate assertion R. The rule is repeated to provide any number of intermediate assertions that will help prove that the exit assertion must derive from the input assertion (or vice versa).

The next rule (or more accurately, pair of rules) allows the assertion that precedes a segment to be replaced by a stronger one and further allows the assertion that follows a segment to be replaced by a weaker one. We can write these *rules of consequence* as

if $P\{Q\}R \wedge S \Rightarrow P$ *then* $S\{Q\}R$
if $P\{Q\}R \wedge R \Rightarrow S$ *then* $P\{Q\}S$

Since "stronger" propositions imply "weaker" ones, from $X \Rightarrow Y$ we can always infer that X is the stronger. Another way of looking at this is that if the execution of Q results in the truth of the assertion R, then it also results in the truth of every assertion that is logically implied by R, as in the second rule, where $R \Rightarrow S$.

We now deal with the *rules of selection*: *if-then* and *if-then-else*:

if-then: P{*if* C *then* Q}R
if-then-else: P{*if* C *then* Q_1 *else* Q_2}R

where C is the branch condition.

Superficially, it may seem odd that a single-result proposition can apply to a program segment with two output branches. However, R is formulated to include in its scope the result of both satisfying C and not satisfying C. For example, for the construction

```
if I = 0
  then X: = 0
  else X: = K + 1
```

an output assertion could be represented by

$$[(I = 0 \wedge X = 0) \vee (I^\neg = 0 \wedge X = X + 1)]$$

Note that this pair of rules provides an axiomatic definition of the two selection constructs.

With a *rule of iteration*, we shall complete a minimum set of inferences with which programs may be logically defined:

$$\textit{if } P \wedge C\{Q\}P \textit{ then } P\{\textit{while } C \textit{ do } Q\} (\neg C \wedge P)$$

If the assertion P is true and the condition C is true before entering the loop and P remains true after each iteration of the body of the loop (Q), then upon completing execution of the loop structure the condition must be false while P remains true. Unlike the other rules, this one has but one assertion, P, that is true before, during, and after execution of the loop segment or body. Called the *loop invariant* (among other names), its specification is one of the major difficulties of formal verifiation. One must find loop invariants that are at once sufficiently general to stipulate the invariant relations and sufficiently strong to imply the output predicate.

Note also that P is a loop invariant IFF $P \wedge C\{Q\}P$ holds and that P is not a function of Q. Although every loop invariant that satisfies these conditions is a loop assertion, as Basu and Misra showed,[5] not all assertions are necessarily strong enough to qualify as loop invariants. We shall return to the problem of forming loop invariants at the end of this section.

Simplifying the rule somewhat, we can let the external condition be understood and simply write the rule of iteration as

$$P\{\textit{while } C \textit{ do } Q\}(\neg C \wedge P)$$

These four rules are quite nearly enough to provide an axiomatic basis for proving correctness by using first-order methods. We need only one more: a rule for assignment. Although every programmer has a correct intuitive understanding of the effect of an assignment symbol, the operation must nevertheless be defined within the overall logical scheme. The *axiom of assignment* is written simply as

$$P_0\{x_i := f(X)\}P$$

where x_i is a particular program variable and X is a subset of all the program variables. X may or may not include x_i. This may be interpreted as follows: If P is true of x_i after the assignment is executed, it must also have been true of the expression f before execution. That is, to derive P_0, for all occurrences of x_i in P substitute f.

An example. We now have a sufficient basis from which we can prove a program correct. For an example, we shall take multiplication by successive addition.* The procedure to be verified forms the product Z of the factors X and Y by setting Z to zero and then adding Y to Z a number of times equal to X, where X is specified as ≥ 0. As in the informal proof of Wensley's algorithm, the assertions have been explicitly placed in the program text and, for later reference, labeled. The proof can be argued without the inclusion of assertions in the text, but as before this has been done in anticipation of the discussion of proof mechanization, without which formal proofs of even simple procedures are beyond reasonable consideration.

```
procedure MULT(X,Y,Z)
  assert X ≥ 0                          ; assertion P
K:= 0
  assert X ≥ 0 ∧ K = 0                  ; assertion I₁
Z:= 0
  assert X ≥ 0 ∧ K = 0 ∧ Z = 0          ; assertion I₂
  assert Z = K * Y ∧ K ≤ X             ; assertion I₃
while K < X do
  assert Z = K * Y ∧ K < X             ; assertion I₄
  Z:= Z + Y
    assert Z = (K + 1) * Y ∧ K < X     ; assertion I₅
  K:= K + 1
    assert Z = K * Y ∧ K ≤ X           ; assertion I₃
endo
  assert Z = X * Y                      ; assertion R
end MULT
```

Following the method used by Stanat and McAllister[3] and others, we divide the proof into the proof of two lemmas, $\ell 1$ and $\ell 2$. That is, the proof of P{MULT}R will be formed from the proofs of P{$\ell 1$}I and I{$\ell 2$}R and the rule of composition.

$\ell 1$:   P{K:= 0; Z:= 0}I_3
$\ell 2$: I_3{while K < X do Z:= Z + Y; K:= K + 1}R

To prove $\ell 1$, we start with assertions P, I_1, and the axiom of assignment: P{K:= 0}I_1. Substituting into this, we have

$$X \geq 0\{K:= 0\}X \geq 0 \wedge K = 0$$

---

* With apologies for the triviality of the program. I have observed that, in the literature of correctness proofs, multiplication by successive addition and division by successive subtraction (used by Hoare[4]) are by far the most popular examples. The consensus seems to be that proofs themselves demand enough of the reader's concentration to make it unwise to use as a first example an algorithm that is not immediately obvious.

Next, we deal with I_2 by writing $I_1\{Z:= 0\}I_2$ as

$$X \geqslant 0 \wedge K = 0 \ \{Z:= 0\}X \geqslant 0 \wedge K = 0 \wedge Z = 0$$

The intermediate assertion I_1 may henceforth be ignored by the rule of composition:

$$P\{K:= 0; Z:= 0\}I_2.$$

With some arithmetic and the hypothetical syllogism of Table 6-1,*

$$I_2 \Rightarrow I_3$$

Accordingly, we can apply the second rule of consequence to the last theorem, giving us

$$P\{K:= 0; Z:= 0\}I_3$$

That is, the segment of MULT up to the *while* loop is proved correct with respect to assertions P and I_2.

The proof of $\ell 2$ resolves to proving $I_3\{loop\}R$. We start with the iteration:

$$I_3 \wedge K < X\{Z:= Z + Y; K:= K + 1\}I_3$$

To execute the bracketed statements, it is necessary that $K < X$. Since

$$Z = K * Y \wedge K \leqslant X \wedge K < X \Rightarrow Z = K * Y \wedge K < X$$

we may use the first rule of consequence to replace the first instance of the loop invariant in the iteration:

$$I_4\{Z:= Z + Y; K:= K + 1\}I_3$$

As we did in Section 6.1, let us write the value of Z after assignment as Z'. Assertion I_5 then reads

$$Z' = (K + 1) * Y \wedge K < X$$

The conjunction of $Z = K * Y \wedge K < X$ and $Z' = Z + Y$ implies the revised I_5, or $I_4\{Z:= Z + Y\}I_5$. Now we represent K' as the value of K after the second assignment statement in the loop and rewrite I_3 as

$$Z' = K' * Y \wedge K' \leqslant X$$

Returning to the text,

$$(Z' = (K + 1) * Y \wedge K < X \wedge K' = K + 1)$$
$$\Rightarrow (Z' = K' * Y \wedge K \leqslant X)$$

---

* To avoid obscuring the proof, further references to the rules of inference of Table 6.1 will be omitted but their application understood.

from which $I_5\{K:= K + 1\}I_3$ holds. We can apply the rule of composition to infer

$$I_4\{Z:= Z + Y; K:= K + 1\}I_3$$

Since we have proved that the rule of iteration holds, we may use it to form

$$I_3\{\textit{while } K < X \textit{ do } Z:= Z + Y; K:= K + 1\}I_3 \wedge K \leqslant X$$

We escape the loop for $K \geqslant X$. Since $I_3 \wedge K \geqslant X \Rightarrow R$, $\ell 2$ is proved by the second rule of consequence.

Applying the rule of composition to $\ell 1$ and $\ell 2$, we have $P\{MULT\}R$, the proof of MULT's correctness with respect to P and R.

Application to real problems.   The proof we have just concluded (often referred to as a Floyd-Hoare proof because Hoare's axiomatic treatment was based on Floyd's method of inductive assertions) is quite obviously tedious and error-prone. The point has been made by several of the early researchers (Hoare, Dijkstra,[6] Wirth,[7] London,[8] Gries[9] and I believe others as well), either explicitly or by example, that these proofs should be developed concurrently with the program or even as a means by which the program is derived.* However, the use of verification systems or symbolic execution to implement proofs (see Section 6.4) is applicable to completed code.

The number of steps required for the proof of MULT raises the question of how a more typical procedure can be proved; one with many more statements and with nested loops and branches. In fact, one rarely tries without mechanical theorem provers (Section 6.4, again). Beyond providing assertions of the input and output conditions, one strategy is to associate one assertion with each sequential group of assignment statements, one for each branch and one (the loop invariant) for each loop while in all cases making certain that no statement falls outside the range of a provable $P\{Q\}R$ theorem. This would seem to be inconsistent with the proof of MULT, wherein each statement was replaced by an equivalent assertion, but the legality of this approach is implied by the rules of composition and consequence (assuming it is done correctly). Attempts to prove that a given assertion can be proved from others will indicate whether the theorem prover needs the help of additional intermediate assertions.

The proof of MULT was in the forward direction; that is, the proof proceeded in the same directions as the sequence of executions. As was implied earlier, proofs may also proceed in the direction opposite that of execution. At each step of these "backward" proofs one attempts to prove that the preexecution assertion is the necessary precondition of the pro-

---

* In fact, this was an essential part of Dijkstra's concept of structured programming.

gram vector for the program segment to have resulted in the given postexecution assertion.

Strategies for the handling of calls to other procedures are based on the presumption (by prior proof) of the called procedure's correctness with respect to its formal parameters. Of the several possibilities for the use of this presumption, one is to replace the called procedure with its input assertion (but with the formal parameters replaced by those in the program vector of the calling program) and prove that the input assertion is satisfied. The called procedure's output assertion may then be treated as a proved lemma.

Recursive routines present a singular problem. How can one previously have proved a recursive routine correct without previously having proved it correct? Formal methods of dealing with this can lead us into further depths of the predicate calculus. For most purposes, it suffices to synopsize the process as one in which an induction over the span of the routine is formed and in which the routine's correctness is assumed. If the proof fails, it is evidence that the assumption does not hold. The method of subgoal induction (see Section 6.3) lends itself to deterministic approaches to setting up the verification conditions for calls to recursive functions.

Total correctness. We have yet to discuss termination as we did in Section 6.1. The proof of a program with respect solely to the program's execution and postexecution assertions is generally referred to as a proof of *partial correctness*. Add to partial correctness the proof of termination and we have a proof of *total correctness*. In the last steps of the proof of MULT, after proving that the rule of iteration holds, we rather glibly stated that the loop is escaped for $K \geqslant X$. We did not, however, prove that the condition $K \geqslant X$ was a necessary consequence of the program.

Proof of program termination nearly always is equivalent to proof of loop termination, proof that the loop exit condition must be satisfied. In the case of MULT such a proof requires an ancillary procedure that proves that repeated incrementing of K must necessarily raise K to the value of X. This really implies futher axiomatic rules to be applied to the behavior of the computer hardware as well as the language constructs. For example, given that a value X can be represented as greater than K, if both X and K are elements of the same set of numbers (data type), repeated execution of $K := K + 1$ will eventually raise K to a value equal to or greater than X provided that $K_0 < X$. In short, we have an argument rather like the $P\{Q\}R$ theorem, but where P is the hypothesis $K_0 < 0$ *and* the conditions on the behavior of the computer, Q is the iterated operation $K := K + 1$, and R is simply $K \geqslant X$.

Although ad hoc methods may be used to prove termination, more elegant approaches have utilized Dijkstra's *predicate transformer*.[6] The idea here is to so define semantics that, working backwards from the system state desired after execution through the executed segment, an initial system state defined to guarantee termination is proved. The predicate transformer, the calculus for deriving programs that it leads to, and its guarantee of termination are beyond our scope. However, two references at the end of the chapter, 10 and 11, describe total correctness methods of proof employing the predicate transformer concept.

More on finding invariants. Determining suitable invariants is probably the thorniest problem attending correctness proofs. The methods for finding invariants can be divided into two classes: algorithmic and heuristic. In the former, deterministic rules derive invariants directly from program semantics. Heuristic approaches accept weak predicates supplied by the programmer or potentially usable loop invariants produced by some incomplete algorithmic technique and "strengthen" or complete the candidate by one procedural method or another. One can think of these two classes as bottom-up and top-down, respectively.

Algorithmic approaches include the work of Basu and Misra,[5] who posited that there exists for any given loop an assertion, related to the function computed by the loop, that is necessary and sufficient for proving correctness and moreover, that several loop invariants can be formed for any loop. For loops exhibiting closure with respect to global variables, they define the form of a predicate P strong enough to prove that the loop performs a function F:

$$P(X, Y) \land \neg condition(X) \Rightarrow X = F(Y)$$

where X is the set of global variables and Y is a set of variables external to the loop.*

Basu[12] uses a specific deterministic method to find invariants for programs that compute output by accumulation during iterations over the input data structures (the class of accumulating programs).

Another algorithmic approach is that of Katz and Manna,[13] who also developed a heuristic. Their algorithms combine the separate generation of invariants from the assignment statements and the test statements of a loop. Wegbreit,[14] who also developed both algorithmic and heuristic methods, based his algorithm on "weak interpretation." That is, he found that certain classes of predicates could be found when the program was evaluated on a simplified model specific to the subject class.

Wegbreit's heuristic method works the output predicate backwards

---

* This conclusion actually relates to theory captured by the functional correctness method, which is briefly discussed in the next section.

through the program while modifying it piecewise to produce candidate loop predicates. Several heuristics are provided for rejecting and strengthening these candidates. The method accommodates the acceptance of inductive assertions supplied by the programmer.

The heuristic method of Katz and Manna[13] is similar. Candidate predicates are subjected to heuristics to strengthen them, weaken them, produce new candidates at antecedent points in the program, produce new candidates at succeeding points, and produce new candidates by restricting the domain of the program variables. Katz and Manna combine both the algorithmic and the heuristic methods into a composite approach.

Thus far we have ignored the problem of finding loop invariants where arrays are involved. The problem here is that invariants that must deal with the relations between arrays or between array variables and scalar variables must take into account the state of array indexes; this despite the fact that an assertion particularized for an index cannot by definition be an invariant. Several methods for handling arrays have been proposed, and we shall briefly look at an overview of one that derives from much of the work previously remarked on in this section.

Assume that a fictitious loop index variable or counter is inserted in each loop. For a single loop, letting k represent the variable, the ith indexed variable will take on the values

$$x_i(k) \qquad i = 1, 2, \ldots n$$

at the control point of the loop. This leads to

$$x_i(k + 1) = f_i[x_1(k), x_2(k), \ldots, x_n(k)]$$

where f_i is the result of analysis of the body of the loop. The loop entry conditions are of the form $x_i(0) = a_i$. Solving the equations in $x_i(k + 1)$ yields a system of equations

$$x_i(k) = g_i(k, a_1, a_2, \ldots, a_n)$$

This system can then be solved to eliminate the variable k, resulting in a new system

$$h_j(x_1, x_2, \ldots, x_n, a_1, a_2, \ldots, a_n) = 0$$

These h_j are invariants at the loop control point, and their conjunction is used, in Ellozy's method,[15] as a candidate inductive predicate. Ellozy then goes on to compare the candidate — possibly strengthened by further consideration of the loop's structure — with the proposed output predicates and then to restrict it by the input predicates.

The above are references to only a portion of the work that has been accomplished toward solving the problem of finding invariants for real-life programs. In general, we can say that heuristic approaches lend themselves quite well to interactive schemes, as do methods combining heuristics with deterministic algorithms. However, practical (mechanized) applications of heuristics require heavy use of theorem provers. Also, heuristics are less successful as the depth of loop nesting increases. It remains that finding suitable loop invariants for real programs constitutes a major hinderance to the wider use of correctness proofs.

6.3   Other Models

In addition to the Floyd-Hoare proof of correctness, methods employing other systems of logic have been developed. In this section we discuss two of them, which are selected because they are similar in concept to the axiomatic model. Both avoid the difficult problem of finding suitable loop invariants, but not without the expense of new problems. Like the axiomatic model, both intrinsically are models of partial correctness. Since the flavor of formal proofs has already been illustrated by the axiomatic model, these two models are discussed only briefly.

Functional correctness.   This model departs in several interesting ways from that of Section 6.2. As succinctly stated by Basili and Noonan, "The goal is to produce loop-free, branch-free, and sequence-free descriptions of the effects of programs on data."[16] The functional correctness approach allows the analyst to *derive* the functions that the program performs and then compare them with the external specifications for the program.

Functional correctness derives from the early work of Mills,[17] which included theorems for composition, *if-then-else,* and iteration. In each, only the function of the construct is material; that is, no variables local to it enter into the derivation of the computed functions. The theorem for iteration is the most interesting, since it obviates the need for a loop invariant. To minimize the introduction of new mathematical notation, it can be stated in the following way:

Given f and a set of ordered pairs (x, y) such that $y = f(x)$, we can write

f = *while* p *do* g

To prove this, we must show that the iteration terminates for every (x, y) pair in f and that

$$[p(x) \wedge y = f(g(x))] \vee [\neg p(x) \wedge y = x]$$

That is, while the condition holds, the body of the loop transforms the state of the data within the domain of f, and when the condition no longer holds, it can have no effect on the state of the variables. The verification condition requires that the loop be closed over the domain of f.

Although functional correctness does away with the need for finding loop invariants, it does require that the intended function of a loop be formed as above; no easy task either. Interestingly, Basu and Misra[5] and also Dunlop and Basili[18] suggest that functional correctness procedures can be used as a heuristic for deriving loop invariants, presumably to continue an axiomatic proof stymied by the inability to find a loop invariant. However, use to this purpose assumes cases in which formulation of the loop function is not equally difficult.

Other salient differences between the axiomatic and functional models are in the mathematics used (the predicate calculus for the former and formal notations for composition and equivalence for the latter) and in the range of specifications required by each (assertions for axiomatic proofs may have to include the effect of previous transformations while functions are local to the segment they are describing).

Subgoal induction. A correctness model similar to the preceding one was developed by Morris and Wegbreit[19] on foundations laid by Manna and Pnueli.[20] Directing their attention to recursively defined functions for LISP-like programs, Manna and Pnueli presented the proof of correctness as a matter of proving the validity of a first-order formula for a program's execution. They developed an algorithmic technique for deriving the formula directly from the program's specification.

Let us look at Morris and Wegbreit's rule for iterative constructions of the form

$$\textit{while } \neg P(X) \textit{ do } X := N(X)$$

where X is an input state vector and N(X) is the transforming body of the loop. For the loop there are two verification conditions in the subgoal induction model:

$$P(X) \Rightarrow \psi(X; X)$$
$$\neg P(X) \wedge X' = N(X) \wedge \psi(X'; Z) \Rightarrow \psi(X; Z)$$

where X' is the altered value of X at the loop control point, (X; Z) is the desired input-output pair, and ψ is a predicate. The concept of subgoal induction is to construct these verification conditions directly from the specification for the loop. It must, of course, be proved that the input-output specification $\psi(X; Z)$ is sufficiently strong, and Morris and Wegbreit present criteria for testing it. Finding adequate input-output specifications is equivalent to constructing adequate loop functions in the functional model.

Morris and Wegbreit remarked on an essential difference between subgoal induction and the method of inductive assertions (which is embodied in the axiomatic model). After noting that the latter leads to the programmer's concentration on the things his program does not change (invariants), they go on to say, "The method of subgoal induction suggests that he concentrate on the dynamics of program segments, i.e. the relation between the current state and the result to be computed."[19] This, too, applies to the functional model, further adding to the sense of equivalence between the two. Finally, Dunlop and Basili observed[18] that subgoal induction can be viewed as the more general case of the functional model, one that applies to a general input-output relation but yields no conclusions if the verification conditions are invalid.

Although the distinction between the subgoal model and the axiomatic model appears clear enough in theory, in practice it may be difficult for even the experts to perceive, at least when recursion is involved. J. C. King, referring to proofs (obtained through symbolic execution) that had been thought to be based on the axiomatic model, wrote, "It was apparent that for simple recursive programs the proofs using the system were proofs by subgoal induction."[11]

6.4   Deus ex Machina

It has already been remarked that attempts to prove correctness entirely by manual means are impractical for any procedures for which one might care to have a proof. This applies to proofs constructed concurrently with code, and not just those attempted after the fact, since a proof typically takes many more steps than are contained in the program being proved. (To say nothing of trying to find adequate inductive assertions or functional or input-output specifications.)

We need not totally despair. Much work on the development of computer-aided verification has been accomplished; it ranges from the restricted goal of helping to find loop invariants to complete verification systems. Before proceeding, however, let it be understood that none of these mechanizations have yet reached a maturity sufficient to encourage the routine use of program proofs.

The synthesis of inductive assertions.   In theory, the programmer should have to supply only the input and output assertions and a loop invariant for each loop of the program. A theorem prover can then generate a proof over the entire space of the program. In practice, any additional assertions the programmer can provide will be greatly appreciated by the theorem prover — or at least by whomever is paying for computer time, since theorem proving is a slow operation. The theory is of little help, with or without programmer-determined intermediate assertions, if forming the loop invariants is a nearly insurmountable problem.

As we saw in Section 6.2, various techniques have been developed to help generate loop invariants. We note two of them that have been automated to one extent or another. ADI[21] mechanizes the combined heuristic and algorithmic techniques of Katz and Manna.[13] Written in QLISP and INTERLISP, ADI, still under development at the start of the 1980s, finds as many invariants as it can and then applies heuristics (including rules beyond those of Katz and Manna) to generate adequate inductive assertions from the conjunction of the invariants. ADI is interactive and uses a theorem prover developed at the Stanford Research Institute (SRI).

VISTA[22] extended the work of Wegbreit.[14] It generates certain inductive assertions automatically and extends other, partial, ones supplied by the programmer. Its theorem prover is one developed by Deutsch at Berkeley as part of his automatic program verifier PIVOT, the subject of his doctoral dissertation. One of the features of VISTA is its use of symbolic execution (in the weak interpretation of Wegbreit's method) to derive simple assertions from the program text.

Apart from its use in a larger system, symbolic execution may be used as an independent technique to aid the programmer in forming loop invariants. A loop may be executed with various symbolic input selected to evaluate the loop's behavior over its full domain. Observation of the algebraically simplified state of the variables at the same point within the loop (normally, the loop test) for the several test cases may provide insights into the invariant relations among the set of variables.

Before leaving systems specific to the synthesis of assertions, let us note that Dershowitz and Manna[23] have developed an experimental system that combines features from systems already discussed to annotate a program with invariant assertions. Operating on the program text, an input specification, and an output specification, the system iteratively generates invariant relations of the program without regard to whether the program is correct. Even without further processing, inspection of these invariants may reveal that the program is not constructed as the programmer had intended.

Verification systems.   We have had several references thus far to the use of theorem provers. Theorem provers, which mostly work either by trying to find contradictions in the proof of negated theorems or by using various deductive methods, are one of the principal components of verification systems. Mostly, these systems comprise verification condition generators, facilities for simplification, and theorem provers, although these functions may not necessarily be implemented as separate components.

Continuing in a general way, verification conditions essentially are lemmas of the kind used in the proof of MULT. Verification condition generators combine assertions and the text following each to produce the conditions. Simplification is the process of reducing complex expressions by one mechanism or another within the semantic reference of the verification system. Theorem provers mechanize the process of proving the truth of an assertion.

Among these "classic" systems are the early verifier reported by King[24] for operating on ALGOL-like programs of restricted data domain and Deutsch's interactive PIVOT, previously remarked on. Another classic example is that of Good, London, and Bledsoe[25] of the University of Southern California. Based on LISP, their system operates on Pascal-like programs. The verification condition generator is based on the axioms and rules of inference of the axiomatic definition of Pascal. The verification conditions are produced with reference to the variables appearing in Pascal text and in assertion statements. The simplification functions include the use of a symbolic evaluator to reduce expressions within the verification conditions and an interactive routine that allows the programmer to simplify the verification hypotheses by substitution. The theorem prover also is interactive.

Continued research at USC has resulted in the AFFIRM[36] system, implemented in INTERLISP. Remarked on in Section 2.1 as a specification language, the system also accepts Pascal-like programs, for which it provides a verification condition generator that not only is a successor to the earlier one but also supports subgoal induction.

Still another classic system is the Stanford University system reported by Suzuki.[26] An interesting feature is that the programmer is given the capability to extend the language (Pascal) with new symbols of intuitive meaning to express variable relations beyond those feasible in the first-order predicate calculus. Let us look at this more closely. Functions, such as the mapping of the elements of one array into another, are handled with excessive verbosity in first-order systems. Second-order logic, which allows quantification of the symbols for predicates and functions,* is much more powerful. For example, the principle of mathematical induction, expressed by an infinite number of first-order axioms, is given in second-order logic by a single axiom:[1]

$$(\forall P)[P(0) \wedge (\forall X)(P(X) \Rightarrow P(X + 1)) \Rightarrow (\forall X)(P(X)]$$

Unfortunately, second-order logic is much more difficult to work with than first-order logic. One approach to taking advantage of the precepts of second-order logic, without having to actually work in the system, is to permit substitution of the predicate and function variables. This is the technique used at Stanford, in which new symbols (e.g., "ordered" and "biggest") appear in the assertion statements.

Although the programmer supplies predicates in terms of these intuitive

---

* For example, the symbol $\forall$, meaning "for all" or "over all."

symbols, he must also supply their meaning in the first-order calculus as well as rules for their use. The verification conditions generated by the system are output in terms of the symbols. Among its other merits, this permits easier interpretation of the lemmas for the manual refinement of trial predicates into proper loop invariants. Polak[27] demonstrates the Stanford verifier on a nontrivial, if small, program: Knuth's permutation program.

As may be inferred from the preceding paragraph, the Stanford system does not automatically solve the problem of supplying loop invariants. None of these verification systems do. However, the interactive ones offer assistance by presenting the derived verification conditions for the programmer's interpretation and by offering the services of a theorem prover.

Before leaving verification systems, let us pause to observe two extremes in mechanical aids to verification. The research group that invented the language Euclid specifically for development of *verifiable* systems software has now achieved a verification condition generator for Concurrent Euclid.[28] In contradistinction to axiomatic language definitions, a verification condition generator has been built for a dialect of Fortran containing the full repertoire of *goto* statements.[29] The availability of verification systems may yet be routine.

Symbolic execution revisited. In Chapter 5 symbolic execution was introduced as a method for evaluating the behavior of a program with respect to classes of input conditions, that is, with symbolic input rather than actual data. Symbolic execution systems were described as having the capability of evaluating the response of each program statement when given algebraic expressions for the variables of the statement. Thus, the predicate $A > B$, which in actual execution might compare the integers 7 and 75, in symbolic execution might cause the system to determine whether $X + Y$ is greater than $X - Y$.

This suggests that symbolic execution can be a mechanism to determine whether the text of a program is consistent with assertions of what that text should represent. If a symbolic execution system can evaluate a boolean expression (i.e., find it true or false), it can evaluate an assertion with respect to its variables. For example, *assert* $A > B$ can be evaluated with respect to the symbolic values (algebraic expressions) of A and B, and the results can be output. In the most simple case, if the programmer has run enough test cases to "execute" each possible path to the assertion and if the assertion proved true in each case, this is tantamount to proving correctness with respect to that one assertion.

It is necessary to evaluate the assertion in terms of the path actually traversed. When several paths terminate at the same point, it would appear that the programmer has to construct a different assertion for each.

This can be avoided if, in addition to being able to prove the hypothesis that the terminating assertion holds true, the system can also establish verification conditions consistent with the input assertion and the statements within each path.

Thus, given assertion statements as part of the semantic content of the programming language, a symbolic execution system augmented by a theorem prover can be employed to assist in proving correctness. This statement approximates the description of both SELECT[30] and EFFIGY.[31,32] The former, developed at the Stanford Research Institute, operates on a LISP-like language. The second, invariably associated with J. C. King, its principal researcher, operates on a simple PL/1-like language. Although the two systems were developed independently, they are quite similar, and we need only remark on the characteristics of one of them to impart a sense of this form of correctness proof.

In EFFIGY, input and output assertions are encoded as *assume* and *prove* statements, respectively. Each has a boolean argument [e.g., *assume* $(A > B \wedge B > 0)$]. The *assume* statement can be used to constrain the paths that will be symbolically executed. For example, if the program contains the statement

```
if A < 0 then A: = 0
```

an input predicate constraining A to be greater than or equal to 0 will force the false path.

Generally following the concept used by Deutsch in his interactive program verifier, the actual generation of the verification conditions is done by the symbolic execution of the path. During the execution, an increasing number of stipulations concerning the input variables are conjoined to the "path condition," initially a function of only the *assume* statement, to define the path domain through the program statements that are encountered. The *prove* statement attempts to prove the theorem that the value of its argument is implied by the path condition, also a boolean expression of input symbolic values. If so, it prints "verified." EFFIGY automatically modifies the path conditions to force all of the paths within the domain constrained by the *assume* argument. If each of these test cases results in the theorem's proof, if the boolean argument of the *assume* statement derives directly from the input specification (no other programmer-supplied constraints), and if the argument of the *prove* statement derives directly from the output specification, correctness has been proved.

Intermediate assertions, required for each loop, are handled by the *assert* statement. This statement undergoes a metamorphosis during symbolic execution. When first encountered, it is treated as an *assume* statement that provides an input assertion for the loop. When encountered the next time, it is treated as a *prove* statement to verify that the loop predicate has held; and then it is used again to assert the input conditions for the next iteration.

Specifying the input and output assertions remains a difficult task. Moreover, lengthy verification conditions can tax the theorem prover. By using the input assertion to place restrictions on the input conditions beyond those found in the procedure's input specification, the domain of the program can be reduced to subdomains that ease the task of forming the output predicates and improve the likelihood of success of the system's theorem prover. Although the set of disjoint proofs so produced is less satisfactory than a complete proof, defects can be found in this way.

Now for the bad news. Symbolic execution does not relieve the programmer from having to form sufficiently strong inductive assertions. Moreover, the problems attending symbolic execution (as noted in Section 5.3) remain when the system is used to aid program proving. Finally, symbolic execution research has focused on languages of limited utility.

Concerning the last, rules of inference that derive from symbolic execution methodology have been developed to define a language containing multiple exits from loops and procedures and expressions with side effects.[33] The evaluation by symbolic execution of programs in this language has been formally described in an attribute grammer, and a verification condition generator has been built on the basis of the rules of inference. Recall the concluding remarks under Verification Systems. Symbolic execution technology may also be maturing to such point that we shall see it available for proving programs written in the more common languages.

Miscellaneous systems.   Mechanical aids to proving correctness are not limited to those that assist in implementing Floyd-Hoare proofs. In particular, Boyer and Moore[34] have used a model known as *structural induction* for a system that proved a variety of recursive LISP functions. More recently, working in INTERLISP, they have demonstrated that if the statement of correctness for a given metafunction is proved, the code derived from the definition of the function can be used as a new proof procedure.[35]

6.5   Some concluding observations

At the current (early 1980s) stage of development, none of the formal correctness schemes offers the facility of use that would permit its application in a production environment. Not even if we accept that the principal benefit is adding to the programmer's insight as the code is generated, as opposed to applying proofs to completed code, can the mostly manual procedures be productively applied to more than the smallest (most critical) part of a large software system.

Verification systems and symbolic execution systems would seem to lend themselves to ex post facto proofs. However, the use of these systems (which may have matured to the point of real, not academic, utility by the time this is read) still requires considerable programmer labor. This, too, precludes use for more than a few critical procedures in a large system.

We have also to recognize that all the theory is directed toward finding inductive assertions and verification conditions in a correct program. If the program contains a bug, the proof will fail and reveal the bug quite handily. However, the proof will also fail if the assertions were not properly constructed, except that incorrect assertions — chiefly loop invariants — may produce the illusion of correctness by their incompleteness. Moreover, given a correct program and correct (and adequate) assertions, the proof may still fail because of a mistake (even one made by a mechanical theorem prover) in the proof procedure.

From these arguments, we must conclude that, even under ideal circumstances, formal proof of correctness best serves to bolster confidence in the correctness of a program, precisely what the name implies.

All is not grim. With whatever mechanical aids one has, certain useful conclusions can be drawn. The inductive assertions found may well indicate to the programmer that the code is not what was intended. If loop invariants for a symbolic execution cannot be found, then the system may still be run with what the programmer intuitively feels are assertions characteristic of the required behavior. Call this partial partial correctness if you will. A symbolic interpreter may also be run with deliberately incomplete output assertions to avoid investigation into areas the programmer is entirely certain of or to reduce the difficulty of the theorem prover's task.

Nor should we forget the business of informal proofs, the substance of Section 6.1. Especially if restricted to only transformations of which there can be some doubt, informal proofs are not as difficult or time-consuming.

For formal proofs to play a bigger part in computer programming, considerable progress in their mechanization is required. Expectations that this may happen are more than wishful thinking. In addition to the interest in artificial intelligence heretofore held mostly by the universities, we are now seeing interest expressed by industry. As new developments in AI evolve for commercial use, we should see some fallout accrue to the benefit of theorem provers and the synthesis of inductive assertions. Moreover, we should witness the migration of these mechanizations from academe to industry. Indeed, the following programmer's fantasy may finally be realized:

> My routines are the pride of my heart.
> Each attests to the state of my art.
> It's as easy as pie
> To prove naught is awry:
> My machine's artificially smart.

6.6 Summary

1. Proof techniques make use of assertions of the relations that exist among the program variables at key points in the program. Other than informal proofs, arguing the truth of the assertions is performed within a formal system of mathematics.

2. Most of the research on proof of correctness has focused on the axiomatic model, which provides axioms and rules of inference for the semantic content of programs.

3. Proofs in the axiomatic model use the theorem-proving methods of the first-order predicate calculus. The program is modeled in terms of axioms and theorems that are then used to prove that the output assertion holds true if the input assertion is true or, alternatively, that the input assertion must be true for the outut assertion to be assumed true.

4. Induction over the number of executions of a loop requires the programmer to provide an invariant assertion for the loop that holds true before, during, and after the loop's exit. Forming these loop invariants is often extremely difficult, although several techniques have been devised to make the problem more tractable.

5. Proving that a program is correct with respect to its input and output assertions is referred to as partial correctness. For a proof of total correctness, one must also prove that the program will terminate.

6. Similar in concept to the axiomatic model are the functional and subgoal models. These avoid the need for finding loop invariants, but only at the expense of introducing new problems.

7. Failure of a proof may indicate not that the program was wrong, but that the assertions were not properly constructed or that a mistake was made in the theorem-proving process.

8. Computer programs to mechanize the proof of programs include those that help synthesize inductive assertions, generate verification conditions, and prove theorems. When the last two are combined with a simplification facility for reducing logical propositions, one has a complete system to help prove the truth of programmer-supplied assertions. Few languages are supported by these aids, nor is success always realizable.

9. Another form of mechanization is the use of symbolic execution equipped with the capability of evaluating assertions. Going a step further, symbolic execution systems have been augmented by theorem provers that can prove verification conditions with respect to the symbolic execution.

10. The versatility of symbolic execution lends itself to the use of several work-arounds to the problems of proving correctness. Although they may result in less than complete proofs, defects can be found in this way.

11. Even with mechanical help, proving program correctness remains a tedious (read expensive) task.

12. In general, the use of program proofs is most appropriate when it is concurrent with program construction. However, employing verification systems and symbolic execution on completed procedures may be planned as part of the defect removal process for the critical kernels of software systems.

References

1. B. Elspas et al., "An Assessment of Techniques for Proving Program Correctness," *ACM Computing Surveys*, vol. 4, June 1972, pp. 97–147.
2. R. W. Floyd, "Assigning Meanings to Programs," *Proc. Symp. Appl. Math.*, American Mathematical Society, vol. 19, 1967, pp. 19–32.
3. Donald F. Stanat and David F. McAllister, *Discrete Mathematics in Computer Science*, Prentice-Hall, Englewood Cliffs, N.J., 1977.
4. C. A. R. Hoare, "An Axiomatic Basis for Computer Programming," *CACM*, vol. 12, October 1969, pp. 576–583.
5. S. Basu and J. Misra, "Proving Loop Programs," *IEEE Trans. Software Eng.*, vol. 1, March 1975, pp. 76–86.
6. Edsger W. Dijkstra, "Guarded Commands, Nondeterminacy and Formal Derivation of Programs," *CACM*, vol. 18, August 1975, pp. 453–457.
7. Niklaus Wirth, "On the Composition of Well-Structured Programs," *ACM Computing Surveys*, vol. 6, December 1974, pp. 247–259.
8. Ralph L. London, "A View of Program Verification," *Proc. 1975 Internatl Conf. Reliable Software*, IEEE Cat. No. 75CH0940-7CSR, pp. 534–545.
9. David Gries, "An Illustration of Current Ideas on the Derivation of Correctness Proofs and Correct Programs," *IEEE Trans. Software Eng.*, vol. SE-2, December 1976, pp. 238–244.
10. S. Basu and R. Yeh, "Strong Verification of Programs," *IEEE Trans. Software Eng.*, vol. SE-1, September 1975, pp. 339–345.
11. James C. King, "Program Correctness: On Inductive Assertion Methods," *IEEE Trans. Software Eng.*, vol. SE-6, September 1980, pp. 465–479.
12. Sanat Basu, "A Note on Synthesis of Inductive Assertions," *IEEE Trans. Software Eng.*, vol. SE-6, January 1980, pp. 32–39.
13. S. Katz and Z. Manna, "Logical Analysis of Programs," *CACM*, vol. 19, April 1976, pp. 188–206.
14. Ben Wegbreit, "The Synthesis of Loop Predicates," *CACM*, vol. 17, February 1974, pp. 102–112.
15. Hamed Ellozy, "The Determination of Loop Invariants for Programs with Arrays," *IEEE Trans. Software Eng.*, vol. SE-7, March 1981, pp. 197–206.
16. V. Basili and R. Noonan, "A Comparison of the Axiomatic and Functional Models of Structured Programming," *IEEE Trans. Software Eng.*, vol. SE-6, September 1980, pp. 454–464.
17. Harlan Mills, "The New Math of Computer Programming," *CACM*, vol. 18, January 1975, pp. 43–48.
18. D. Dunlop and V. Basili, "A Comparative Analysis of Functional Correctness," *ACM Computing Surveys*, vol. 14, June 1982, pp. 229–244.

19. J. Morris and B. Wegbreit, "Subgoal Induction," *CACM,* vol. 20, April 1977, pp. 209–222.
20. Z. Manna and A. Pnueli, "Formalization of Properties of Functional Programs," *JACM,* vol. 17, July 1970, pp. 555–569.
21. Moshe Tamir, "ADI: Automatic Derivation of Invariants," *IEEE Trans. Software Eng.,* vol. SE-6, January 1980, pp. 40–48.
22. S. German and B. Wegbreit, "A Synthesizer of Inductive Assertions," *IEEE Trans. Software Eng.,* vol. SE-1, March 1975, pp. 68–75.
23. N. Dershowitz and Z. Manna, "Inference Rules for Program Annotation," *IEEE Trans. Software Eng.,* vol. SE-7 March 1981, pp. 207–222.
24. James King, "Proving Programs to Be Correct," *IEEE Trans. Computers,* vol. C-20, November 1971, pp. 1331–1336.
25. Donald Good et al., "An Interactive Program Verification System," *IEEE Trans. Software Eng.,* vol. SE-1, March 1975, pp. 59–67.
26. N. Suzuki, "Verifying Problems by Algebraic and Logical Reduction," *Proc. 1975 Internatl Conf. Reliable Software,* IEEE Cat. No. 75CH0940-7CSR, pp. 473–481.
27. Wolfgang Polak, "An Exercise in Automatic Program Verification," *IEEE Trans. Software Eng.,* vol. SE-5, September 1979, pp. 453–458.
28. H. C. Holt, "A Short Introduction to Concurrent Euclid," *Computing Surveys* and *SIGPLAN Notices,* ACM, vol. 17, May 1982, pp. 60–79.
29. R. Boyer and J. S. Moore, *The Correctness Problem in Computer Science,* Academic Press, New York, 1981, pp. 9 –101.
30. R. Boyer et al., "SELECT — A Formal System for Testing and Debugging Programs by Symbolic Execution," *Proc. 1975 Internatl. Conf. Reliable Software,* IEEE Cat. No. 75CH0940-7CSR, pp. 234–245.
31. James C. King, "Symbolic Execution and Program Testing," *CACM,* vol. 19, July 1976, pp. 385–394.
32. S. Hantler and J. King, "An Introduction to Proving the Correctness of Programs," *ACM Computing Surveys,* vol. 8, September 1976, pp. 331–353.
33. R. Dannenberg and G. Ernst, "Formal Program Verification Using Symbolic Execution," *IEEE Trans. Software Eng.,* vol. SE-8, January 1982, pp. 43–52.
34. R. Boyer and J. S. Moore, "Proving Theorems about Lisp Functions," *JACM,* vol. 22, January 1975, pp. 129–144.
35. R. Boyer and J. S. Moore, *The Correctness Problem in Computer Science,* Academic Press, New York, 1981, pp. 103–184.
36. David R. Musser, "Abstract Data Type Specification in the AFFIRM System," *IEEE Trans. Software Eng.,* vol. SE-6, January 1980, pp. 24–32.

Dynamic Testing

Matters of Strategy

Let us begin these chapters on active testing with the observation that the greatest value received from a test is its disclosure of existing defects. I have several times argued this point with people who held the opposite view: that the purpose of a test is to demonstrate the capabilities of a program. The fallacy of the second position is that every defect not exposed by a test, regardless of the specific operation successfully demonstrated, will eventually manifest itself as a degradation of performance. Admittedly, at some point one needs to assess the extent to which performance objectives have been attained. This is especially true of qualification testing, when compliance to specified performance requirements must be demonstrated. Nevertheless, the fewer defects the operational software product has, the more satisfied will be its users, and dynamic testing represents the last opportunity to remove latent defects from the programs delivered to users.

Accordingly, in planning a testing program the emphasis should be on defect removal. This implies the efficient utilization of a variety of test techniques and implementation tactics directed to the purpose of defect removal; a strategy that must address such issues as

- Determining where each test technique shall be applied
- Forming objectives for each test series
- Planning for the timely availability of hardware, software, and human resources required to meet test objectives
- Choosing reliable test cases

This last requires some explanation. Goodenough and Gerhart define test reliability in terms of a data selection criterion C:[1] "In short, to be reliable C must insure selection of tests that are consistent in their ability to *reveal* errors, as opposed to necessarily being able to detect *all* errors."

Much of the modern testing theory has been directed to the determination of sets of tests that are reliable in this sense. Although these chapters on dynamic testing are built on a foundation of modern testing theory, we shall not dwell on theoretical aspects but shall concentrate on practical measures that, in the aggregate, are consonant with the theoretical objectives. Test theory is very difficult to directly translate into test cases, often because it requires information that is too time-consuming to come by and too arduous to use if you have it. With respect to test planning, practical interpretation of testing theory reduces to forming a strategy that will maximize the rate of return (measured in detected defects) for the amount of testing performed.

In planning a test program, it would be of inestimable help if we knew just how many defects lie hidden in freshly minted code. Besides helping us plan the duration and use of personnel for testing, the number would also tell us when we need no longer test for bug removal (given the optimistic assumption that no new bugs will be introduced in the process). Unfortunately, we shall never be able to get an accurate estimate of the bug count, but before confronting the central issues of test strategies, let us digress to examine techniques that can provide some inkling of the number of defects *ab initio.*

7.1   Defect Estimation

At the start of testing, the number of bugs is related to:

1. Size
2. Complexity
3. Software development environment, methodology, and languages
4. Programmer competence
5. Passive defect removal procedures previously performed
6. Stability of requirements and top-level design

Assuming items 3, 4, and 5 are fairly consistent from project to project, in theory we should be able to perform regression analysis on items 1, 2, and 6 — by using some modeling technique for each — to estimate the number of bugs that will have to be removed. The theory can further be extended to gauge the reliability of the estimate from the regression coefficients. However, item 6 is not readily quantifiable by any theoretic technique, although we can settle for counting the number of change notices applied to requirements and design documentation. Still, this fails to take into account the level of significance of the changes. Perhaps the most realistic approach to item 6, given still vivid memories of whatever turmoil attached to the early development stages, is to upgrade the number of bugs estimated from items

1 and 2 by some intuitive ratio. For example, add 20 percent because half the top-level design was reworked when the requirements tardily reached the usual state of maturity.

What we are left with, then, is a formula in which

Number of bugs = F(complexity, size)

The quantified measure of complexity would, of course, be normalized for size.

Deriving the formula presents several problems. For a statistically significant history to which we can apply regression analysis, we require a number of projects to have been completed (and measured) while factors 3, 4, and 5 remained stable. Since the completion of large projects takes many months, during which practices are upgraded and personnel are changed, and since few programming installations have more than a handful of large projects concurrently in progress, the number of samples to analyze will be small.

As a practical matter, it is unlikely that a formula for the number of bugs as a function of complexity and size can be formed except by averaging the normalized history of a very few relevant projects, with size and complexity considered independently. Then one can go with whichever of the two seems the more consistent.

This seems most unscientific, but it represents a major improvement over the usual practice of making no estimates at all.* Let us, then, look at the measurements of size and complexity.

Measuring program size.   The simplest measurement of size is the number of lines of code (LOC). Since we are much less concerned with annotation defects than program faults, more useful is the count of noncomment source statements (NCSS). Unfortunately, even the latter fails to account for statement density. One program may have a preponderance of short, simple statements, which will preclude sensible comparison with programs with long algebraic expressions and compound predicates.

Of the measures of size that are attempts to deal with these variables, none has achieved more prominence than Maurice Halstead's measures.[2] The core of the family of these programming yardsticks is based on four variables:

n_1 = number of unique operators in a program
n_2 = number of unique operands in a program
N_1 = total count of the use of all operators
N_2 = total count of the occurrence of all operands

---

* Besides being unscientific, it presupposes the existence of historical data, which is to say measurement. More on this in Chapter 10.

From these, the *vocabulary* of the program is defined to be

$$n = n_1 + n_2$$

The *length* is defined as

$$N = N_1 + N_2$$

The *volume* is defined as

$$V = N \log_2 n$$

Halstead also goes on to derive other measures, but they are based on less easily quantified matters such as language levels and the rate at which programmers can make mental discriminations. To the critical observer, they seem to be as much the product of divination as of technical causality, although some success has attended various attempts to validate these derivative models. (Unfortunately, as Gillian Frewin and Peter Hamer showed in an internal ITT memorandum, the validation experiments seem to be chronically beset by deviations from the scientific method.)

At any rate, both Halstead length and volume have at least intuitive appeal as size measures, although his nomenclature may seem arbitrary. They may even have a foundation. Halstead also gives an alternative formula for estimating length:

$$N = n_1 \log_2 n_1 + n_2 \log_2 n_2$$

Although Halstead offers no derivation of this equation, Laemmel and Shooman[3] show that their translation of Zipf's laws of natural language* into computer programs provides a theoretical basis from which this alternative form of N can be derived. Thus, the basic Halstead measures have a more satisfactory meaning than intuition alone can provide.

Unfortunately, the Halstead length and volume are often viewed as measures of complexity. This does not at all correspond with the commonly shared perception that complexity has something to do with interactions, path divergence and convergence, and so on. For a complexity model, we should want something that correlates better with intuition.

Measuring complexity. Models for estimating program complexity have been based on nearly every aspect of program structure and semantics imaginable. Quite a few of them are described in a recent survey.[4] Two that were not included, but are interesting because of their use of information entropy, are those of Berlinger[5] and Mohanty.[6] There are still more, but to

---

* Laws having to do with the statistical occurrences of words in natural languages. These laws have been successfully validated for a number of languages.

illustrate the concept of complexity measurement, we shall use only the one that has probably gained the greatest acceptance, McCabe's cyclomatic complexity measure.[7] I suspect that the relative popularity ("relative" because few programming installations make any attempt to measure complexity) derives from the ease of application and the intuitive appeal of a model based entirely on the decision structure of a program. As simple as the model is, there is scant evidence that attempts to refine it by further structural considerations provide any closer correlation with experience.

The McCabe model is expressed by the simple equation

$$V(G) = e - n + 2p$$

where $V(G)$ = graph-theoretic cyclomatic number, used here as the measure of complexity

e = number of edges (or statement-to-statement arcs) in the program

n = number of vertices (or nodes) in the program

p = number of connected components (essentially, the number of independent procedures if each has its own graph)

In the calculation, a directed graph is assumed; that is, each edge is unidirectional. If control can flow both ways between two nodes, the two nodes are connected by two edges.

Figure 7.1 is the program graph for the procedure COMP of Section 4.2. The numbers identifying the nodes are the statement numbers of the program text. To make the graph more obvious, we can *reduce* it by combining with their successors the nodes (except for the entry node) that have only one edge as an output. This leads to the reduced graph of Figure 7.2, which has 9 vertices and 14 edges. Since it has but one component, its cyclomatic number is

$$V(G) = 14 - 9 + 2 = 7$$

Assume that a program about to be tested comprises m procedures, or connected components. To form the gross complexity measure, we simply sum each of the m $V(G)$ calculated as above. Alternatively, we drop the 2p term of the calculation for each and form the gross complexity from

$$V(G) = \sum_{i=1}^{m} V_i(G) + 2m \qquad V_i(G) = e_i - n_i$$

The two methods are equivalent.

There are, of course, limitations to the ability of this model to represent complexity accurately. The model does not account for the difficulties intrinsic to different types of structures. For example, quoting Bill Curtis et al., "Further, neither Halstead's nor McCabe's metrics consider the level of nesting within various constructions (e.g., three DO loops in succession will result in metric values similar to those for three nested DO loops). However, nesting may influence psychological complexity."[8] And psychological complexity influences defect production.

Moreover, it is impossible for the McCabe model to consider the complexity associated with interaction with the outside world, including the

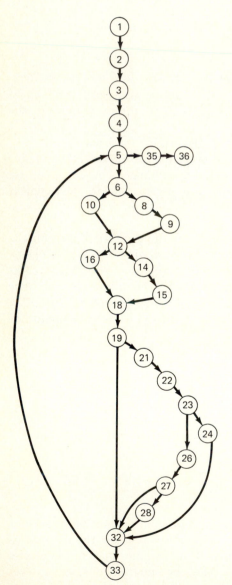

Figure 7.1   Directed graph of COMP.

effects of response time dependencies. Nor does it account for either the complexity of data definitions or the level of abstraction of the coding language. Assembly language offers the hazards of access to the program counter and various registers; a risky business that is spared programs written in compiler language.

Still, the emphasis on the decision structure is borne out by other experiments. Here is an example. In a linear regression analysis of software problems with respect to measures of program properties, Lipow and Thayer[9] initially used nine independent variables as program descriptors:

1. Number of branches
2. Number of calls to application routines
3. A complexity measure based upon the number and levels of nesting of *if* statements
4. Number of assignment statements not involving arithmetic operations
5. A loop complexity measure based on the number of levels of nesting
6. Number of calls to system or support routines
7. Number of I/O statements

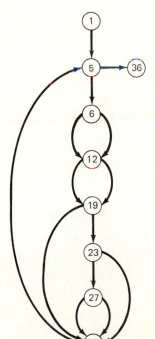

Figure 7.2 Reduced directed graph of COMP.

8. Number of assignment statements involving arithmetic operations

9. Number of nonexecutable statements (but not including comments)

In attempting to correlate these descriptors with failures, the last five were quickly eliminated on the basis of statistical zero influence coefficients. With just the first four, R^2, the square on the multiple correlation coefficient, was calculated as .967. Using stepwise minimization, the number of variables was reduced to just the first, with R^2 diminished by only .008 (to a value of .959). The suggestion that the number of branches alone is a good defect predictor seems to corroborate the McCabe measure.

Interestingly, Lipow and Thayer also attempted to correlate problems with the total number of statements (over 300K machine language instructions divided among 25 functions), which resulted in R^2 of .941, less convincing than that obtained from just the number of branches.

Whatever measures of size and complexity are used, and assuming there also exists a history of the number of defects found in dynamic testing and operational use of previous projects, one can apply past experience to the present work to arrive at a rough estimate (perhaps ± 30 percent) of the testing job at hand.

7.2   Incremental Test Strategies

However many bugs we expect, we know better than to attempt to purge them in a single, monolithic, series of tests. Rather, we divide the testing period into several more or less sequential stages to which different objectives have been assigned. Not all programs have the same defined phases of testing, since the latter reflect the type of program at hand. Further, we neither have nor need a doctrine that there is but one way to segment the testing applicable to a given type. Table 7.1 compares a phasing strategy

Table 7.1   Possible Incremental Testing Strategies for Two Types of Programs

Automated office system	Embedded system
Unit test (module level)	Unit test (module level)
Integration (modules operating together)	Software integration (modules operating together)
System test (evaluate system against external specifications)	Software test (evaluate program against its external specifications to the extent possible)
Volume test (stress program)	Hardware-software integration (resolve hardware-software interface inconsistencies)
Qualification (test program in end-use installation with real data and actual operators)	Qualification (test hardware-software system against its external specifications)

applicable to automated office software with one that might be used for embedded software.

The comparison illustrates only a single possible strategy for each of the two program types. For the automated office system, one could also include an installation test before qualification; for the embedded system one might consider a separate phase for stress testing rather than imply incorporation of that testing in hardware and software integration or qualification or both. Less of a variation is the use of alternative names: string test instead of integration, acceptance instead of qualification, procedure or module test instead of unit test. No matter. The idea of gradually building a system in an incremental fashion is the important thing.

The basic philosophy of incremental testing is to reduce the uncertainty in the location of the faults responsible for failures. Thus we start with unit test. If a test is directed to the operation of a single element of the program, we can be fairly confident that a problem that develops is in that element.

Confident, but not certain. It might be in the test harness. In top-down testing, wherein the element is first tested in an evolving system, the defect may be in a previously tested unit or in the mutual interface. Even here, however, the scope of uncertainty is reduced by the limited size of the test driver or the known path taken through the partially integrated program. In general, the test stages are so defined as to reduce the range of diagnostic searches, but no division can restrict them as much as one would hope.

Within an incremental strategy, integration largely becomes a matter of testing software interfaces, which, by implication, also means testing the overall program structure. Section 7.3 will have more to say about integration.

Extrapolating from unit test and integration, we see the progression of the testing stages toward ever-increasing levels of abstraction. Each one entails more pieces (software, hardware, people, whatever), with the consequence that diagnosing the cause of failure becomes more difficult and expensive. Moreover, as the system grows, the cost of library control associated with the removal of a defect increases. At the module level, there is no library control overhead associated with each change (although once the module is released, its design documentation will be updated). At the other extreme, during qualification each change in the program is attended by the approval of a change board. Finally, the amount of retesting increases with the level of abstraction. Repeating all unit test procedures after a change is not always necessary, and at worst rarely exceeds an hour; a change during qualification requires total test regression.

All of which is to say that, like the argument for defect removal at each stage of the development process, starting with requirements, early defect removal is cost- and quality-effective. This is the fundamental rationale for incremental testing. Incremental testing lends itself to the use of the right technique at the right time. Incremental testing decreases the number of bugs for users to find. Incremental testing is cost-effective.

None of which is news. Most software managers are aware of the advantages. Nevertheless, there are many projects in which one or more stages are bypassed as the project begins to run out of time or funds. The usual excuse for skipping a given test series is that any bugs it would have revealed will be found in the following test steps anyway. We know this to be counterproductive. How, then, can it be prevented? What is required is a test plan outlining the scope of each of the stages, a plan drawn and approved well before dynamic testing starts. Also required is a reporting mechanism to make higher levels of management aware of deviations from the plan. (This is another way in which quality assurance engineers can pay their own way.)

Beyond defining the kinds of tests that specify each of the test stages, the contents of the test plan should identify the hardware and software test fixtures required for each phase, the people needed to participate in each phase (and their responsibilities), data reduction procedures that will be used, and — unless included in a separate configuration management plan — the library control procedures applicable to each stage.

Clearly, each test plan should be based on a logical strategy that exploits the benefits of incremental testing. One such strategy that can satisfy most needs, independently of the class of program, is a strategy based on verification.

A verification strategy.   Recall the definition of verification given in Section 2.5: procedures that attempt to determine that the product of each phase of the development process is an implementation of a preceding phase, that is, satisfies it. Thus, the design of the components of a system are examined to see if they meet the external characteristics specified for them in the top-level design.

If we let the definition of "development process" encompass testing,* we can then define each stage of testing in terms of the immediate objectives of a corresponding stage of design or code generation. A strategy so conceived requires that the testing stages be identified with respect to the earlier paper stages. This would seem to raise the risk of contriving the test plan to fit some arbitrary or artificial constraints. Fortunately, this does not present a material problem. The stages of testing so defined generally seem quite reasonable.

---

* Occasionally, the term is used to refer to those phases in which programs are created, in contradistinction to those in which programs are tested.

As an example, we shall take an embedded software development project comprising the following paper phases:

1. Project initiated by receipt of system performance specification
2. System designed to the extent that various functions are assigned to elements of hardware and software, and their interfaces loosely defined
3. Detailed system design resulting in performance specifications for hardware and software
4. Software top-level design consisting of data structures, architecture, and control mechanisms
5. Module-by-module detailed design and coding

These sketchily defined phases comprise the upper half of Figure 7.3. In the lower half we see the five testing stages, applicable to embedded programs, that are identified in Table 7.1.* In this schematic representation of the verification approach to an incremental strategy, we assign to the unit test stage the development of experimental evidence that each module satisfies the external specifications established for it by the top-level design. Of course, unit testing is not only concerned with demonstrating that performance specifications are met; it also includes the tests required to show that the code conforms to the design.

Software integration verifies that the architecture of the program, outlined by the top-level design, works, that the interfaces and data structures implied by that design were correctly executed. Software integration is also a test of the validity of the overall program logic. For example, integration may also reveal that the performance stipulated for a procedure does not permit the procedure calling it to correctly perform its assigned function. In this respect we have to recognize that to some extent integration tests also verify the program against its overall performance specifications. However, this is incidental to the purpose.

The more formal demonstration of compliance with overall software specifications is reserved for the stage identified as software test. Although the objective may have been partially accomplished in integration testing, this is where pains are taken to make certain that performance features are evaluated with specific reference to their documented requirements. For embedded software — our example — the satisfaction of some of these requirements may not be feasible without the use of hardware components of the total system. As an example, consider a closed-loop control system in which the sensitivity of data-gathering hardware is con-

---

* Admittedly, no coincidence.

trolled by the computer to keep the amount of data fairly constant from one second to the next. Incorporating a suitable simulator in the software test driver may not be economically justifiable when compared to the alternative of completing this aspect of software testing during the following phase.

That phase is the integration of the program with hardware components. Analogous to the software integration test stage, this is a series of tests designed to test the correct execution of the interfaces between hardware and software implied by the overall system design. It may also be a test of certain hardware-to-hardware interfaces, especially those that could not have been accomplished earlier without the use of the computer program as a hardware test driver. This raises a point unique to embedded software (which is one reason why it was chosen for the illustration). When newly minted computer programs and electronic devices are married, it often is very difficult to determine whether problems that arise are in the hardware, are in the software, or are evidence of incompatibility in their individual external specifications. Nearly always the software temporarily becomes the diagnostic mechanism to locate the problem. This may mean that temporary patches or special compilations will be made and, further, that the test programmers will assume the principal role in diagnosing what really are system ills. We shall return to this in Chapter 9, where the consequences and the solutions to this nettlesome testing phenomenon are more closely examined.

Finally, Figure 7.3 shows system qualification as the verification that

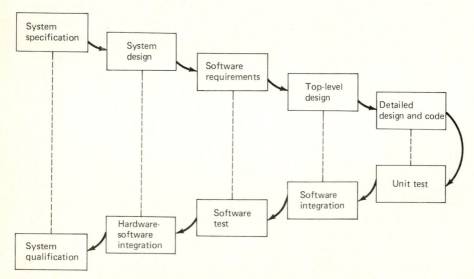

Figure 7.3   A verification strategy for embedded software.

the fully integrated system satisfies the specifications with which the development project was initiated. If it is in hardware-software integration where the two are married, it is in qualification that that marriage is consummated.

Looking back at these stages of testing as they were defined, it is clear that a bottom-up strategy was implicit in the illustration. One can also start from the top by singling out specific features (threads) and employing skeletal versions of both hardware and software. One cannot start at the top in the sense that the first testing series is that of system qualification, but it is feasible to start with hardware-software integration. This approach, however, is rarely used, partly because hardware stubs are difficult to come by and partly because the process is somewhat unwieldy.

However, with respect to software only, top-down integration is practical, as is top-down testing in the sense that no tests of modules in isolation are conducted. In top-down testing, the objectives of module testing remain intact; the only difference is that satisfaction of the external specifications for each module is verified, as are the software interfaces in the path to that module. The temporal division of the test stages is not significant; only the purposes are.

7.3 Integration

The preceding discussion brings us to the subject of how one integrates software components into a working whole, a topic of much discussion and controversy. The divisive issue is top-down or bottom-up. Bottom-up integration builds a software pyramid as a pyramid should be built: starting with the building blocks in contact with the ground and, layer by layer, working up to the capstone. Advocates of top-down testing argue that programs are not pyramids, notwithstanding the analogy suggested by schematic representations of their architecture, and that it makes more sense to start with the metaphorical capstone. Apart from the issues exclusive to testing, in a complete top-down production method the choice of top-down testing (wherein top-down integration subsumes unit testing) is necessarily made. All other production methods permit a discretionary selection.

The arguments.   One of the points made by the top-downers is that stubs are easier to construct than test drivers. This is a weak argument. Except for stubs that do little more than return as soon as they have been called, the size and complexity of stubs can easily approach — and sometimes surpass — that of drivers. There are equivalencies at every level. For the stub that provides a rote response to a predetermined invocation, there is the driver that provides a single static input. For the driver that sweeps through a range of input, there is the stub that returns a fixed sequential set of responses.

More important are the distinctions that attend the emphasis one wishes to place on test objectives. In a properly designed system, control more or less monotonically decreases from the top of the structure to the bottom. If it is desired to expose the conditions of program control to as many variations as possible, it makes good sense to start at the top and work down. In this fashion, the upper modules get more exercise than the ones that have less influence on program flow.

Alternatively, greater importance may be given to exercising computational kernels at the bottom of the structure. Thus, one would want to put these in place first and work upward, thereby exposing the hierarchically disadvantaged modules to new input stimuli each time a relevant module at a higher level is introduced. There is no guarantee that the input conditions will differ from previous ones, but in a large system the likelihood is fairly good, especially with regard to erroneous calling parameters. We may note also that if reused or remanufactured modules* form part of the program, a certain amount of bottom-up testing is inherent.

As a corollary to its emphasis on testing control mechanisms, top-down integration lends itself more easily than does bottom-up testing to the production of incremental builds. Bottom-up integration requires a new set of tested top-level control functions each time a new performance capability is delivered, with the risk that previous builds have to undergo complete retest as a result of upper tier changes. Not so for top-down, where these functions are among the earliest tested.

If top-down integration is selected, further strategic matters must be addressed. To reduce the complexity of the scaffolding, in top-down integration one wants to assign priorities to the order in which modules are selected so that input and output routines can be incorporated as quickly as possible, that is, to have available the built-in mechanisms for inserting test data and evaluating the results by the time complicated test cases are needed. At times, however, this advantage of top-down integration must be weighed against the desire to quickly plunge to lower-level modules of critical importance, a consideration that may force a different set of priorities.

One of the disadvantages of top-down integration that is often ignored is the occasional difficulty in providing the desired test conditions. Let us look at a bottom tier procedure to form the inverse of a matrix. If we want to evaluate the procedure's performance in the region about singularity, we

---

* Reused modules are borrowed from previously developed programs. Remanufactured (or "reengineered") modules are slight modifications of those that have been used before.

must provide to the module a number of test cases bearing specific relations among the rows or columns of the matrix. If, however, these test data are seen by the procedure only after a number of intervening operations at higher tiers, it may be all but impossible to fashion the test cases without laboriously engineering the system in reverse.

Another consideration is whether we want to wrest new-born code from its programmer's grasp by letting an integration test team have first go at module testing. If, for psychological motives only, we want to give the programmer the opportunity to do some testing in some private, dark corner, we shall have compromised the strategy of top-down testing.* The compromise is more in form than fact, though, if the test team applies its own set of test cases once it gains control of the code.

As much for managerial convenience as for any other purpose, it is not uncommon for programming shops to define modules as bundles of structurally related procedures and to stipulate them as the entities that are handed over to the top-down integration test team. If not the product of a single person, each module is developed under the supervision of a designated leader who decides when the module is "deliverable." In either case, bottom-up versus top-down decisions have to be made for the internal integration of the module before the module is handed over to the test team. This approach suggests the following compromise.

A hybrid strategy. In view of the need to consider the several facets of the top-down–bottom-up choice, it seems shortsighted to take a doctrinaire position. There is room for each strategy. Indeed, the greatest room seems to be allocated to judicious combinations of the two tailored to issues specific to the subject program. For example, one attractive method is to have the integration test team start at the top and work downward while incorporating input and output routines as early as possible. At the same time, in several thoughtfully designated integration activities that are performed, substructures of individual procedures are formed for subsequent integration into the top-down structure. These substructures may be built either top-down or bottom-up. Also, they may occur at any level of the system hierarchy, although the lower levels house the more promising candidates. This hybrid approach to integration takes careful planning, but not much more than is required for any successful integration effort.

Bottom-up, top-down, or both, let it be clear that, whatever strategy is adopted, it should be incremental. Any attempt to implode all of the pro-

---

* Whoever does the testing, the author of the code is the person best able to fix the bugs found by testing.

gram elements at one time (a common practice some years ago) will lead to much waste of labor-hours in the diagnosis of failures.

Software integration has been singled out for this lengthy discussion of methodology not only because there has been so much debate on the issue, but because for most development projects this is where the greatest number of test hours are expended. (To be consistent with the earlier example, let us note that it is hardware-software integration that accounts for the lion's share of the testing of embedded software.) Solve the integration problem successfully, and productivity will enjoy a marked increase.

7.4   Testing Black Boxes and Testing Glass Boxes

The term "black box testing" refers to testing programs with respect to their external specifications. Some software engineers like to restrict the meaning of external specifications in this sense to the specifications of performance requirements, but we shall include in the category any design specifications that are externally applied. For example, if the external specifications include the rules for manipulating a given file, compliance with the rules must be demonstrated as part of black box testing beyond examination of the state of the file following execution. Black box testing is equivalent to functional testing, which demonstrates that the program properly performs each function stipulated for it. "Black box testing" is one of those happy locutions that says it all: We pretend not to know the contents of the software black box (a truly independent test team may, indeed, be ignorant of how the program works), but we know how to determine if it does what it is supposed to do.

The semantic opposite to black box testing is "white box testing," and this term is sometimes used. However, the more descriptive "glass box testing" serves intuition better. Here the testers know everything there is to know about the program. Nothing is hidden; not the code, the data structure, nor the design documentation. In glass box testing, not only are the external specifications theoretically irrelevant, but their consideration may escape even the people designing the tests. Tests of the glass box are directed to operations along specific program paths and to the selection of those paths. Apart from procedures used during the diagnosis of test failures (debugging), an equivalent to "glass box testing" is the more formal "structural testing."

Although it has little relevance to the planning of tests, we digress for a philosophical observation of some importance: Functional unit tests are structural tests of a complete program. The most prominent aspect of the program visible through the glass walls is the modular architecture. Tests that each module correctly performs the functions assigned to it by the grand design are no less than tests of that structure.* Thus, the hybrid integration approach of Section 7.3 will be effective to the extent that testable external specifications exist for the designated substructures.

For the most part, structural testing (in the usual sense of path and branch testing) is confined to small components of a program: individual procedures or modules comprising several procedures. However, many integration tests will involve structural analyses to invoke specific interfaces.

A Paradox. Most of the theory developed for software testing is directed at structural testing. Most of the advanced tools specific to testing support structural testing. Most of the software engineering literature that is concerned with testing relates exclusively to structural testing. Most of the tests actually performed are functional tests, without regard to structure.

We cannot presume with any certainty to know why this paradox exists, but a few guesses suggest themselves. That software engineering emphasizes research into structural, rather than functional testing, should not be all that surprising; the former is the more mathematically tractable. With regard to the functional tests that experience tells us are favored by programmers, we might consider the following possibility. At the module level, in one form or another, the programmer is given a specification of what the module is to do. The measure of job performance is the satisfaction of that specification. Unless the scope of the task has been defined to include not only program performance matters but also specifics of how the program is to be tested, tests directed to the specification are all that are required for the programmer to demonstrate that the assigned task has been properly performed.

At the program level, the same situation prevails. The programming team has had the task of meeting external specifications, and if it (in contrast to an independent test team) is charged with testing the program, it will place its emphasis on demonstrating that it has correctly done the required job. Even an independent test team may be handed the external specification and tasked to "Test the program until every function is working."

---

* Howden[10,11] formalizes this notion (along with formalism in the selection of functional test data). He divides functional testing into four categories: requirements-based (at the program level), general computational design functions, detailed computational design functions, and control design functions. These last three are much the same in concept as the low-level black box tests (and the reference to them as structural tests in the large) of our strategy.

This is bottom line thinking in the best tradition of some quarters of government and business management. Whether or not it is appropriate to all business matters, it most certainly is not to computer program testing.

Both glass box and black box tests are needed. Before getting into particulars, let us synopsize the case for conducting both glass box and black box tests. The argument can be made that we should be satisfied with functional testing alone, since if the program or module satisfies the expectations for it, there is no need to care about its construction. Unfortunately, except for rare instances at the level of individual procedures, no combination of test cases can expose the code to more than a statistically insignificant part of its domain. Testing at the functional level will leave many paths totally unexercised. Yet the selection of these dormant paths may well be made by real data at some time in the future.

If all the paths can be shown to execute correctly, why not leave it at just structural testing? As we shall see in Chapter 8, structural testing in practice is directed at assuring the testing of a given percentage of structural elements, for example, decision-to-decision paths. Testing a high percentage of end-to-end paths is not feasible. Also, computations can give the correct answer, but for the wrong reasons. Moreover, that a path was executed does not tell us that it was executed *when* it should have been.

More on structural limitations. Goodenough and Gerhart[1] identify three types of program faults: missing control flow paths, inappropriate path selection, and inappropriate or missing action. Clearly, the first cannot reliably be found by path testing. If no path exists to take defensive action on an attempt to divide by zero, no set of structural tests will reveal that the path is missing (except by luck). With regard to inappropriate path selection, simply exercising every path and branch condition in a module will not reveal an incomplete predicate; for example, *if* A rather than *if* A *and* B. For the third defect class, observe that the erroneous statement Y:= X * 2 cannot be distinguished from the correct statement Y:= X ** 2 if the path containing the fault is only so executed that X has a value of 2.

These examples of the incompleteness of structural testing are very simple ones. A more subtle illustration that 100 percent path and branch testing may not expose every bug is borrowed from Goodenough and Gerhart:

```
if (X + Y + Z)/3 = X
  then print (''X,Y,AND Z ARE EQUAL IN VALUE'');
  else print (''X,Y, AND Z ARE NOT EQUAL IN VALUE'').
```

Both paths can be taken without revealing the fallacy.

Before leaving structural testing, we should not forget that no programmer, on the basis of path and branch testing alone, would ever have the courage to face the user and state that the program has been demonstrated to meet the user's requirements.

More on functional limitations. Let us take a few simple examples of the inadequacy of the other extreme, all functional and no structural testing. Initialization faults that materially affect only input data of small magnitude will go unnoticed if a series of input data starts off with large values. Error traps that transfer control to the wrong place may never be found if the traps are only for internal protection (e.g., guarding against zero divisors) and dependent on combinations of input data that are not easily deducible from the specifications.

Here is an illustration of the indeterminacy of the fractional part of a program that is covered by functional testing. Consider the root of a quadratic equation:

$$X = \frac{-B \pm SQRT(B^2 - 4AC)}{2A}$$

If after testing for $A \neq 0$ and forming $B^2 - 4AC$, the segment tests for a zero radicand and immediately assigns to the vector X two identical real roots ($-B/2A$), and if no functional test data are used that do not satisfy this condition, both the path for two-valued real roots and the path for complex roots will go untested. It is almost impossible to presumptively know that the set of functional tests — assuming that this segment lies in a large program — will explore only one of the three possible solution sets for the segment.

Perhaps most important of all, independent of the number of paths that can be exercised by black box testing, even the number of combinations of discrete input may be impossibly large. Consider a video game in which the effect of joy stick movement is constrained by the current location of six seemingly independent monsters with respect to a grid of 10 vertical positions and 5 horizontal partitions. If the 2 million and then some combinations are ever to be functionally tested, it certainly will not be with joy stick movement.

Finally, functional test case design can only be directed to less than half of the code of a program. For most programs, depending on the language used, more lines of code are devoted to housekeeping affairs than to the identifiable performance of stipulated functions.

Using both kinds of tests. In the preceding section, with top-down and bottom-up integration each offering important advantages, a firm position was taken to equivocate. Specifically, combination strategies were endorsed. Here, although we face the opposite situation in that both structural and functional testing have important restrictions, we arrive at the same conclusion: there is nothing for it but to plan on using both.

Structural testing is most productive on small units of code. Accordingly, it can be weighted heavily at the unit test level and in the early stages of integration — although scarcely to the exclusion of functional testing. Conversely, the later test stages will be dominated by tests directed to the program's requirements.

By now it should be obvious that the verification scheme of Figure 7.3 really addresses black box testing. However, this does not contradict the position that both black box and glass box tests should be used. The argument for a verification strategy was based on producing results for each test phase that can be easily measured against documented expectations that already exist. To include glass box tests, we simply extend the task descriptions for unit and integration test (and possibly hardware-software integration if applicable) to encompass measurable structural testing (of which more in the next chapter).

With this strategy, both structural and functional testing will contribute their share of inducing failures, *and in approximately equal numbers*. There has been a great deal of research on this subject and partisans of both structural and functional testing can find experimental results favoring their cause.

> The fact is that at least a third of all defects can be found by either technique. More likely two-thirds. There is also a pessimistic extreme: perhaps as few as 20 percent will be found by functional testing only and another 20 percent exclusively by structural testing. All these numbers are subject to wide variation, but the conclusion is irrefutable: both kinds of tests are required.

Thus far the term "exhaustive testing" has been assiduously avoided. When used carefully, it generally has the structural connotation of testing all end-to-end paths in a program. However, some careful software engineers use it to mean that a program has been forced into all of its latent discrete states; also structural but with a hint of functionality. The two definitions are much the same. More important, since neither is possible, software engineers raise the notion of exhaustive testing only in the context of an unattainable goal. This, however, does not stop programmers and software marketeers from speaking of a program product's having been exhaustively tested, whatever that might mean. Tested until the programmers were too tired to enter another test case, I suppose. This ambiguous use of the term is the reason I avoid it. Of course, even if a marketeer knew what it meant, he might use it anyway. Imagine, if you will, a marketeer standing with his hand resting on a stack of program listings, and, without a blink's loss of eye contact, saying something like

Here's a zillion and six nifty states
Not including a dozen odd waits.
We'll test all without rest
(And our tests are the best)
While maintaining our low thrifty rates.

7.5 Summary

1. The ultimate strategic objective of test planning is to maximize the number of defects found for the amount of testing performed.

2. Within a given programming installation, the variables influencing the number of defects in the untested code of a specific project are size, complexity, and project stability. Although the last does not lend itself to quantification, the first two do and can be modeled from semantic and structural properties to improve estimates of the test requirements.

3. Size and complexity models are typified by the well-known ones of Halstead and McCabe, respectively.

4. Testing should be viewed not as a monolithic phase of development, but as a sequence of stages designed to minimize the total time spent in diagnosing failures.

5. One technique toward achieving the objective of (4) is to divide the test activity into phases that can provide incremental verification against prominent milestones belonging to the period between the inception of the project and the production of code.

6. The costliest stage of testing is integration. Two fundamentally distinct approaches to integration have received much attention: top-down and bottom-up. Most projects are best served by judicious combinations of the two.

7. Strategic planning must also resolve the dichotomy between black box and glass box testing: testing to specifications and testing to design details. On examination of these two philosophies, it is evident that neither one is sufficient to detect all kinds of faults. Moreover, one cannot presumptively determine which will find the greater number of faults in a given project.

8. Although the test strategy must encompass both black box and glass box tests, it should be noted that the usefulness of glass box testing decreases as the time to final product acceptance nears, whereas black box testing necessarily becomes more prominent with time.

References

1. John Goodenough and Susan Gerhart, "Toward a Theory of Test Data Selection," *1975 Internatl Conf. Reliable Software,* IEEE Cat. No. 75CH0940-7CSR, pp. 493–510.
2. Maurice Halstead, *Elements of Software Science,* Elsevier–North Holland, New York, 1977.
3. A. Laemmel and M. Shooman, *Software Modeling Studies: Statistical (Natural) Language Theory and Computer Program Complexity,* Polytechnic Institute of New York, issued by Rome Air Development Center as Report RADC-TR-784, April 1978.
4. W. Harrison et al., "Applying Software Complexity Metrics to Program Maintenance," *Computer,* September 1982, pp. 65–79.
5. Eli Berlinger, "An Information Theory Based Complexity Measure," *Proc. 1980 Natl Computer Conf.,* AFIPS Press, 1980, pp. 773–779.
6. Siba Mohanty, "Models and Measurements for Quality Assessment of Software," *ACM Computing Surveys,* vol. 11, September 1979, pp. 251–275.
7. Thomas McCabe, "A Complexity Measure," *IEEE Trans. Software Eng.,* vol. SE-2, December 1976, pp. 308–320.
8. Bill Curtis et al., "Measuring the Psychological Complexity of Software Maintenance Tasks with the Halstead and McCabe Metrics," *IEEE Trans. Software Eng.,* vol. SE-5, March 1979, pp. 96–104.
9. M. Lipow and T. A. Thayer, "Prediction of Software Failures," *Proc. 1977 Annual Reliability and Maintainability Symp.,* IEEE Cat. No. 77CH1161-9RQC, pp. 489–494.
10. William E. Howden, "Functional Program Testing," *IEEE Trans. Software Eng.,* vol. SE-6, March 1980, pp. 162–169.
11. William E. Howden, "Validation of Scientific Programs," *ACM Computing Surveys,* vol. 14, June 1982, pp. 193–227.

Glass Box Testing

Heretofore, "glass box testing," "structural testing," and "branch and path testing" have been used as equivalent terms. Now we shall be more precise. Glass box testing is testing with respect to design details, that is, with full knowledge of the source code and design. (In theory, only the code is necessary, but testers avail themselves of design information to make the design of test cases easier.) Glass box testing encompasses both structural testing and the diagnosis of test failures (debugging).* Except as used in Section 7.4, where functional unit tests were viewed as structural system tests, we use "structural tests" mostly to mean tests directed to forcing some minimum execution coverage measure with respect to the structural properties of programs. The term "coverage-based tests" also is used for them. Coverage-based testing evolves from the primitive but weakly defined concept of "testing the whole program." Although coverage-based testing, alone, can satisfy most of the goals of structural testing, we shall see (in Section 8.2) that the likelihood of finding defects can be improved by using certain deterministic methods. Without execution coverage measurements, however, the handcrafted highly deterministic methods of selecting test cases expose one to the risk of leaving other defect detection opportunities untouched.

Apart from the counting of statements that were executed, with which we shall deal only cursorily, the most commonly used structural properties for coverage criteria are those related to paths or branches or both. Tests of branches are tests of branch conditions and the decision-to-decision seg-

---

* Purists may cringe at this inclusion of debugging under a testing classification. With regard to objectives, debugging (find and remove the revealed defect) most certainly is distinct from testing (reveal that the defect exists). However, many of the practices of debugging are barely distinguishable from those of testing. Who among us does not speak of diagnostic *tests*?

ments they initiate. Path testing refers to testing chains of these segments. The term is frequently used with reference only to complete (end-to-end) chains, but with necessary constraints on the requirements for iteration. In any case, branch (path) testing refers to forcing some percentage of branches (paths) in the program component under test. As noted in Chapter 7, although even 100 percent structural coverage is no guarantee that all defects will be exposed, our confidence in the correctness of a program increases as the coverage increases.

There are other, relatively recent, types of structural test methods allied to coverage testing, one of which — *mutation testing* — will also be discussed in this chapter.

In addition to the semantics of testing, some other terminology will be used more rigorously in this chapter. If we define the domain of a path as the part of the program domain that results in the path's execution, then, using a classification developed by Howden,[1] a *domain fault* is equivalent to an incorrect path domain. Domain faults can be further divided into *path selection faults* — incorrect selection of paths such as those caused by incorrect branch predicates — and *missing paths*. The function computed by the sequence of computations within a path is the path computation, and a fault within that sequence is a *computation fault*.

Modern structural testing implies test instrumentation. The use of test instrumentation is frequently referred to as *dynamic anaylsis*. Section 8.4 (Instrumentation) includes two dynamic analysis techniques, data flow analysis and assertion testing, that can be used independently of execution coverage instrumentation. However, as with the use of deterministic test case selection, use of these analytic methods without coverage measurement leaves one vulnerable to incomplete structural testing.

Since much of this chapter is concerned with the business of execution coverage, we shall start with a discussion of the issues surrounding coverage criteria.

8.1   Measures of Coverage

Apart from mutation testing coverage, which is treated separately in Section 8.5, coverage measures are usually those having to do with statements, branches, and paths. Of these, the simplest (and weakest) is the ratio of executed statements to executable statements. Statement coverage does not account for the structural relations among the statements. Because 80 percent statement coverage cannot mean that 80 percent of the statements in each path were executed (how were the remaining 20 percent avoided?), we must infer that the number of paths that were executed is indeterminate. Since paths, not statements per se, transform input into output, statement coverage is a weak coverage measure.

But then branch testing, although stronger than statement testing, must also be weaker than path testing. It is, but it is much more easily measured because we can arrive at the total number of branches — especially with the help of relatively simple static analysis tools — much more easily than the total number of paths. Moreover, if we recall that a path may include an incalculable number of iterations within its domain, it is clear that, unless we restrict the definition of a path, no path coverage criterion can have much meaning. For example, for a simple loop — one with no predicates within its body — we might define one domain in which the body is not executed at all and a second in which it is executed precisely once. Easy enough for simple loops, but more complex loops require much further definition.

Even branch coverage is not trivially defined, since we should want to account for compound branch conditions. Miller[2,3] has proposed several graded measures to deal with these problems in defining branch and path coverage. The premises of four of them are:

1. At least one result for every branch test (this is equivalent to testing each decision-to-decision segment)
2. At least one result for each branch predicate (similar to the first except that it requires testing elements of compound branch conditions)
3. The number of iterations tested for each loop
4. At least one result for each program flow class (roughly, equivalent paths, of which more shortly)

With regard to path testing, which the fourth item addresses, we may note that, as a system is being built, only sections of the final end-to-end paths can be tested. Yet we are more interested in structural testing during integration than in later test stages when the paths are complete. To account for partial path executions, Phoha[4] has developed the following test effectiveness measure (TEM):

$$\text{TEM(k)} = \frac{\text{number of paths of length k or less executed at least once}}{\text{total number of paths of length k or less}}$$

where a path length of k is a path through k + 1 decision nodes. Note that this, as well as the Miller measures,* give no metric credit for exercising any structural characteristic a second time. *Coverage* means just that: repetition of a segment with different data is not a factor in meeting coverage criteria.

Returning to the business of program flow classes, in his *boundary-in-*

---

* Excluding from the third measure consideration of simple loops.

terior method, Howden[5] puts paths in the same class if the only difference among them is the subpath followed during iterations beyond the first traversal of the loop. The proportion of path classes that are executed defines another intuitively useful coverage measure.

Additional coverage measures may be formed from combinations of all of the above. Whatever measures one uses, the likelihood is that, when first used, the low percentages of coverage that are found will be surprising. Without coverage standards, and using only ad hoc test case selections, few programmers actually exercise more than half of their decision-to-decision paths (or straight-line segments). Various experiments, however, have indicated that 80 to 90 percent decision-to-decision path coverage is economically feasible with systematic methods of test case selection. (A path-testing criterion is not so easily estimated owing to the number of variables involved.)

8.2   Test Case Selection

Second only to the means of measuring test coverage, the subject of later sections, test case selection is at the focus of structural testing. We do not want for methods of selecting test cases, some more systematic than others, and we shall start with the least methodical of all.

Ad hoc methods.   As is true of almost anything in programming, ad hoc methods are the most prevalent. However, when coupled with an execution monitor or analyzer (Section 8.4), ad hoc test design techniques are not necessarily insufficient for the specific purpose of structural testing. The idea is to keep choosing test data until the analyzer shows that the desired test coverage has been attained. The problem is that the test cases chosen may have a high incidence of redundancy. To reach a previously untapped chain of decision-to-decision paths, it may be necessary to repeat another subpath for the hundredth time. Also, the point in running the test is not just to improve one's coverage ratio, but to evoke a failure.* To know that a failure has occurred, the tester needs presumptive expectations of the results of each test, a laborious determination at best but at its worst for ad hoc methods. In this regard let us note that the term "test case" implies not only test data but also the anticipated output resulting from those data.

By definition, it is difficult to characterize ad hoc methods, but they generally take the form of the programmer's studying the text of the pro-

---

* G. Myers feels so strongly about this that he defines a test that reveals a defect as a success and one that terminates with anticipated results as a failure.[6] The temptation to use his terminology in my own conversation and writing is tempered only by the certain knowledge that I would revert to the customary definitions often enough to confuse everyone about me.

gram, arbitrarily selecting a path (or decision point), noting the predicates that define the domain, and fashioning appropriate input data for the predicates. Loops are usually iterated a number of times sufficient to include all of their interior domains. Simple loops are generally iterated once. To avoid overlooking a common source of path selection faults, test cases are also chosen — when logically applicable, as in *do-while* loops — to block execution of the body of the loop.

A problem that frequently arises in path testing is that of satisfying several path predicates that reference the same variable, for example, $X - Y \geq 1$ and, later in the path, $2 * X - Y < 2$.* Simple cases like this easily grow into the solution of systems of inequalities as more predicates referencing X, Y, or both are encountered. Huang[7] suggests an attractive algorithmic solution to the problem, but it is one that can also get cumbersome.

In the very act of determining the input conditions, the programmer may well find an improperly constructed decision point. This raises a fundamental issue: If the tests are constructed to force execution along designated paths, why are not *all* domain faults found in the act of manually determining the requisite input data? The answer is that many are; nevertheless, human fallibility still plays its part, especially with regard to hidden branches and unreachable paths.

There is a distinction between the process for selecting data for path testing and that for branch testing. The choice of a path requires the forcing of sequential branches wherein only one result is desired for each decision point. Assuming that 100 percent testing of a branch is intended, branch testing requires that a path be selected, as before, up to the subject conditional statement but that each — not just one — of the possible conditions at that point then be forced.

With regard to path control, a less deterministic approach — one bordering on functional testing — is to select test input that will result in values at the extremes of all internal ranges (subscripts, control variables, and so on). This is a form of boundary testing that for many programs will provide considerable coverage. Indeed, one should see also that, to exercise error traps, ranges are exceeded.

Heuristic guidelines that exploit our knowledge of common fault patterns also can provide a sense of system to the selection of input data. One such methodology[8] requires that the arguments of each predicate be assigned values such that all logically possible strict ordering relations ($<$, $=$, and $>$) exist between pairs. A second rule demands that a variable required to be less than or greater than a constant be assigned a value such that it differs from the constant by the least possible decrement or increment.

---

* For which one solution is $X = -0.5$, $Y = -2.0$.

These rules will detect many domain faults. A third rule reflects a practice used by many experienced programmers: assign different values (sign and magnitude) to the input variables for each test case. Also, do not assign the same value to two variables.* Finally, make certain that the variables in arithmetic operations will have measurable effect on the output. Although this last, which requires careful examination of variable transformations, seems directed at computation faults, it will pick up domain faults as well because measurable effect on the output often implies logical effect of the evaluation of relational variables.

Using test data of functional tests.   Since functional testing will, in any case, be performed, an attractive idea is to see if functional test cases can serve simultaneously as structural test cases. Assuming that execution (or coverage) monitors (or analyzers) are used, this is trivially accomplished. Section 8.4 will have more to say on these tools. For the present, we need only know that they can report the decision-to-decision (and sometimes longer) paths actually traversed or, even better, those not executed. Thus, one can run functional tests with the tools switched on, as it were, and examine the results later to determine if adequate coverage has been achieved. When functional testing includes copious use of random data, as in volume tests, extensive coverage is quite likely.

Since the coverage will seldom achieve the desired level, additional test cases will be constructed by using, singly or in combination, any of the other techniques discussed here.

Graph-based methods.   The use of program graphs for manual test case selection is rather like life imitating art in that the methods are intensively used by static analysis systems for the same purpose (see below). In any case, the fastest way of manually identifying the paths in a program is by inspection of the program graph. A reduced graph, as was illustrated by Figure 7.2, is the easiest to use. If static analysis tools are not available for generating program graphs, this method is, of course, attended by the overhead of having to draw the graphs manually. However, if mechanized graph generation does not exist, it is likely that coverage tools are not available either, in which case the manually produced graph may be used for the collateral purpose of recording the paths that have been executed.

A fundamental problem with this secondary use of program graphs is that the record will show the paths that were intended, not necessarily those that were actually traversed, given the presence of domain faults. Domain faults will generally cause the results to be different, so that the

---

* This rule should not be followed so faithfully that it rules out certain boundary conditions.

tester, in diagnosing the problem, will be alerted to the need to correct the record. However, faults that produce coincidental correctness remain a problem.

The ad hoc approach to the number of loop iterations is repeated for graph-based methods, except that in this case recognition of interior domains is more apparent. Less obvious, however, is the determination of which of the domains are the ones that most warrant directed testing. An excellent criterion is to completely test those having the greatest cyclomatic complexity.

Mechanization of test selection. Beyond the module level, manual methods become so arduous to apply that high coverage measures are unlikely. Even at the module level, their inefficiency may preclude economical testing to coverage criteria. Clearly, mechanization is called for. Section 5.4 noted that static analysis systems that have the capability of generating program graphs also have the potential for determining structural test data. Although determining test cases for end-to-end logical paths remains a formidable task, generating test data for exercising each decision-to-decision path is relatively tractable.

Where static analysis has been used to automatically generate test conditions, a recurring problem has been that of infeasible paths. These are paths that exist structurally but cannot be executed because of mutually exclusive conditions. An example is given in Section 5.4. The graph traversal algorithms used for test data generation cannot distinguish between feasible and infeasible paths without evaluating the path predicate. This is less significant for manual graph-based test case selection, since the programmer does evaluate predicates in the course of determining the expected output.

Help from symbolic execution. As in the selection of test cases for dynamic testing, one also has to select test cases for symbolic execution. However, the latter chore is eased by the mechanisms of the symbolic execution system itself. Moreover, symbolic execution systems have also included the capability of generating test data subject to user-defined constraints, as we saw in Sections 5.3 and 6.4. All of which raises the suggestion that static testing be run more or less concurrently with dynamic testing for the selection of structural test cases.*

---

* A different view is taken by Howden,[9] who has had much experience with use of the DISSECT system. His position is that symbolic execution is not useful for automatic test data generation, partly because the symbolic execution required for generating feasible paths precludes the need for actual execution. On the other hand, he notes that symbolically evaluated systems of predicates have value for the programmer who is generating test data for functional structured testing (i.e., testing with respect to computational and control design functions).

A good example of the help available from symbolic execution has been documented by Lori Clarke,[10] based on experience with the ATTEST symbolic execution system, which maintains a history of path traversals. Upon encountering a conditional statement, both the current path status and the history are used to select the branch next to be executed. When multiple choices remain, the selection is made on the apparent potential for achieving additional coverage. This potential may be influenced by weights, previously supplied by the programmer, for statement coverage, branch coverage, and loop boundary conditions.

The proposed Automated Test Case Generator,[11] which in one version would support the Air Force's Jovial Automated Verification System (JAVS), also uses symbolic execution in its algorithms. One of these, based on negating previous constraints, first uses a partial symbolic execution of the last path that was executed to determine an approximation to the path condition of that test case. In the next step, the test data selected are those that violate at least one test constraint in each of the previous path conditions.

Finite domain strategy. Fairly recent methods have been developed to provide high confidence levels for the detection of domain faults. Concentrating on the boundaries of path domains, these strategies attempt to minimize the risk of letting domain faults go untested, although they have a collateral capability of finding computational faults as well. The domain faults addressed are those of path selection, to the exclusion of exposing paths that are missing. Restrictions in the seminal research of White and Cohen,[12] applied to the programming language, allow no reference to arrays within predicates and allow no subroutine or function calls.

Exposition of the strategy is well beyond our scope. To summarize the method, let us define a *border* as a single simple predicate in the boundary of a path. *Closed borders* are those formed by the relationals $\leq, \geq$, and $=$ (to the exclusion of *open borders*, which are formed by $<, >$, and $\neq$). A *border shift* (a domain fault) results in a displaced domain, or set of elements placed in an incorrect path domain. The domain strategy leads to the selection of test points on or near the closed borders, so as to detect border shifts or to provide limits on the maximum displaced domain. A measure for the maximum displacement is the *domain error magnitude.*

More recent work by Clarke, Hassell, and Richardson[13] indicates that the White and Cohen strategies can result in undefinably large border shift errors. These are the least upper bounds of a geometric interpretation of undetectable border shifts. Clarke et al. have proposed alternative path domain strategies that improve on the error bound.

Finite path domain strategies are currently experimental and subject to restrictions that are not always tolerable; they must, in any case, be integrated with other structural test cases. However, the concept of deliberately choosing test data along the closed borders of path domains can be applied to other test case selection precedures. Execution monitors do not analyze the significance of the coverage reported, but we are fully aware that certain segments of code are more likely than others to have faults.

Combined methods.   All of the above methods for selecting structural test stimuli can be combined, and in a diversity of ways. In most cases, combinations will be required to meet predetermined coverage goals greater than 80 percent. Moreover, regardless of the basic method used, selection of tests specific to domain faults or complex substructures leads the programmer to consideration of the issues that attach to the domain strategy, ad hoc heuristics, and graph-based methods. An overall strategy will depend on one's tools; principally the availability of static analysis in any of its forms.

In the most general case, in which symbolic execution or automated test case generators are not available and not even any support for test case generation is forthcoming from static analysis, the most attractive strategy is the one previously suggested: tabulate the results of execution monitors following the completion of a *functional test* series and then fill in by using combinations of the manual methods.

If no execution monitors are available, the conscientious programmer tester, after threatening his supervisor with resignation if such tools are not available in time for the next project, can still perform some coverage-based testing. It has already been suggested that marked-up program graphs can substitute — sort of — for monitors. Also, a common practice, which had its origin in debugging, is to place coded output messages at procedure calls and returns, entry points of *case* construct selections, and other critical points. Another common practice is the use of coded loop counters. These are not useful for branch testing (too many are required) and only provide rough measures of path testing, but they can support ad hoc measures similar to path testing.

It logically follows that we should now turn our attention to execution monitors and the other forms of program instrumentation, but putting first things first, we shall digress for a quick survey of the general testing environment.

8.3   The Basic Test Environment

The basic test tools surveyed in this section are not unique to glass box testing but also apply to black box testing. Not included here are the tools peculiar to structural testing (see Section 8.4) or debugging (Section 8.6).

Elements of test control.   Other than a computer on which to exercise the code, the most basic tools of all are those that provide test stimuli, act as surrogates for missing components, and record the results. Since these tools are in universal use, there is no need to describe them here. Rather, we can consider their organization in a manner that will improve the productivity of the tester and the effectiveness of the defect removal process.

The number of stubs required for top-down integration or testing has, as its upper limit, the number of modules less 1. This can be a very large number. Maintaining the stubs and ensuring that the latest edition of each stub is available to a link editor will easily get out of hand in the absence of some form of data management system, essentially a program library. One of the more descriptive terms for such a system is "scaffold," recalling the temporary members of a building under construction.

The term "test driver" is most often used to describe the mechanism for applying stimuli to a module under test (prior to integration) and outputting the module's response. Many of us also speak of test drivers as the source of test input for partially integrated programs. In that sense, the capabilities of a driver increase with time to expand the repertoire of test cases. For bottom-up integration, a family of test drivers is required. That family, along with recording devices, is frequently referred to as a "test harness," a term that is occasionally extended to include test stubs as well, as in top-down–bottom-up combination methods. Organized into a harness, these elements of "throwaway code" can be placed under library control to enhance the likelihood of developing complex drivers on the foundations of the simpler drivers used earlier.

For certain kinds of testing, it is impossible to automatically record the results of tests. Examples are when the output is measured on oscilloscopes or by the observation of phenomena such as oven temperature. Whenever possible, however, an audit trail of both stimuli and results should be mechanized. Moreover, means to automatically compare results with previously recorded output is a significant timesaver during regression testing. That brings us to a further level of organization and control.

Automated test systems.   Systems to manage test input and output can take many forms. A common one is to drive the test program from prerecorded disk data, compare the responses with prerecorded test expectations, and output any deviations in hard copy. This, obviously, does not work for all types of programs. A variant permits the test procedure to be recorded and generates input from that procedure. Panzl[14] describes the use of IBM's Automated Unit Test (AUT) system in a mode much like this. Operating on the object code of individual modules, AUT accepts test procedures in a special interface test language used for the definition of test data, the definition of expected results, and the specification of required stubs. Responses are automatically verified against the expectations. Although the system treats the module under test as a black box, test designers are, of course, free to design the tests with full knowledge of the code.

Unit test mechanization is becoming fairly common. At ITT's Programming Productivity and Quality Conference, June 1983, chaired by Dr. Bill Curtis, three geographically dispersed ITT units demonstrated sophisticated module-level test systems, each tailored to a specific production methodology.

Panzl also describes General Electric's TPL/F system, which is even more applicable to glass box testing. TPL/F tests source code (Fortran) modules, which permits the specification of test cases with reference to internal structure. Any variable can be referenced by the test procedure, and any sequence of statements (which implies path selection) can be specified for execution. A macro capability allows families of test cases to be designed; they are instantiated for specific data by the equivalent of a macro call in the test procedure. A later version of the General Electric system, TPL/2.0, contains a capability for substituting actual results for expected results and thus archiving test cases for subsequent use in regression tests.*

Any number of test systems have been improvised for the testing associated with specific projects. As we might expect, they use a diversity of techniques for generating test data and expected results, evaluating and archiving output from the test program, and providing access to the internal structure of the program. Common to all is the use of some form of data management system.

Environment simulators. At levels higher than individual modules, certainly when testing full programs, it is necessary to dynamically model the outside world for certain types of applications. Simulators are used to represent the performance of missing hardware devices, provide synthetic environmental test stimuli (for example, air traffic scenarios for a controller's console), or both. These simulators, most of which are peculiar to development projects, are noted here only as logical outgrowths of low-level test drivers. Their principal use is in functional testing, and we shall revisit them in the next chapter.

Interpretive simulators and emulators. These tools are used mostly for microprocessor support, in which, at least with respect to glass box testing, we would not expect the target computers to come equipped with the sophisti-

---

* This may not have been the purpose of this feature. Panzl states that its use is to ease the updating of test procedures after module revisions. Nevertheless, the capability recommends itself to retest purposes.

cated operating systems and hardware peripherals required to support the other tools of interest. The lack of these data processing facilities is solved if a more well-endowed host computer system can be made to behave like the naked (target) microprocessor. Thus, emulation or simulation. Although the two words mean much the same thing, most people prefer to reserve "emulation" for the use of techniques incorporating microcode as well as software and "interpretive simulation" to mean step-by-step mimicking of the target instructions using the native architecture of the host machine. We shall return to emulators in Section 8.6 for a discussion of their excellent application to debugging.

As it turns out, simulators can simplify the design of minimum software instrumentation to support coverage-based testing, whether or not the target processor is a microprocessor. Assume that a program occupies the first n locations of memory. Let us zero n contiguous unused memory addresses or, if memory is at a premium, disk locations. Under simulation we can trap the simulated program counter so that at the execution of each instruction we can write a binary 1 into the previously zeroed address equivalent to the contents of the program counter. At the conclusion of each test, a second program is run to output the beginning and end addresses of each block of memory containing sequential 1s. These were the addresses that had been executed. By using the load map and the relative addresses output by the compiler, it is possible to determine which statements were and were not executed. Thus, a cheap and dirty (well, awkward to use) statement coverage monitor. That will serve as an introduction to the tools that are central to testing to coverage criteria.

8.4   Instrumentation for Structural Testing

The earliest forms of instrumentation used for testing were tracing tools (e.g., Fortran's TRACE option that reported the value of each variable after assignment or the value of control variables at decision points), user-controlled breakpoints, and binary patches inserted anywhere for almost any reason. Modern instrumentation does nothing that the primitive methods were unable to accomplish. However, to state that time has brought only convenience to the use of testing instrumentation, while true in a pedantic sense, is so understated as to miss the point that without modern methods the measurements discussed in this chapter would seldom be made.

The instrumentation discussed here starts with that required for coverage measurements, but it continues beyond to include probes that provide further visibility of the behavior of programs when under active test. A term enjoying considerable currency describes program instrumentation and the uses to which it can be put: *dynamic analysis*. That is what this section is really about.

Simple coverage probes. We shall begin by addressing execution coverage in the simplest way. More automatic technology will follow. Simple or advanced, the basic coverage idea is much the same, and it involves four steps:

1. Analyze the program (manually or by static analysis).
2. Instrument the program with probes (manually or automatically).
3. Execute the program to collect data.
4. Interpret the results by using whatever level of mechanization is available.

At the most primitive level of instrumentation, the probes can be as simple as in-line flags, coded in source language by the programmer, of the form

```
if not FLAG(16) then FLAG(16):= true
```

marking that a segment of code has been executed at least once. This is similar in concept, if cumbersome, to the memory mapping with which Section 8.3 ended. The difference is that it permits rapid interpretation of the flags (dumped directly after the test run) in source code.

To provide further information, we can make the probe a counter by incrementing the number of times that the segment has been executed:

```
COUNT(16):= COUNT(16) + 1
```

With this we can gain more understanding of the test case and more understanding of the program, especially with regard to where the real inner loops are.

The amount of manual data entry is reduced if one encodes procedure calls to run time routines for gathering data:

```
call COUNT(16).
```

With this call, the routine COUNT would increment the count of the sixteenth "test point." This is the method generally used by preprocessors for mechanized probe insertion.

For manual insertion, a common practice is to place one probe in each decision-to-decision path. This is easily accomplished with reference to the reduced graph of the program. A static analyzer that identifies all the decision-to-decision paths on a listing of the source code text is even better. The placement of probes for branch coverage has been given considerable attention by designers of static analysis systems that include instrumentation preprocessors, but an algorithm for efficiently finding the minimum number of required probes remains elusive. Reducing the number of probes to be manually inserted is even more pertinent. In any case, 100 percent branch coverage is possible with fewer probes than the number that results from placement in each decision-to-decision path. For example, in Figure 8.1 the count of P4 (probe 4) clearly is the sum of the counts of P2 and P3. Obvious relations among branches such as these can often be used when the form of the text makes it difficult to insert probes manually, as in

```
if A = B
  then X: = X + 1
endif
call ANYPROC
```

There is no convenient way to place a probe in the invisible *else* path to the procedure call. However, if instrumented as

```
call COUNT(18)
if A = B
  then X: = X + 1
    call COUNT(19)
endif
call ANYPROC
```

it can be determined that the else path is traversed COUNT(18) − COUNT(19) times. We might note that if statement coverage rather than branch coverage were of interest, the question would not arise.

Quite obviously, the use of totally manual instrumentation (if we can call it that) requires a considerable amount of labor. The data collection routine (e.g., COUNT in the above example) does not have to be developed anew for each project, but the probes do have to be inserted (and later removed) one by one. More mechanization is called for.

Execution coverage analyzers.   There are three basic elements of analyzers:

1. Automatic probe insertion (based on static analysis)
2. Run time routines to collect data from probes

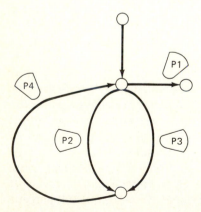

Figure 8.1   Redundant probes.

3. Postprocessors to report collected statistics

Occasionally we see the use of "execution coverage analyzer" or the equivalent "execution monitor" also applied to systems comprising only the last two items.

Analyzers can go beyond placing probes in each decision-to-decision path and then simply reporting which of the paths were traversed. By also reporting the sequence in which the probes were "activated," the user is given direct path coverage information as well as branch coverage statistics. In the method devised by Paige and Benson,[15] each probe is in the form of a procedure call with two arguments. In the general case, these arguments represent program graph nodes straddling the probe and thereby simplifying reconstruction (with reference to the program graph) of the path followed.

One of the earliest well-developed dynamic analysis systems is McDonnell Douglas's program evaluator and test (PET) system.[16] With regard to execution coverage, it reports the number and percentage of all source statements and branches that were executed and also the number of times each was executed. PET operates on Fortran programs, and the branches in this case are of the *if* and *goto* types. The number of iterations of *do* loops can be determined by examining statement counts within the bodies of the loops.

PET has another capability, one that is tied more closely to debugging than to coverage-based testing: It can report the min/max and first/last values assigned to variables by assignment statements and the min/max ranges of *do* loop control variables.

Another well-known analysis system for Fortran programs is the proprietary RXVP80™ of General Research Corporation.[17] It too counts both statements and branches, and it reports not only the number of times each decision-to-decision branch was executed but also the branches that were not reached during the test. Going a step further, the GRC system also provides information on what paths to traverse to get to a previously untried decision-to-decision path. Closely related to RXVP80™ is GRC's SQLAB system, developed for the Air Force. SQLAB also has the capability of operating on a special dialect of Pascal, VPASCAL (verifiable Pascal).

Fortran remains the language of favor for the University of Houston's INSTRU system.[18] The subsystem INSTRU.D., for performing the detection of data flow anomalies (to which we shall return in a few pages), also provides system-inserted counters for decision-to-decision paths. And Fortran continues as the target language for the SADAT system,[19] which has output much like that of the GRC systems but—to get around the infeasible path problem noted in Section 8.2—also incorporates a user-assisted test case generation capability.

The Air Force's Jovial language is supported by an execution coverage analysis system, JVAS.[20] This GRC development is much like RXVP80™ in concept, including the help offered in setting up tests to reach previously untested branches.

The commercial EDP world has not been ignored by dynamic analysis. The people at Management and Computer Services, Inc. have a system called TRACMACS that includes preprocessing, execution, and postprocessing components for Cobol programs. The output includes the sequence of decision-to-decision paths taken, the number of times each was traversed, and the branches that were not executed.

Finally, the LDRA test bed developed by Liverpool Data Research Associates Ltd. in the United Kingdom provides test coverage for several languages: PL/1, Fortran, Cobol, Pascal, Algol68, and the assembler language for the Intel 8080 architecture. LDRA provides coverage measures at three levels: statement, branch, and LCSAJ. The last is a path fragment consisting of a linear code sequence followed by a control flow jump.

Unfortunately, it remains true that commercially available execution coverage analyzers are few in number and peculiar to few languages.

Hardware monitors. One problem with any of the software-based data-gathering methods is that they create a problem for the testing of real-time programs. If the tests entail critical timing response or analysis, the execution time taken by software monitors has an effect rather like that of Heisenberg's uncertainty principle, wherein the energy required to observe the momentum of atomic particles changes the very observation.

The problem of real-time coverage monitoring is not as pressing as it may seem. Recall that structural tests are most appropriate in the early test stages. Unit test and integration of real-time software is most often carried out under simulation (i.e., in an all-software environment) and in circumstances in which execution time is not a major issue. Determining actual real-time performance is another matter, one that will be discussed in the next chapter.

To the extent that there is a real-time monitoring problem, hardware monitors can provide a partial solution by monitoring the program counter and presenting statistics in terms of absolute addresses. This is an all-hardware implementation similar in concept to the all-software monitoring with which Section 8.3 ended. A hardware monitor as primitive as this adds little real-time load; however, it is not easily interpreted in terms of the source code. Hardware monitors that can correlate CPU events with source code need to monitor the execution of interpreted, rather than compiled code, or some near equivalent, which reinvents the timing problem.

Executable assertions. We depart from execution coverage to examine an entirely different kind of probe. Assertions of the relations among elements of the program vector were the building blocks upon which proofs of correctness were constructed, as in Chapter 6. Apart from trying to prove anything formally, the individual assertion statement suggests by its form its use in providing further visibility of the dynamic operation of programs — if, that is, assertions could be executed as are other statements. It is hardly news that the PL/1 language supports executable assertions, that at one time they were included in the specifications of Ada, or that compilers for derivatives of Pascal have been built with provisions for handling assertions.*

Most programmers do not have the advantage of a programming language environment that directly supports the use of assertions. For those programmers, the availability of assertion handling in the dynamic analysis system of their testing environment is an attractive adjunct. Heretofore, we have been concerned with dynamic analysis in terms of probes directed to matters of control flow. We now extend the concept to include probes that can report on the state of data; namely, executable assertions. A source file containing assertion statements is compiled; a source code analyzer constructs an assertion data base; and the compiled code is linked with assertion-handling run time routines for execution.

The use of executable assertions may easily — too easily — be viewed as being more relevant to debugging than to testing, the sort of improvisation a programmer might use to aid in the diagnosis of a failure. However, executable assertions can also expand upon the failure production capability of any test case. We have been considering test cases in terms of known input and expected output, and we have ignored the possibility of internal anomalies that may not affect the output of a particular test only because of the restricted domain of that test. For example, a test case caused a subscript to exceed an array bound, yet the datum used from an adjacent array was coincidentally close enough to the value that should have been picked up that the output was not materially affected. This sort of thing happens all the time in testing when test data are deliberately chosen to ease the calculation of expected results. In this example, had an executable assertion checked the subscript for a violation of its prescribed bounds, the tester would have been alerted to the fact that something was wrong.

---

* Examples are Euclid and the language for the AFFIRM system[21] (which we last saw in Section 6.4 in connection with verification systems). The Euclid language goes beyond allowing programmers to include assertion statements within the source code. The compiler generates its own "legality assertions" when it cannot guarantee, solely from its syntactic analysis, that a language restriction will be met. As reported,[22] however, the number of such assertions can at times be too much of a good thing.

The beauty of the executable assertion is that the programmer can ignore it if the program behaves as asserted. Only if the assertion is evaluated as a false description of the state of the program vector is the programmer's attention diverted. This is in contradistinction to breakpoints and test statements that output a number of variables, when the programmer must in all cases examine the data and compare them to what was expected.

Executable assertions may be divided into two classes: global and local. The latter are similar to the assertions used in correctness proofs in that they are evaluated at their insertion points in the course of execution. Global assertions, such as may be used for checking that a subscript stays within stipulated bounds, are evaluated whenever the variable in question is altered in value. Thus, a single global assertion may cover any number of potential checkpoints.

The classical implementation of executable assertions is that of the previously remarked PET system.[16] Here, the programmer encodes assertions as comments in the source text. For production compilation, the comments are ignored by the Fortran compiler. For testing, however, a preprocessor translates them into language forms recognizable by the compiler. Violations of the assertions during execution, like coverage statistics, are stored in a file for subsequent postprocessing and correlation back to source code. A variety of assertion formats are used. The general local assertion form is

```
assert local (extended logical expression)(control qualifiers)(control
options)
```

Specialized local assertions check variables against legal ranges and/or values, assert variable names to be invariant, locally check subscript ranges against corresponding array specifications, and check vectors for either ascending or descending order. Global assertions can be declared to check new values of variables for validity with respect to predefined ranges, test discrete values or invariant conditions, or perform bounds checking on subscripts. Additional features provide the programmer with considerable flexibility.

We think of executable assertions in terms of compiler languages, but there seems no reason to exclude them from assembly language programs. Traditionally, assembly language programmers have used breakpoints in their debugging, but aside from their being nuisances, predetermined halts lack definitive foreknowledge that the selected locations are those of interest (as, for example, the place where a pointer goes negative). The ALLA-DIN[23] debugging and testing facility allows assertions in the form of conditional (halt if assertion is false) breakpoints. It also permits the stipulation of tests similar to the range assertions for compiler languages. For example, if it is asserted that the program counter is always greater than N, a halt will occur if the computer attempts to execute an instruction in location $M \leq N$.

Data flow analyzers.   Again we turn to a form of dynamic analysis instrumentation outside the realm of execution coverage but well within the interest of the programmer attempting to evaluate the structural soundness of the program under test.

Many domain and computation faults can be detected by the data flow analysis technique. This is one of the more systematic approaches to finding defects, yet one that can be defined quite easily. Consider that the values of the variables during execution of a program are in one of three states:

1. Undefined, as before initialization, or for variables local to a procedure after execution of the *return* statement
2. Referenced, as when on the right side of an assignment statement or in a predicate
3. Defined, as when on the left side of an assignment statement or when returned by a called procedure

Given these three states, we find three anomalous sequences for them:

1. Undefined and then referenced
2. Defined and then undefined without an intervening reference
3. Defined and then defined again without an intervening reference

Chapter 5 noted that Fosdick and Osterweil[24] had used static analysis to exploit the existence of one of the above sequences as a signal that a defect may be present. However, static analysis cannot unambiguously handle array variables, since it cannot dynamically evaluate subscripts. Moreover, it cannot with certainty know the order of procedure invocations. On the other hand, to the extent that paths affecting variable states are executed, these problems are irrelevant to dynamic analysis. Accordingly, data flow anomalies can be detected by probes placed to determine where the states (undefined, referenced, defined) of variables are altered and whether the current state is an anomalous successor to the previous state.

As implemented for Fortran programs by the aforenoted INSTRU system,[18] the probes for data flow anomaly are instrumented by the same subsystem that instruments branch counters. Warnings of anomalies are output during the course of execution as they are detected.

8.5   Mutation Testing

From the point of view of test coverage, we have seen structural testing more a way of determining the effectiveness of test cases than a methodology directed at the specifics of the program under test. The idea of mutation testing carries this a bit further: find out if a slight change in a program will cause the program to fail a test that it previously passed. If the mutant program fails the test, we have greater confidence in the test case. On the other hand, if it passes, it may simply mean that the alteration (really, a seeded fault) did not enter into the program's response to the test input. These alternatives call for the use of a number of mutant programs to be applied to a number of test data sets. The objective is to find output from each mutant program P′ that differs from the output of the original program P in at least one test. The methodology, as implemented, is to form a number of mutants and to continue to execute tests until for each P′ an output is found to be different from that produced by P.

An example will be useful to illustrate the way in which mutation testing can validate the coverage of test sets, and, in the process, uncover faults. The following example is an adaptation of a particularly elegant one used by DeMillo et al.[25] Consider the following program to find the index of the *first* occurrence of the largest element in a vector:

```
procedure MAX(VECTR,N,INDEX)
integer variable N,INDEX,I
integer array VECTR(N)
INDEX:= 1
I:= 1
do while I < N
  I:= I + 1
  if VECTR(I) > VECTR(INDEX)
    then INDEX:= I
  endif
endo
return
end MAX
```

We now test with three test data sets (three sets of the vector VECTR), each a different permutation of three values. This is typical of the test methodology used by programmers.

Test data 1	0,	100,	200
Test data 2	0,	200,	100
Test data 3	200,	0,	100

MAX would successfully return the correct index for each of these tests. But it would also return the correct value of INDEX if the relational operator in the *if* statement were "greater or equal" instead of "greater than." Let us assume that the incorrect relational were in the program and, moreover, had been selected for mutation. Running the program with the relational >* would return the same results as earlier ones, which would cause the programmer to question the fact that the alteration had had no effect. The programmer, in scrutinizing the code, might discover the reason. Alternatively, the programmer might choose more data sets to be run with both P and P'. The choice of (200, 200, 0) would yield an incorrect response.

It is possible for mutants to provide the same result but consume different resources, principally execution time and memory. The mutant may even provide a gratuitous improvement. These *equivalent mutants* lend an obvious element of confusion. Fred Sayward, coinventor of mutation testing, has informed me that good progress has been made toward developing algorithmic methods of recognizing the existence of equivalent mutants.

With regard to test coverage, one can quantify the adequacy of a set of t tests in terms of the percentage of mutants P' of the subject program P for which t evokes responses different from those of P.

Mutation testing requires that a number of elements of the program be altered and, to minimize coincidental correctness, altered one at a time. Even though all the individual mutations are simple ones, the amount of labor required to generate the mutants and test them is clearly excessive if the test is to have any statistical worth. In short, mutation testing requires mechanization. Very simple syntactic and semantic mutation rules are used by an experimental system[26] for Fortran programs. One mutation operator changes a single occurrence of a binary operator to form a mutant that is identical with the original program in all but one symbol. Another operator changes the semantics of a single *do* loop so that it will be interpreted as though it were a *for* loop, with the consequence that precisely one iteration of the loop body might not be executed. And so on.

Used on 11 programs, the experimental system found 20 of 25 known bugs, 12 more than branch testing (alone) would have caught. Again repeating information provided by Sayward, mutation testing has also met with success in the tests of Cobol programs.

As a minor philosophical point, mutation testing seems to straddle the domains of black box and glass box testing. The programmer does not have to know much about the program to form mutant versions, but the testing system does.

Howden[27] has defined a test method he calls *weak mutation*. Here the effect of the mutant is determined by examining the state of the program vector directly upon execution of the mutated statement, rather than comparing final results with previous ones.

The technology of mutation testing is being transferred from the aca-

---

* Which, of course, *we* know to be correct. In the general case, whether or not the altered element is correct, mutations are incorrect.

demic world to that of the software production environment. The LDRA test bed, noted earlier in Section 8.4, also supports mutation testing. Operator intervention in this interactive system is required only for the explicit construction of test data.

Mutation testing is not the only testing scheme that deliberately places faults in a program. Another is random bug seeding. The idea is to estimte the number of real defects remaining at the conclusion of testing by noting the number of seeded ones that were not exposed. Somewhat arbitrarily, but for reasons that will be given there, a more thorough discussion of seeding will be found in the next chapter.

8.6 Debugging

Testing is the process of attempting to induce failures. Debugging is the process of finding the cause of failures. Determining the cause of a single failure may take tens as many labor-hours as setting up the test case that resulted in failure. Debugging, then, should be of acute interest to anyone concerned with improving programming productivity. Unfortunately, the definitive guide to debugging has never been written, nor is it likely to be. A debugging Baedeker is about as plausible a project as a handbook to lead a detective to the efficient solution of problems of the class *crimes*. And for the same reasons.

Despite the absence of a general solution, there is some commonality to the procedures followed by debugging programmers. Although each programmer's procedures are tied to available tools — which topic will occupy our interest in a little while — at least one general observation can be made: Debugging is a procedure of iteratively isolating the location of a defect (notwithstanding the fact that one might get lucky and find it on the first pass through the debug procedure). Rather like the loser's territory in mumblety-peg, the bug's apparent domain is diminished at each iteration.

Debugging = data + analysis. The ad hoc procedures favored by programmers usually involve a combination of several approaches. Attempts are made to work backwards from the observed results of the failed test case to synthesize the program structure that actually exists, in contrast with what was thought to exist. Diagnostic tests are fashioned to narrow the scope of bug pursuit by either the choice of test data, the insertion of special diagnostic output statements, or both. Test data are manually walked through the code (recalling the walk-throughs of Chapter 4) in the forward direction. If necessary, binary patches are used to trap or disable primitive machine functions.

The diagnostic output statements referred to are generally simple: examples are straddling procedure calls ("ANYPROC called with parameters 3.4 and 62," "ANYPROC returned with 14"). In assembly language, however, unless a diagnostic system is available, inserting such messages may be more bother than the messages are worth. Assembly language programmers are more willing than others to call for breakpoint-triggered octal or hexadecimal snapshots or, if it comes to it, dumps set off by aborts. Obviously, octal or hexadecimal is more easily understood in the context of assembly language programs than higher language programs, but even here a formatting tool is a productive adjunct.

The special tests that are run for finding the location of defects have a more restricted scope than those used for exposing the fact that defects are present. The attempt to find information relevant to a specific failure leads quite naturally to test conditions that focus narrowly on specific subdomains. It does happen, however, that programmers are deluded by what they consider appropriately restricted diagnostics. Consider a program in which a contiguous series of records is drawn from a file and the last field of each record is converted to a real quantity and summed with the others. For the test, the file is loaded with five records and the program is executed, returning an incorrect sum. Suspecting the routine that converts strings to reals (because it was written by his worst enemy), the programmer tries a diagnostic run in which the program is left unchanged but the applicable fields are loaded with ASCII zeroes. The computed sum is properly output as zero, thus confirming the programmer's suspicions (there was never any doubt that the bum knew his business when it came to zero).

Of course, what actually happened is that an initialization defect affected the selection of records for processing. Instead of starting at the first memory-image record, the program was starting at the third. The last two records processed by the program were background; specifically, they were the printer buffer for the last job run, which happened to be the validation (for security reasons) of a memory-zeroing program.

Few programmers have not experienced similar frustrating coincidences of their own.

A similar problem can arise when one bug masks another. An illustration of this is given toward the end of the chapter as an example of the difficulties that attend defect removal as contrasted to defect detection. In that illustration, insufficient analysis results in the programmer discarding the results of diagnostic experimentation.

The potential for just such misadventures as these tells us that simply running more tests is not the most productive way to find bugs. Experienced programmers know this and combine diagnostic tests with the previously mentioned analytic approaches.

Then there is the other side of the coin. Although some inexperienced programmers are given to inductive debugging based on running one input data set after another, a second mark of inexperience is to ignore the acquisition of more experimental data and expect that study of the code alone will inevitably lead to the source of the problem. In some cases it does, but all too often it ends with the programmer glassily staring at the source listing while awaiting some sort of epiphany reserved for unresourceful programmers.

In brief, successful debugging should rely on both analysis and the use of diagnostic tests directed toward isolating the bug. Moreover, when inserting diagnostic probes in their programs, programmers should start by getting information at a level as close to the application as possible. Looking mostly at the minutiae of interim calculations and branch predicates far removed from the problem is akin to reading the code for the nth time. The programmer is likely to make the same reasoning mistakes as those made at the time the code was written. Observing more problem-related operations (e.g., seeing which record the pointer is at, not how the pointer was computed) permits the programmer greater opportunity to apply intuition — the most important debugging asset available.

As necessary as they are, diagnostic probes can occasionally prove nettling, as, for example, when insertion of special output messages results in the program producing the correct output. A program comes to a mysterious halt and a set of diagnostic messages is encoded, following which the program runs to completion and even produces the expected results for the several test cases used. Only after hours of analysis is it realized that the problem was a control variable that caused the program to branch into nonexecutable data. Placing the probes in the program resulted in new absolute addresses for the program that coincidentally allowed recovery from the wayward branch. Although this sort of phenomenon is a common occurrence, it usually catches programmers by surprise because it defies logic.

> A rule of thumb learned by many programmers is that elusive bugs are not to be found in the logical place for them.

Not that this knowledge really helps; for where should the programmer look?

We may use the address-sensitive problem just described as an illustration of another point. A type of probe with minimal side effect is the binary patch. Although the testing (for defect exposure) of patched programs must always be regarded as an unsatisfactory last resort, the imputation of patches should not be extended — as has happened — to the use of patches as diagnostic aids.

It should be noted that the use of execution coverage analyzers also changes the state of the program under test. Although it is unlikely that probes and statistics-gathering routines will cause defects to be masked, testers who are given to wearing both belts and suspenders may feel it prudent to repeat the battery of structural tests with an uninstrumented program. An alternative solution is to leave the instrumentation in the program permanently but switched off as with the PL/1 on and off statements.

We can forgive execution coverage instrumentation for having the potential for producing peculiar effects if we recognize that coverage probes can also be used for the purpose of fault isolation. Rather than place trace messages in the program to analyze control flow, if this seems to be the appropriate experimental approach, the programmer can turn to the execution coverage analyzer or to less ambitious branch-testing instrumentation to acquire the desired information.

Another form of instrumentation introduced earlier, the executable assertion statement, is also eminently useful for debugging. Since it only reports violations of the programmer's expectations, it bears directly on the fundamental debugging question: Why did the code not perform as had been thought it would?

Apart from the reuse of testing instrumentation, there are other tools that lighten the debugger's burden. When one considers that it takes many more hours to find (and fix) a bug than it does to expose its existence, the cost-effectiveness of debugging tools makes their acquisition or development even more defensible than that of other testing tools.

Microprocessor debugging tools. Nowhere is instrumentation of greater value than that required to help find bugs in programs intended for execution by microprocessors. Unlike mini- and maxicomputers, it is the rare microprocessor that has the peripheral devices, operating system, and memory that ease the pain of debugging. Which is to say that there are many more microprocessors in use than there are microcomputer systems. Microprocessor development systems provide some of the amenities found on larger systems. Offered by several microprocessor and test equipment manufacturers, these development systems either work in concert with the target microprocessor, mimic it with "in-circuit emulation" for total test control (the emulator may even use the same kind of chip as the target processor), or have the capability of operating in both modes.*

Development systems for microprocessors are used not only for debugging but for testing as well. The application as a test vehicle is simply to provide the testers with the run time environment of larger computers. As instrumented for debugging, however, many microprocessor development systems have interactive features that in some ways exceed those found on most console-equipped minis and maxis. These include commands to ex-

---

* See the discussion in Section 8.3 on interpretive simulators and emulators.

amine or modify the contents of registers and memory locations, various options for setting breakpoints and outputting sets of instructions immediately antecedent to them, register and bus traces (listings of the sequence of transactions on each), and provisions for triggering external equipments (such as oscilloscopes) for analyzing traffic on the buses.

Many of the microprocessor development systems can also support symbolic, or source-level, debugging to one extent or another. In the modest range of symbolic features, displays of instructions — as in a register trace — can be in assembly language if the system contains an on-line disassembler. The name given to more ambitious (and increasingly common) systems suggests human abilities: symbolic debuggers. Used for a compiler language program, these debuggers work with compilers and link editors to reference the names and location of data assigned during the translation and linking procedures. With the debugger controlling the execution processor and drawing upon files produced by the compiler and link editor, programmers can set breakpoints or change the contents of memory or registers entirely in the language of the source program. Programmers not only may request the values of variables under the name of their source file mnemonics, they may also specify the formats (e.g., octal, decimal, character) to be used for display.

Symbolic debuggers are commercially available not only for microprocessor development systems but also for cross software operating on host machines (more often than not the DEC VAX systems). Offered by the manufacturers of microprocessors, by test equipment manufacturers, and by independent software houses as part of more comprehensive microprocessor tool chains, symbolic debuggers are now available for several languages, most commonly Pascal, C, and PL/M.

One weakness of debugging systems that applies to mini and maxi computers as well as microprocessors is the inability to control and monitor real-time programs without affecting the timing of the process. Although the problem is not unique to microprocessors, it seems to draw the greatest attention there, probably because so many of the larger programming systems installed on microprocessors are for real-time operations. To report on-line events (as one does for programs embedded in instrumentation systems) such that they can be interpreted at the level of source code, it is necessary to steal time from the on-line process, that is, to introduce delays. We saw this in the discussion of hardware monitors in Section 8.4.

In a solution to the problem that has been proposed,[28] a FIFO buffer isolates the target processor from the execution monitor. The buffer transfers from the target processor descriptions of the transactions that modify the target processor's state. With the monitor and its debugging package operating asynchronously with respect to the target process, the buffer behaves as a variable delay line, always lagging the actual process by an amount of time determined by the length of the FIFO stack but leaving that process unaffected.

Traces. The use of execution trace tools dates back to early computing times. Their value to the debugging process was so well recognized that even then some compilers included traces as standard features incorporated in the program load by compile time directives. For example, the Fortran trace utility gave the programmer the option of printing the result of every arithmetic assignment statement or the arithmetic evaluation of control expressions or both. The only operational problem attending such trace tools is the need for the programmer to correlate the long lists of unidentified output with the source statements that generate each item.

When programs are prepared for translation by interpreters, in contrast to compilers and assemblers, tracing is much easier to use. Since the interpreter has the source code available at all times, it is relatively simple to display source statements along with the results of their execution. Also, run time monitors that trap underflows, overflows, out-of-range subscripts, and the like can output the last statement executed rather than cabalistic messages of the ilk of "abnormal halt in location F6F6." Since even personal computers have source-level debugging systems, it seems odd that the person debugging a program to reconcile check registers with bank statements may have more mechanized assistance than the programmer developing an electronic funds transfer system.

A different kind of trace is directed to control flow. Rather than output 7.2 as the result of the execution of A:= B/C, as would the previously remarked Fortran trace, a *symbolic trace* outputs A:= B/C. That is, the source statements of linear segments are printed as those segments are executed. Control statements (other than unconditional branches) are output as they are evaluated. For example, *if* X.LT.DELTA *goto* 20 might be printed as either .NOT.X.LT.DELTA or X.LT.DELTA and, in the latter case, would be followed immediately by the listing of the statement labeled 20 and any linear segment started by it. Succinctly defined as "listings of the source statements and branch predicates that occur along paths through a program,"[29] symbolic traces can tell programmers just what paths were taken to produce an incorrect result while directing the programmer's attention to the concatenation of decision-to-decision paths that occurred.

As implemented in INSTRU.S,[18,30] trace output is generated by the expansion of source segments. For example, the statement X = A + B would be produced by the preprocessor as

```
    X = A + B
    WRITE(OUT,101)
101 FORMAT('X = A + B').
```

Branches are instrumented in terms of the evaluation of the branch predicates. For example, the three-way branch *if* (I) 10,20,30 would result in

```
      IF(I.LT.0) WRITE(OUT,101)
101   FORMAT('I.LT.0')
      IF(I.EQ.0) WRITE(OUT,102)
102   FORMAT('I.EQ.0')
      IF(I.GT.0) WRITE(OUT,103)
103   FORMAT('I.GT.0')
      IF (I) 10,20,30
```

For I = 5, this results in execution trace output of I.GT.0

```
30    text of statement 30
```

Each of the other control structures (computed *goto*'s, *do* loops, and so on) is in a fashion that has source-level meaning for the programmer. Summarizing, symbolic trace permits the programmer to see his earlier logical thinking unfold, and in the process he may learn of a junction where he was less than noble in reason.

Bug removal. Defect removal means fixing bugs as well as detecting them, and only retest can confirm the success of a fix. This is no small matter, since the experience of many programmers indicates that perhaps half the bugs revealed in testing are improperly identified during the search for them and that, of those finally found, half of the fixes do not really work. An example of this was given in Section 2.6.

A common cause of the low success rate is that test failures often result from a combination of defects. Consider this outline for a loop in which all variables are reals:

```
until A = B loop
       .
       .
   A: = A * 2
       .
       .

end loop
```

We have two bugs here: a domain fault and a computation fault. The loop predicate makes no allowance for round-off or truncation errors. It should be of the form

```
until ABS(A — B) < EPSILON loop.
```

Also, let us assume that the arithmetic assignment of A should have been A:= A**2. As a result of the first defect, some test inputs will cause infinite looping and others will not. The second defect may coincidentally give the correct answer for some, if not for all, test input. It may be that it took the combination of the two bugs to result in the observed infinite loop. This raises some interesting possibilities. Let us assume that the programmer fixes only one of the two bugs — the most likely case. When the test that originally failed is rerun, it may again fail. Moreover, it may fail with more severe symptoms than the original failure. In that case, the programmer may even undo the partial fix made earlier, especially if he feels that diagnosis was made hastily. A remote possibility? Scarcely. I have observed this several times (as well as sharing in the culpability). With the pressure of schedules or the knowledge that machine time must be surrendered in 30 minutes, the progammer may very well jump to a false conclusion, try out a fix without proper analysis, discover that things only get worse, and remove the fix even though it was a correct (if incomplete) action.

This sequence of events can occur also when a single bug accounts for a failure. Removing one bug may at any time open a path to a new source of defects of greater observable severity.

Other than the use of analysis sufficient to give the programmer confidence in his fix, the only relief from this fairly common and always vexing problem is to temporarily retain code changes unless they have no effect on the outcome of the test. After the failed test is rerun, all the diagnostic cases that can easily be reconstructed should also be executed a second time. Since the programmer knows what to look for in them, there is a good chance of verifying that the fix made was sound while, at the same time, observing any anomaly that has become more obvious as a result of the modification.

Suppose, however, that the incomplete fix worked. The programmer should, in any case, suspect there is another bug nearby.* Retest in the neighborhood of the domain of the bug that was removed should also be used. For fixes that involve control flow problems, additional test cases should be run to exercise the alternative outcomes. Fixes having to do with software interfaces should be retested with procedure calls that stress the interfaces.

Always, programmers should be wary of adverse effects incidental to *any* fix. One thinks immediately of side effects as in the example given in Section 2.6, where the removal of a seemingly redundant procedure call produced incorrect results, but there are any number of ways that a modification to a program can cause failures not directly connected to the failure

---

* For mysterious reasons, bugs tend to occur in groups. Chapter 10, in discussing failure-prone modules, remarks on the macrocauses of unstable requirements and matters having to do with personnel but offers little else in the way of explanation.

that led to the fix. Very rarely can one feel confident that repetition of previous, successful cases is unnecessary. Whether or not it makes sense to perform 100 percent regression testing depends on the test phase one is in (doubtful for integration, but almost a certainty for qualification) and the specifics of the bug removed. For example, discovering that input data were improperly scaled would seem to call for 100 percent retest, whereas reformatting an error message certainly would not. The economics of regression testing will also be influenced by the tooling to support retest. (See Section 8.3.)

It is tempting to wait until the end of a test phase to perform regression testing; that is, rather than rerun all previous tests of the series after each fix has been made, at the end rerun all up to the last failed test. If we assume one fix were required for each of N test cases and further assume that all previous test cases were successfully rerun once after each fix, the total number of retests would be $(N^2 + N)/2$. On the other hand, if no tests are repeated until the very end, only N tests need to be repeated. Unfortunately, experience demonstrates that previous tests frequently do not run successfully, that a fix made for one test often degrades the performance with respect to other tests. This is, after all, why regression testing is performed. Moreover, the density of regression test failures is an indicator of the extent to which the program structure has been eroded by successive fixes. Thus, prudent managers will want to do at least some regression testing after each fix and have the option to leave most of it for the end if the tests go well.

We can easily understand the unpopularity of regression testing. It is redoing what has been done before; it conforms to no one's idea of progress. And it is costly, which is why a policy of deferring some retesting to the end frequently makes sense. The worst of it, as so often happens, is that the last few tests are jammed up tightly against the committed completion date. Unless each test case is stored and test control is automated, the eleventh hour is not the time to learn that a complete retest is necessary, which is what happened to some friends of mine this afternoon:

> Testing structure and function and stress,
> They roared on like the Highball Express,
> But today brought bad luck
> When a fix came unstuck
> And it's back to square one they'll regress.

8.7   Summary

1. Glass box testing mostly includes testing to test coverage criteria and debugging. The tests executed to satisfy coverage criteria may be designed for the purposes of functional testing or dynamic analysis.

Alternatively, dynamic analysis may be conducted as a by-product of coverage-based testing.

2. Coverage criteria are generally based on the number of statements executed, the number of branches selected, or the number of paths traversed. The first is the weakest. The last is the strongest, but it is also the most difficult to determine.

3. The most prevalent methods of selecting glass box test cases are based more on the programmer's intuition than on anything else. For coverage-based testing, these methods tend to be inefficient because of redundant execution.

4. Unmechanized ad hoc test case selection may require fairly laborious examinations of program structure and the satisfaction of multiple path predicates that reference the same variable.

5. Test cases directed at the boundaries of path domains and various heuristic techniques involving internal stress testing or knowledge of common fault patterns increase the effectiveness of coverage-based testing.

6. A more systematic way of designing coverage-based tests is based on analysis of the program graph. This may be mechanized by static analysis systems, but at the expense of introducing the problem of infeasible paths. Another way to mechanize test case selection is through the use of symbolic execution.

7. Where mechanization is weak, the most efficient way to select test cases for coverage-based testing is to perform functional testing first and then use any other feasible method to fill the coverage holes reported by execution monitors.

8. The efficiency of testing can be improved by organizing collections of stubs, drivers, and test record files in data management systems.

9. Automated test systems provide a more efficient way to define test cases and perform regression tests.

10. For measuring execution coverage, probes in the form of counters or procedure calls are inserted in the program. Following execution, the contents of counters or records built by data collection routines are output as reports of branch coverage.

11. Manual probe placement is made more efficient by reference to the program graph or static analyzer reports.

12. Execution coverage analyzers automatically insert coverage probes and provide various decision-to-decision coverage reports at the conclusion of execution.

13. Another type of probe is the executable assertion. Executable asser-

tions can provide internal tests of the relations among program variables while tests for expected output are in process. If not a feature of the compiler language, executable assertions can be translated into compilable constructs by a preprocessor.

14. A novel form of dynamic analysis is the detection, by probes, of anomalies in the sequence of variable states (undefined, defined, redefined). The presence of a data flow anomaly can lead to the exposure of a fault.

15. Mutation testing is a way of measuring the effectiveness of test cases for finding defects. Simple alterations of the program are made to determine if the test cases can evoke different responses. Mutation testing requires mechanization of the mutations for their number to be great enough to produce statistically significant results.

16. Debugging, or finding and fixing the cause of a test failure, is an iterative process that should include both analysis and the collection of experimental data. Elusive bugs are not to be found in logical places.

17. The use of diagnostic probes can alter the state of programs in a way that makes bugs harder to find.

18. Microprocessor development systems not only offer the programmer of a microprocessor the facilities of larger computers, they are commonly instrumented to provide superior source-level debugging. Unfortunately, source-level debugging does not lend itself well to real-time operations, for which many microprocessor programs are destined.

19. Trace tools that can report variable assignments and predicate evaluations in source-level terms are invaluable debugging aids. A variant of the trace concept is the symbolic trace, which outputs source language statements and control predicates as they occurred during execution.

20. Bugs may be erroneously identified or fixed. Not only the failed test should be repeated after a fix but also other tests that provide visibility into the effect of the fix or that might indicate the presence of other, nearby, bugs. To one extent or another, previously successful test cases should also be repeated (regression testing).

References

1. William E. Howden, "Reliability of the Path Analysis Testing Strategy," *IEEE Trans. Software Eng.,* vol. SE-2, September 1976, pp. 208–214.
2. Edward Miller, "Introduction to Software Testing Technology," *Tutorial: Software Testing & Validation Techniques,* IEEE Cat. No. EHO 138-8, 1978, pp. 3–14.
3. Edward Miller, "Program Testing: Art Meets Theory," *Computer,* July 1977, pp. 42–51.
4. Shashi Phoha, *A Quantifiable Methodology for Software Testing: Using Path Analysis,* The Mitre Corporation, 1981, released by the USAF Electronic Systems Division, Hanscom AFB, as Report ESD-TR-81-259.

5. William E. Howden, "Methodology for the Generation of Program Test Data," *IEEE Trans. Computers,* vol. C-24, May 1975, pp. 554–559.
6. Glenford J. Myers, *The Art of Software Testing,* Wiley-Interscience, New York, 1979.
7. J. C. Huang, "An Approach to Program Testing," *ACM Computing Surveys,* vol. 7, September 1975, pp. 113–128.
8. Kenneth A. Foster, "Error Sensitive Test Cases Analysis (ESTCA)," *IEEE Trans. Software Eng.,* vol. SE-6, May 1980, pp. 258–264.
9. William E. Howden, "An Evaluation of the Effectiveness of Symbolic Testing," *Tutorial: Software Testing & Validation Techniques,* IEEE Cat. No. EHO138-8, 1978, pp. 300–313.
10. Lori A. Clarke, *Final Scientific Report for Development of a Program Testing System,* Air Force Office of Scientific Research, Report AFOSR-TR-81-0803, May 1981.
11. Daniel Leach and Sukhamay Kundu, *Automated Test Case Generator,* Rome Air Development Center Report RADC-TR-80-31, February 1980.
12. Lee White and Edward Cohen, "A Domain Strategy for Computer Program Testing," *IEEE Trans. Software Eng.,* vol. SE-6, May 1980, pp. 247–257.
13. Lori Clarke et al., "A Close Look at Domain Testing," *IEEE Trans. Software Eng.,* vol. SE-8, July 1982, pp. 380–390.
14. David J. Panzl, "Automatic Software Test Drivers," *Computer,* April 1978, pp. 44–50.
15. M. R. Paige and J. P. Benson, "The Use of Software Probes in Testing FORTRAN Programs," *Computer,* July 1974, pp. 40–47.
16. Leon Stucki and Gary Foshee, "New Assertion Concepts for Self-Metric Software Validation," *Proc. 1975 Internatl Conf. Reliable Software,* IEEE Cat. No. 75CH0904-7CSR, pp. 59–71.
17. W. Dehaan, *RXVP80™ A Software Documentation, Analysis, and Test System,* General Research Corporation, Santa Barbara, Calif.
18. J. C. Huang, "Experience with Use of Instrumentation Techniques in Software Testing," *Proc. NSIA Natl Conf. Software Tech. and Measurement,* National Security Industrial Association, Washington, October 1981, pp. D1–D10.
19. Udo Voges et al., "SADAT–An Automated Testing Tool," *IEEE Trans. Software Eng.,* vol. SE-6, May 1980, pp. 286–290.
20. E. R. Miller, *Methodology for Comprehensive Software Testing,* General Research Corporation, 1975, released by Rome Air Development Center as Report RADC-TR-75-161.
21. David R. Musser, "Abstract Data Type Specifications in the AFFIRM System," *IEEE Trans. Software Eng.,* vol. SE-6, January 1980, pp. 24–32.
22. David B. Wortman, "On Legality Assertions in Euclid," *IEEE Trans. Software Eng.,* vol. SE-5, July 1979, pp. 359–367.
23. Richard E. Fairley, "ALLADIN: Assembly Language Assertion Driven Debugging Interpreter," *IEEE Trans. Software Eng.,* vol. SE-5, July 1979, pp. 426–428.
24. L. D. Fosdick and L. J. Osterweil, "Data Flow Analysis in Software Reliability," *ACM Computing Surveys,* vol. 8, September 1976, pp. 305–330.
25. R. A. DeMillo, R. J. Lipton, and F. G. Sayward, "Hints on Test Data Selection: Help for the Practicing Programmer," *Computer,* April 1978, pp. 34–41.
26. T. A. Budd, R. A. DeMillo, R. J. Lipton, F. G. Sayward, *Theoretical and Empirical Studies on Using Program Mutation to Test the Functional Correctness of Programs,* Georgia Institute of Technology, February 1980. This report is also found in the *Conference Record* of the *Seventh Annual ACM Symposium on Principles of Programming Languages,* January 1980, pp. 220–233.
27. W. E. Howden, "Weak Mutation Testing and Completeness of Test Sets," *IEEE Trans. Software Eng.,* vol. SE-8, July 1982, pp. 371–379.
28. Bernhard Plattner and Jurg Nievergelt, "Monitoring Program Execution: A Survey," *Computer,* November 1981, pp. 76–93.
29. William E. Howden, "Proving Properties of Programs from Program Traces," *Tutorial: Software Testing & Validation Techniques,* IEEE Cat. No. EHO138-8, 1978, pp. 46–56.
30. J. C. Huang, "Instrumenting Programs for Symbolic-Trace Generation," *Computer,* December 1980, pp. 17–23.

Chapter

9

Black Box Testing

Since black box testing is directed at the external specifications of computer programs, it would seem that there should be little one can say about it. Just identify the applicable specifications and see that a test case is designed for it, right? The premise is right, but only if there is no question of what the external specifications are, and at that only if the goal is solely to demonstrate that a work task has been completed as defined.

As it turns out, for many programs it is impossible to define the input domain completely. Worse, it is not always clear what the program is to do with the input, and the consequence is that black box testing often has to include "tuning." An example of this is a computer-controlled rapid-transit system, wherein dynamic interaction of brake mechanisms, wheel friction, and the effect of curves may not be sufficiently known to allow precise definition of the constants in the programmable part of a control loop. Moreover, especially at the full program level, black box testing may well include calibrating the performance of the program, not just satisfying a set of numbers.

With regard to the second provision, demonstrating that a job was well done, we know that the primary goal of testing is to find the bad, not to prove the good. In practical terms, this means that we cannot be satisfied with the minimum set of test cases required for function coverage, but must run additional tests to explore the corners of the program's functionality.

Clearly, the dominant issue of black box testing must be the design of the tests, and that is where we shall start.

9.1 Test Case Selection

In this section we shall address the design of tests in which specific test input are chosen point by point to achieve specific test objectives as distinguished from testing with random input, the subject of Section 9.2. Recall that in a similar section (8.2) in the preceding chapter, the several methods of glass box test case selection were presented as options for the test designer's choice. All of the techniques presented here, however, should be used, at least to the extent that they apply to a given test phase.

Finding the function. The first problem to be solved is determining the applicable specifications to test against. At the level of the complete program, this is a matter of isolating individual functions embedded in the overall specification set. During integration or unit test, we are concerned with extracting the subfunctions that apply specifically to the code under test. Here we find the traceability tools of Section 2.3 invaluable. At any stage of test, the functions to which the code should be evaluated fall directly out of the traceability scheme. Such functions may include algorithms, file transformations, processing time, and so forth, all directly related to the prime specifications set. From these, test input and expected output are determined by instantiating the identified input and output domains at a number of points.

Determining these points is beyond the scope of the traceability technique itself.* As is usual, the most prevalent selection is by ad hoc methods. At the system level, testers use what they presume to be typical operational conditions pertaining to each function; at the procedure level, typical interface conditions. None of this is systematic, save for the trivial case of one arbitrary point per function. The methods that follow attempt to add some sense of system to providing coverage of each functional domain.

Functional partitioning. Functions identified in the external specifications generally lend themselves to being partitioned into classes. Two test cases are members of the same functional class if:

- The same input variables are relevant to each.
- The same types of transformations will result.
- The same output variables are affected by each.

Iteratively, subclasses are formed by using the same definition. For an example, we shall consider an inventory control system. Inquiries of the status of the master file of items (e.g., electrical parts) form one class. This class is divided into two subclasses: valid and invalid inquiries. Invalid inquiries include those that are unrecognizable and those for items not inventoried (e.g., soup). Another functional class comprises transactions

---

* Although Myers[1] describes a variant of the traceability concept, *cause-effect graphing*, that derives test cases directly from specifications. The method looks attractive for those who have access to proprietary IBM programs that partly mechanize the process.

that modify the master file. This in turn is divided into the subclasses of invalid transaction classes (e.g., input codes for which there is no identified transformation), inventory additions, withdrawals, and alterations. Each of these is further subdivided. For example, the subclass *alterations* may resolve to:

- Changing the values of minimum and maximum quantities to be stocked for an item
- Changing the base cost of an item
- Correcting the number of the item currently in inventory
- Changing the identity of the supplier for reorder
- Invalid alterations

The last of these is further subdivided. For example,

- Specifying the maximum to be less than the minimum
- Reducing the balance to a negative number
- Attempting to alter the record for an item not in the file

Given the complete partitioning of a function, it now remains to select one test case for each subfunction at the lowest hierarchical level of the partitioning. Beyond the more obvious possibilities of defect exposure, it is likely that one will learn that the program does not guard against at least one of the invalid classes. Of course, if the partitioning is performed by the person who prepared the requirements specification or designed the program (or relevant section of the program), the existence of these classes will probably not be recognized.*

As a test selection technique, partitioning has its limits. Consider a routine to form the tangents of angles. Angles in the first and third quadrants would seem to belong to one class, angles in the second and fourth to a second class, and $\pi/2$ and $3\pi/2$ to be single-point classes, but what is to be done with angles beyond 2π radians? If we knew how the code handled them, it might be possible to lump them all into a single partition, but in black box testing we are ignorant of the code.

Although defining one test case for each lowest-level partition is more systematic than most test design practices, we can further exploit defect detection opportunities within these partitions by using the supplementary methods that follow.

Sensitivity analysis.   Over the full domain of many functions or subfunctions, the output does not vary linearly or even smoothly with the input. For

---

* This is one of many aspects of the argument that functional tests should be designed by people independent of the development process.

simple illustrations we immediately think of algebraic or trigonometric functions for which discontinuity (e.g., tan x, x $= \pi/2$) is the extreme case. For a less obvious example, we have a production-planning system in which is buried a matrix inversion routine used to solve linear programming problems. In this system, certain ratios of available machine time to the time required to manufacture a single article may invoke the matrix inversion routine with values close to singularity and cause odd perturbations in the computed allocations of machines.

The potential for discrepant program behavior may be uncovered in certain cases by varying the input over the full allowable range and looking for unexpected roughness in the graph of output versus input. On encountering a region where small changes in the input cause major changes in the output, additional test cases are designed to populate the region more densely. This is done even though no output is found outside tolerable limits.

As an alternative to increasing the number of tests, one can always stop testing and analyze the program. However, analysis may take longer than running a few more tests. Of course, if one of the tests does evoke an actual failure, analysis will be required as part of the debugging process.

A more exact approach to sensitivity analysis can be based on the use of predictor algorithms. Fairly simple algorithms using first and second differences will account for most program behavior with respect to natural continuous phenomena. Deviations from the nth predicted value beyond some predetermined allowance are regarded as symptoms of sensitive regions. One such algorithm[2] estimates the next computed value from

$$\hat{y}_{n+1} = y_n'' + y_n' + y_n$$

where y_n' and y_n'' are the first and second partial derivatives of the output with respect to the varying component of the input data for the nth iteration of the program cycle.

The use of sensitivity analyses suggests a comment on the use of prepared test specifications to the exclusion of impromptu functional testing. Although functional tests — especially functional qualification tests — should always be conducted on the basis of previously prepared descriptions of the test conditions, it is always good practice to depart from a planned test series to explore promising defect sources.

Boundary tests. Recall the finite domain strategy (Section 8.2) for selecting test cases along the boundaries of path domains. Similarly, we need to test not only at typical points within each function partition but also at its boundaries. As a simple example, if a procedure is called with an integer variable that is supposed to be in the range of -10 to $+10$, test inputs are used at -10 and $+10$ as well as at some intervening point (and also at 0 simply because we always worry about zeros).

Boundary testing also applies to the output domain. The extremes of the specified output may not always have an obvious correlation to the range of the input. For example, the maximum braking force demanded by the program of the earlier example of a closed-loop rapid-transit system may result from various combinations of measurements input to the program.

Returning to input data, we should want to test not only at the extremes of the specified input ranges but a little beyond as well. The inability of a program to protect itself from invalid data is a defect. Note that values that exceed stipulated ranges may often be explicitly declared as partition classes, in which case test input for the tests will have previously been specified.

A different kind of boundary test is the process of calibrating the performance envelope of a system. The measure of the average time it will take for a time-sharing system to respond to a carriage return command, given 25 active terminals, 50 terminals, 75 terminals, and so forth, is a form of exploratory boundary test.

Boundary tests dealing with amounts of data rather than their values are frequently referred to as *volume tests*. In a system for handling contract files, we might want to test with every contract option exercised and with every possible endorsement added. A printed-wiring-board program can be tested with every available component and connector position occupied and with increasing numbers of interconnections. As the board gets increasingly dense, the ratio of incomplete to complete connections is calculated as the measure of performance.

Stress tests. Analogously to the way boundary tests deal with values or volumes, stress tests are directed at the edges of the available computation time. Stress tests are akin to the way one tests the tensile strength of fishing line: by adding more weight to the bottom of the line until the line finally parts. To determine the rate of traffic a message-switching system can bear before the wait queues fill up, one gradually increases the rate of data input. The number of aircraft an air traffic control system can handle without falling behind real time is determined by gradually increasing the number of tracked targets.

The distinction between stress tests and boundary tests is not always clear. For example, in calibrating the job mix that a virtual system can handle before thrashing occurs, are we in boundary test or stress test? Calling it a stress test seems the more natural, since the time spent in paging is the real measure, but a good case can be made for viewing the jobs being processed as the values presented to the system under test. Quite obviously, the distinction is immaterial. Whatever we call it, programs should be pushed in any applicable dimension to determine the point of fracture and to find the limits of usable performance.

9.2   Tests Using Random Input

A random test point is one of many uncorrelated points chosen not by the tester but by a force beyond the tester's control. Mathematicians may cringe at this definition, but it is as precise as we want it to be for the purpose of testing. The tester chooses an interval (e.g., the range of values over which all input data are valid), but the actual data points within that interval are determined by some pseudo-random process. Intuitively, this suggests a test process that is more likely than predetermined test case selection to represent an operational environment: the real world is full of surprises, and random functions are the quintessence of surprise.

To speak of "forces beyond the tester's control" sounds somewhat metaphysical or, perhaps, derivative of science fiction. More mundanely, the forces are those of programmed random function generators, special machinery, or data reduced from natural phenomena. Since these sources can produce copious amounts of input data, random input has the further advantage of providing a great number of test points at low cost. The tester merely specifies the interval for the input variables, draws upon the source of random numbers, and, if necessary, provides appropriate mechanisms for shaping the random function into the desired frequency distribution.

In one sense, random input fits the notion of black box testing better than test cases selected for specific points in the input domain. Even the testers most removed from the design process often have some knowledge of the structure of the code they are testing. That is, somewhere in the back of each tester's head is an educated guess of the basic structure or of key algorithms. Random processes do not have the ability to speculate.

Strictly speaking, it is incorrect to refer to random test cases. The term "test case" implies expected output, not just input. To determine the expected output from random input, one has either to laboriously work each input point by hand or run the same input through some kind of prototype program that is known to be absolutely correct. The former nullifies the advantage of voluminous test input at bargain prices, and the latter is seldom available. Accordingly, most of the time we speak of random test input rather than random test cases. However, there are many uses for random test input in which the output can be validated by inspection. In the three examples of random testing that follow, the results of each test may be checked without recourse to prior calculations or simulation.

A general sort routine.   This is a simple application for random testing. A programmed random function routine generates a stream of numbers. The numbers are sieved, and those representing valid alphanumeric codes are concatenated into input strings. A preprocessing routine or test driver forms a new input record or table entry each time a string grows to a given length. That length is determined by a separate random function sequence shaped to provide some desired median value. The result of all this is a record or table of input that looks like anything but the outcome of conscious thought. It may look odd, but it is irrelevant to the purposes of testing whether a delinquent account bearing the unlikely name of Vgotq Iauekklz will ever be sorted.

As was noted earlier, the specification for the test would not have included the expected output values, that is, an exhibit of the correctly ordered input. This presents no problem. Validation is accomplished simply by printing the sorted data and checking to see if it is in alphabetical order.

A printed-wiring-board layout program.   Programs to interconnect the components that will be mounted on a printed-wiring (or printed-circuit) board are large systems, usually interactive. The number of interconnect patterns that they are capable of generating approaches the number of paths in the structure of a computer program. Moreover, for each set of components and interconnection specifications, there generally are several correct, if possibly incomplete, solutions. The kinds of boards most commonly used in computers have a number of "pads" arranged in regularly spaced rows and columns; each pad is a double row of electrically conductive holes into which the connector pins of a component fit.

The program devises conductive paths to connect $P_{i,j}$ to $P_{k,l}$, where $P_{i,j}$ is the jth conductive hole (pin) of the ith pad. A uniformly distributed random function is used to generate a sequence of 4-tuples i, j, k, l. The values output for j and l are integers scaled to the maximum number of pins per pad, and the values for i and k are scaled for the maximum number of pads. If there is a constraint on the maximum number of connections that can be made to a single pin, the preprocessor that generates the input problem set rejects any 4-tuple violating the constraint. The number of interconnections in the problem set can also be randomly determined, but it is more likely to be manually specified to allow testers the capability of testing the program against boards of varying density.

Validation is manually accomplished by visually examining the output diagram, making certain that each input connection pair is realized (or counting those that are not) and that there are no unspecified connections (short circuits) between pins. Note that not only is it unnecessary to have an expectation of the exact solution, it is impossible, since a correct software solution and a correct manual solution would be the same only by coincidence. As a matter of interest, one might want to have a manual solution generated by an expert designer for the purpose of evaluating the program for efficiency — as measured by interconnection path lengths, for example. But this would most likely be a deterministic test case; specifically, it would be one based on a previously designed board.

A signal-processing system. For the last example we shall consider a program for which random input can be supplied by both software and hardware random function generators. In a sense, this illustration cheats, because it has to do with noise, itself a random process. However, it is a common application for random testing. The example is that of a program to separate, in real time, periodic electrical pulses of interest from ambient noise pulses. To simplify the example (but to make things more difficult for the programmers), we assume that the electrical properties of all the pulses are too much alike to be used as distinguishing criteria.* This is a real application, as might be encountered in radar systems, radio telescopes, and many kinds of communications systems.

In the software solution for random testing, the pulse interval of the signal to be extracted would most likely be manually selected but varied slightly from pulse to pulse to account for equipment irregularities. The amount of variation (jitter) is determined by a Poisson or normal random distribution. Noise pulses are produced by distributions representative of the type of noise from which the program is trying to extract data. Note that in this illustration the random data generated by software are in the time domain.

Once the subject program is integrated with the associated receiving equipment, it is possible to use a hardware noise generator (as based on a gas discharge radio tube, for example) of preset average amplitude. The output of this generator is electronically summed to the output of a stable pulse generator of controllable pulse repetition interval. Communications systems are often modeled in the frequency domain rather than, or in addition to, the time domain. Hardware noise generators calibrated for power density (frequency) spectra also are available. If one wants to test the system with respect to its ability to extract signals from noise of known stochastic frequency characteristics, the hardware solution is the easier to implement.

Whether software or hardware sources of random input are used, as earlier, validation is once again performed by inspection. The number of pulses recovered over both short and long periods of time is compared with the number available for recovery, which provides an evaluation of the performance of the system against known noise environments.

---

* For black box testing, we are unconcerned with how a program distinguishes between signal pulses and noise. However, for those whose interest is piqued by the problem, solutions generally either take the mathematical forms of correlation or convolution or employ heuristic multiple associations to form chains of data approximately equispaced in the time domain.

Random notes on random testing. Each of the examples referred to random input, not arbitrary input. A fairly common misconception is that random testing means testing with "any old input." Not so. Any old input is still sufficiently influenced by the tester's prejudices or awareness of the program structure to vitiate the value of random testing — especially with regard to functional coverage — and as we saw, random functions are always at hand.

More on software random function generators. There are a number of techniques to simulate a random process within a computer: use of Fibonacci numbers, methods based on mathematical congruence, the power residue method (actually, a special case of congruence methods), and so on. Of these, the power residue method is by far the most popular. It is fast, and it performs well with respect to most statistical tests of randomness.

One warning applies to the use of the power residue method. Unknown to many of its users, its period is fairly short. That is, given a machine word length of q bits to represent positive numbers, the sequence of random numbers repeats after 2^{q-2} numbers have been generated. This must be taken into account when designing tests using random input.

Most random function generators, including the power residue method, generate a uniform frequency distribution. That is, the probability of producing one number in the stipulated range is the same as that for any other number. To produce a different distribution, one has to "shape" the random function. For example, to produce an exponential distribution, one can use, not the random number x_i produced by the generator, but $-\log_e x_i$.

Random testing can mean many tests. The generation of test input using random processes not only constitutes a convenient source of voluminous input data, it also eases the task of executing a large population of tests — both tests requiring many input values (the sort routine) and tests conducted with a single input value.

Random testing may mean many tests, but it does not have to mean tests evenly spread over the input domain. To expose defects before the users find them, one is tempted to favor — by choice of input interval or frequency distribution — test input most likely to be experienced in actual use. This is not necessarily wrong. Our intuition is supported by a probabilistic analysis[3] which demonstrates that an essentially uniform distribution is optimum for large numbers of tests, but for relatively small numbers of tests (but not so small as to be statistically insignificant) it is better to favor the inputs most likely to be used and most likely to result in failure.

The fact that random testing can mean many tests has led some people to confuse random testing with stress testing. The notion here seems to be that if you hammer away at a program hard enough (read, many tests), you will have stressed it. That the program will have been given considerable exercise is indisputable, but this is not stress testing in the sense previously defined. More important, accepting for the moment a more general connotation of the term "stress testing," the simple fact that many tests have been run provides no assurance that the functional test objectives discussed earlier will be met. Of this, more shortly, when we look at combining random methods with the others.

Recovering test input.   One problem with random testing is that it does not have pretest documentation to describe the exact input used for each test. This can lead to inefficiency. On encountering a failure, it may be difficult to recreate the exercise for the purposes of debugging. It is not impossible, if a software random function generator is used, since the random sequence will repeat if given the same seed.* However, this may require either that all previous tests in the random sequence be repeated or that the test driver be modified to default execution of the tests that preceded the one that failed. If a hardware source of random data is used, it definitely will be impossible to recreate the input condition.

Although sometimes ignored when testing with random data, logging the input data of each test is always advisable. This permits the test to be run again, whether for debugging or regression, while using the recorded input as one would with predetermined test data selection. When random data derived from hardware are used to simulate a stochastic process extending over many instances of the input variables, as in the earlier signal-processing example, it may be necessary to settle for repeating the aggregate characteristics (e.g., mean, variance) in lieu of the exact set of input values.

Combining random and preselected test data methods.   The attractive qualities of random testing can best be exploited in conjunction with the methods of Section 9.1. For example, one can select the functional partition to be tested and then apply random input within that partition rather than data manually selected. But this should be a substitute for test case selection only if successful execution can be confirmed without calculating the expected output for each input point.

Similarly, one can select intervals in the region of the functional boundaries for random testing. In the earlier example of calibrating the performance envelope of a time-sharing system, rather than have all 25, 50, or 75 terminals doing the same thing, one can randomly assign them tasks from a catalog. Stress tests can also be enhanced by random processes. The example of determining the maximum traffic rate of which a communications switch is capable is often accomplished by using Poisson-distributed

---

* Unless the seed comes from an unlogged real-time clock or some other fortuitous source.

random input to provide a synthetic, but credible, operational environment.

Random input is less useful for sensitivity analysis. Since sensitivity analysis depends on smoothly varying input, it lends itself to random testing only if observation of apparent anomalous behavior pertains to the statistical, or aggregate, properties of the random input. For example, again returning to the signal processing illustration, if the ratio of recovered to lost data pulses suddenly drops when the pulse repetition interval approaches a multiple of the median pulse repetition interval of the noise pulses, we can suspect the existence of a problem.

9.3   Automated Test Systems

Other than tools to manage test execution and interpret test procedures prepared in special languages, as previously discussed in Section 8.3, little exists to mechanize functional testing. What one wants most is a system to automatically generate test data from the external specifications of the functions to be performed. Given a program to perform a mathematically defined function — say, to evaluate a trigonometric function — it is a simple matter to write a driver that will automatically step through a user-specified range of values. One would scarcely call this test automation, but even at this fribbling level it demonstrates two problems. First, the mechanization provides test input only; to generate expected results, the system would need the complete capability of the program under test. Second, to be capable of generating sensitivity, boundary, or stress tests, the system would need capabilities many times those of the program under test, capabilities we are not even certain we know how to build.

Now let us compound the problem by considering the more realistic condition of testing a program with several independent input variables. To cover the input domain properly, an automatic test system needs to generate the countless number of combinations of input values. Worse, most of these combinations may be invalid, with the result that a hopelessly large number of tests will be run outside the range of greatest interest. In short, automation for functional testing must be defined on fairly narrow grounds.

Obviously, any automatic system will have to be guided by the tester. Let us not view this as an obstacle to be overcome. Nearly all of the tools used for active or passive defect removal are interactive. More importantly, any automation beyond the level of test management will have to have some capability of operating in the nebulous realm of functional requirements, which means that at the most modest level it will be costly. Mechanization developed for testing a single software system makes financial sense only if the system is destined to go through many modifications during its life, each one requiring new sets of functional tests.

A more likely candidate for development is an automatic test system that can be applied to the functional test of a number of different programs having in common a given class of performance characteristics. From the data generation properties reflecting those characteristics, the tester chooses input values and, in effect, particularizes the test system for the program under test and the function to be demonstrated. This is the capability offered by the environmental simulators discussed in the next section. For example, the U.S. Air Force has developed radar threat generators capable of evaluating a number of different jamming systems. These simulators fail to achieve a more ambitious definition of automatic test systems, however, since they have only weak capacity for evaluating the extent to which a test has succeeded. We must really regard these simulators as elaborate test drivers.

Another class of programs that would seem to be amenable to automatic test generation is that of compilers. The syntax and semantics of grammars are well-bounded, and it should be possible to automatically generate compilable and intentionally noncompilable test programs over the full domain of the compiler. This is precisely what has been accomplished for languages that can be described in tabular form by using a formalism similar to that of context-free grammars.[4] In this system, the algorithm that generates the test input accepts user commands to restrict the complexity and length of the test programs, suppress specified code productions, limit the number of identifiers and types, and limit the number and types of fields within a record for the formal parameters within a procedure. The system has been used to test several Pascal and PLZ compilers.

The use of a formal language specification to drive the generation of test data suggests that functional specifications written in an axiomatic or operational requirements language, such as the ones remarked in Section 2.1, are likely candidates for automatic test generation, especially when given restrictions to bound program classes. However, there appear to be no successful experiments to demonstrate this.

9.4   Special Problems of Embedded Software

Section 7.2 raised the problem of testing programs operating on line with newborn hardware. Test failures may result from design faults in the software, design or fabrication faults in the hardware, or incompatible software and hardware external specifications. Consider a simple closed control loop as in Figure 9.1. The indicated physical process may be the braking system of an electrical locomotive, a nuclear power plant, an oil refinery, a milling machine, or even a microwave oven. In addition to the computer program, the full system includes the computer, the sensors, and the computer-driven control actuators.

Individual specifications unique to this system describe each type of

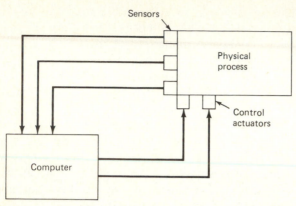

Figure 9.1 Closed control loop incorporating a computer.

sensor, each type of actuator, the computer, and the computer program. There may also be specifications defining installation and adjustment procedures for the sensors and actuators. The full set of specifications may be viewed as a model of the physical process. When the temperature in the reactor rises to T°, increase the amount of cooling water proportionally to the temperature increase observed during the last measurement interval. Expressed as a continuous function, we have a simple differential equation. The correct solution depends not only on the accuracy of the program but on the linearity of the sensors and the electrically controlled valves as well. If a valve is slightly sticky, performance will be erratic. A sensitivity test, such as the tests defined in Section 9.1, might lead one to believe that a fault exists in the program — anything from a structural defect to round-off error.

The solution is not to eschew sensitivity analysis or any of the other functional test types, but to implant system diagnostic messages in the program. Unlike the diagnostic messages used for debugging, these are planned during the software design process. It is not a question of dark forebodings: Difficulties in system integration are inevitable, and the computer in the system can perform — indeed, will be called upon to perform — as an ideal built-in diagnostic tool.*

Programmers are really protecting themselves when their design includes every conceivable system diagnostic. Nearly every system problem will immediately be referred to the programmers, since they control the central diagnostic tool. Each built-in diagnostic avoids the need for a patch

---

* Many embedded programs are installed with code for testing, either periodically or on command, the continued soundness of the system hardware. Some even have routines for isolating hardware failures to a specific component or group of components.

or special compilation to try to isolate the problem. Assuming the software has undergone reviews or walk-throughs, static testing, and the full set of glass box and black box tests possible without the use of actual system hardware, the number of problems traceable to program bugs will be fewer than half. Nevertheless, the programmers will be the people on whom the finding of a sticky valve devolves. Worse, the time spent in finding system problems may be disproportional to that spent in debugging. There are any number of projects in which up to 80 percent of the time spent by the software test team was connected with system or hardware design faults or hardware failures.

The reference to prior software tests without the use of system hardware recalls the environment simulators previously discussed. Considerable confidence that the program conforms to its external specifications, including those of timing or speed of response, can be gained by first driving it with simulators that provide accurate representation of the outside world. For a closed-loop control system, such as that of Figure 9.1, a simulator must be able to replicate the transfer function of the process, a fairly expensive matter. Simulators are more commonly found for open-ended systems, especially for the generation of input data for testing. Here one uses several remotely controlled electronic signal generators — pulse generators, waveform generators to modulate the pulse generators, noise generators, whatever — operating under the control of a computer. For maximum versatility, the simulator's software system contains drivers for each signal generator, all taking their cues from an executive program (or scenario translator). The most useful systems have an operator interface to allow on-line entry and modification of the script.

Closed-loop simulators must go beyond the relatively simple environment simulator to interpret the results of the program's actions and modify the simulated signals as would the actual process being modeled. Simple processes that can be modeled with straightforward mathematical operations are not all that much of a problem. It is a different matter when the simulator must produce output that is dependent on a number of discrete control signals generated by the program under test, especially when time delays are involved. Simulators used to evaluate radar-jamming equipment (the simulated radar signals must be altered according to the signal output of the computer-controlled jammer, thus forming a virtual closed control loop) are controlled by computer programs that approach and even surpass in size the programs in the jamming equipment. If we consider these simulators to be test drivers on a grand scale, we have drivers that represent a larger software development project than that which culminated in the program under test. It must be concluded, analogously to the earlier discussion of environmental simulators as approximations to automated test systems, that testing embedded programs in an all-software environment will in many cases be feasible only when the simulator can be applied to a class of similar programs or to individual programs expected to undergo many future modifications.

9.5   Criteria for Verification

Recalling the verification test strategy of Section 7.2, each stage of testing is defined in the context of demonstrating that a set of external specifications has been satisfied. The scope of unit testing is determined by specifications for individual modules, integration testing by the top-level design specification, and so forth. Thus, in addition to meeting structural testing criteria for a module under test, we need criteria for verifying that the module meets its functional specifications. So too for the other stages of testing.

A simplistic criterion is that one has successfully completed running the full set of planned tests.* Unfortunately, this ignores the opportunity to learn from the tests themselves how well they were designed to uncover latent defects. Moreover, it fails to account for the inability to successfully complete all tests.

With regard to using functional tests to measure themselves, there is little on which we can build a firm foundation for measurement. The EOR (defined in Section 1.7 as the ratio of defects removed to those present at the start of the test series) is unknown until the completion of all testing — more precisely, until the program has matured during operational use. Using estimates of the number of bugs (see Section 7.1) has merit in verifying test planning and may be used to bolster or reduce one's confidence in the tests just completed, but it is too imprecise to use as a firm completion criterion. Reliability growth models, which will be discussed in the next chapter, have a place in test planning too, but they also lack the precision necessary for service as standards of test completion.

The plain fact is that black box testing does not have a mathematically based criterion for completion comparable to the coverage measurements of structural testing. However, it is possible to judge the usefulness of functional tests in a manner recalling the technique of mutation testing (Section 8.5) — specifically, by seeding the program with deliberate faults.

Fault seeding.   The earliest suggestion of seeding seems to be that of Harlan Mills in about 1970. Seeding is related to the tagging procedures followed for many years by state fisheries. In what is also referred to as the capture-

---

* Simplistic, but at least a step up from the criterion that testing is complete when the schedule says it must be.

recapture process, a number of fish in a lake are netted, tagged, and returned to the lake. A second fishing expedition nets a second catch, and the ratio of tagged to untagged fish is noted. The estimate of the total number of fish is formed by dividing the size of the second catch by this ratio.

The programming equivalent of tagging uses two testers. Each finds a certain number of defects. Tester A finds a set of n defects and tester B finds m. The number of defects common to the two sets is c. These are analogous to tagged fish. The estimate for the total number of defects that existed at the start of testing is

$$\hat{N} = \frac{n \times m}{c}$$

The tagging process is equivalent to the classical statistical experiment of sampling without replacement. This experiment produces a hypergeometric distribution of the probabilities of finding a given number of tagged fish. As shown by Rudner[5] and also by Schick and Wolverton,[6] the maximum likelihood estimate (MLE)* for the total number of initial defects more formally derived from this distribution is essentially the same as the expression given above.

The tagging model requires two programmers operating independently for some period of time. The result is an estimate of the number of faults requiring removal. This has value for estimating the remaining amount of testing that will be required, but it does not help us to gain confidence in the tests that have been conducted. For that, we turn to a variant of tagging: seeding. In seeding, a number of defects are deliberately implanted in the code at the start of a test series. To determine the effectiveness of the tests, we can interpret the previous equation, $\hat{N} = (n \times m)/c$, as follows:

$\hat{N}$ = estimated total number of real and seeded faults
n = number of faults that had been seeded
m = total number of faults exposed during testing
c = number of seeded faults that were exposed.

The evaluation of the effectiveness of the tests is gauged by the size of the ratio $(m - n)/(\hat{N} - n)$. Assume that 50 faults had been seeded and that at

---

* The MLE is common in reliability engineering.[7,8] Given a random sample $x_1, \ldots, x_n$ from a population of probability distribution frequency (pdf) $f(x, \theta)$, one seeks an estimator $\hat{\theta}$ for the parameter θ. The *likelihood function of the sample,* defined as

$$L(x_1, \ldots, x_n; \theta) = f(x_1; \theta) \cdots f(x_n; \theta)$$

is the a priori probability of obtaining the x_i that constitute the observed sample. MLE then resolves to the determination of that θ that maximizes L. The definition extends to the estimation of more than one parameter.

the end of functional testing 240 faults had been found, 40 of which were seeds. This yields $\hat{N} = 300$ for an estimate of 250 unintentional defects of which only 200 had been found. The ratio computed from this is 0.76, somewhat less than the ratio of recovered seeds. In general, a ratio below 0.9 suggests that more tests need to be run, and a ratio of 1 (all seeds found) provides high confidence in the effectiveness of the tests.

The use of seeding as a measure of the usefulness of a set of functional tests is predicated on how closely the implanted defects resemble the real ones and how randomly they were seeded with respect to the domain of the program. Although techniques may be devised to evaluate the latter, we have no presumptive way of knowing how representative the seeds are.* Accordingly, results obtained from seeding should be regarded as a guide toward determining whether sufficient testing has been performed, not as an absolute criterion.

Let us digress briefly to distinguish between mutation testing and seeding and, in the process, reveal the basis for including the former in the chapter on glass box testing and the latter here. Mutation tests the adequacy of test cases to reveal faults. It closely relates the structure tested (program domain) to the test input used. Thus, it serves much the same end as coverage-based testing.

Seeding also does this, but with less exactness. It is more difficult to relate the arbitrary seeding to structural coverage, unless, of course, an enormous number of seeds is used. On the other hand, if a programmer familiar with both the program structure and its functional specification implants defects with respect to the functions performed, seeding can be used to guard against a battery of functional test cases that result from too narrow an interpretation (by the test designers) of the external specifications.

Criteria for qualification.   Although completion or pass criteria need to be established for every stage of functional testing, they are most critical during qualification testing. This is, after all, the last opportunity to remove defects before they fall into the unwary hands of the user. On a less lofty

---

* In a recent conversation, Bill Huber, of Norden Division of United Technologies, suggested that for integration testing one might seed by refraining from the removal of all of the bugs found during module testing. Unlike other direct adaptations of the capture-recapture of fish, this technique avoids the duplication of test personnel (although it presupposes an independent test team) yet reduces the seed credibility problem to that of determining which defects to leave in, a more restricted decision domain. Whether this is a more tractable approach remains to be seen, since the suggestion came too late in the preparation of this manuscript to be tried out. In any case, the technique would militate against the appearance of nonrepresentative, contrived seeds.

plane, qualification may be the basis for contractual acceptance or some equivalent rite of passage. The acceptor needs reassurance that the program does what it is supposed to do. For that matter, the developers need to be told that they are discharged from further responsibility (save for that associated with a warranty or the preservation of goodwill). This usually implies an acceptance test procedure (ATP) written by the user's representative or prepared by the user in advance of the performance of the tests. The tests specified in the ATP are nearly always functional tests, although documented evidence of earlier structural testing may also be stipulated. Notwithstanding the amount of testing accomplished in earlier test phases, full functional performance must be demonstrated here.*

Unlike the other testing procedures that have been discussed, the primary purpose of qualification testing is not defect removal, but demonstration of performance. Indeed, to most faithfully imitate the operational use of the program, no alterations to the program are permitted in the course of the qualification tests. Thus, in theory at least, defect removal is impossible. However, if severe defects are uncovered during the qualification tests, or if there is an excessive number of minor problems, the program may be judged unacceptable, a judgment as likely to be made by the developers as by the users. Under these fairly common circumstances, the disclosed faults are then removed and the exercises started anew. This can be viewed either as a condition of 100 percent regression testing or as two separate phases of testing: a qualification dry run followed by the qualification exercise, proper.

Since certain tests may not be precisely repeatable with respect to input values, there is no guarantee that the final run through the test series will not produce problems previously unseen. Taking into account the time required for the qualification testing of a large system (two or three months is not unheard of), it may be impractical to demand total test success as measured by perfect performance. Accordingly, it is prudent to establish, in the acceptance test procedure, criteria for acceptance that accommodate the possibility that qualification testing may be imperfectly concluded.

Apart from problems of testing, another reason to entertain delivery of a program with known problems is that the system may be too complex to ever be entirely bug-free — or at least predictably so. For such programs, one may recognize the presence of a defect but choose not to attempt to remove it for fear of creating five more. Of such pusillanimity are born the caveats in user manuals. A typical example is a large operating system, some specimens of which have dozens of known bugs when first released.

---

* As a matter of form, we might observe that qualification tests are more a matter of validation than they are of verification.

A number of acceptance criteria have been used in lieu of unblemished test results. Among them, used singly or in various combinations, are:

- Number of defects uncovered but not removed per thousand lines of code
- Ratio of failed tests to successful tests
- Ability to run with random or arbitrary input for n consecutive hours without incident
- Number of undiagnosed failures per thousand lines of code

To all of these must be attached levels of severity. For example,

1. Inability to complete an operation (e.g., system crash for an operating system or nose dive for an autopilot)
2. Inability to complete an operation within specified tolerance (accuracy of solution, response time, etc.)
3. Inconvenience to the user

The severity levels are used to weight the numerical criteria. For example, the computation of the ratio of failed tests to successful tests might consider a failure of the second severity level to be only half a failed test case, a failure of the third severity level to be only an eighth a failed test case.

Quite obviously, the choice of criteria to be included in the acceptance conditions must reflect the purpose of the software under test. A 24-hour endurance run makes a lot more sense for an airborne navigation system than it does for a first-stage rocket guidance system.

With regard to the actual numbers used, one has to consider what is actually usable software and what is not. Nor does it hurt to prejudice oneself with the knowledge that large software systems are frequently delivered with up to three defects per thousand lines of code, including this time-sharing system:

> There's a system installed in Lucerne
> That gives users grave cause for concern.
> At their first compound branch
> They're logged out in Romansch
> For no reason the Swiss can discern.

9.6   Summary

1. At all levels of test, traceability tools direct the tester to the functions that need to be tested.
2. Devising a minimum set of functional test cases can be approached by iteratively decomposing the input domain into partitions sharing equivalent characteristics.

3. The technique of sensitivity analysis finds areas within functional domains for which a greater density of test cases is appropriate.

4. Boundary tests are used to exercise programs at the extremes of the input and output domains. Boundary tests directed at amounts of data rather than their values are called volume tests.

5. Stress tests are analogous to boundary tests, but they explore the edges of performance in the time domain.

6. Random tests are those using input from random processes over which the tester has only gross control.

7. Since testers do not have foreknowledge of individual test points, random test input is a closer approximation to operational use than are other test selection methods.

8. The sources for random data may be either software or hardware random function generators.

9. For greatest effectiveness, random test points are confined within the bounds established by other test data selection methods.

10. Functional specifications are not documented in forms that allow mechanized deduction of test case properties. However, it is possible to define classes of programs — compilers, for example — for which automated test case generation is feasible.

11. To monitor the behavior of programs embedded in instrumentation systems, it usually is necessary to implant diagnostics to report the program state.

12. Testing embedded programs with environment simulators before joining the programs to actual system hardware improves the effectiveness and efficiency of functional testing.

13. Unlike structural testing, functional testing does not lend itself to statistical completion criteria. However, fault seeding protects against the use of a battery of functional test cases that have limited functional coverage.

14. Statistical defect, failure, or endurance criteria may have to be established to qualify programs that are of a size and complexity that defy 100 percent bug removal.

References

1. Glenford Myers, *The Art of Software Testing,* Wiley-Interscience, New York, 1979, pp. 56–73.
2. Marvin Watkins, "A Technique for Testing Command and Control Software," *CACM,* vol. 25, April 1982, pp. 228–232.
3. Arthur E. Laemmel, *Software Modeling Studies, A Statistical Theory of Computer Program Testing,* Polytechnic Institute of New York, 1981, released by Rome Air Development Center as Report RADC-TR-81-183, vol. IV.

4. F. Bazzichi and I. Spadafora, "An Automatic Generator for Compiler Testing," *IEEE Trans. Software Eng.,* vol. SE-8, July 1982, pp. 343–353.
5. B. Rudner, *Seeding/Tagging Estimation of Software Errors: Models and Estimates,* Polytechnic Institute of New York, 1977, released by Rome Air Development Center as Report RADC-TR-77-15.
6. George Schick and Ray Wolverton, "An Analysis of Competing Software Reliability Models," *IEEE Trans. Software Eng.,* vol. SE-4, March 1978, pp. 104–120.
7. Martin Shooman, *Probabilistic Reliability: An Engineering Approach,* McGraw-Hill, New York, 1968.
8. David Lloyd and Myron Lipow, *Reliability: Management, Methods, and Mathematics,* 2d ed., published by the authors, Redondo Beach, Calif., 1977.

10

Analysis of Defect and Failure Data

Systems analysts and programmers are seldom given to contemplating their errors. Faults, once found and corrected, are forgotten as attention is redirected to forward progress. Failures are regarded as unscheduled impediments to the completion of testing; certainly nothing one would want to dwell upon. Yet, analysis of all three — failures, the faults that cause them, and the errors that underlie faults — are an inseparable part of modern programming. Examination of defect and failure data leads to the detection of modules that have an untoward potential for producing failures, helps to reckon the amount of testing that remains before an acceptable level of failure-free performance is achieved, and yields information useful in the improvement of both productivity and quality for future projects.

We would much rather review our successes than enumerate our failures. Our predisposition in this respect is scarcely peculiar to programming, nor is it born of our time. Thucydides had thought it necessary to advise, "The wise ensure their safety by not making too sure of their gains, and when disasters come they can meet them more intelligently." Within the context of computer programming, the second clause may be a bit extravagant, but not entirely farfetched. So much for philosophy: the fact remains that analysis of software failures and defects (both the fault itself and the circumstances of the error) is performed on a minority of projects, when it should be undertaken on all.

More tangible than our distaste for raking over bad news are the obstacles that seem to hinder the accumulation of defect and failure data. Accordingly, although the greater part of this chapter is given to analysis itself, we shall start with its necessary antecedent, the collection of defect and failure data.

10.1   Data Collection

Certain of the defect data are available from vehicles that previously were discussed. Chapters 3 and 4 noted that the minutes of requirements, design, and code reviews are mostly the lists of items requiring correction. This applies also to walk-throughs. At the very least, it is a trivial matter to tabulate the number of defects found in each review or walk-through. This information will subsequently be used for the improvement of the development process. It will also be used to calculate the EOR (defined in Section 1.7) of the reviews.

With a little more effort, defects exposed in reviews of requirements and design can be classified according to categories of the sort suggested by Section 1.3 (missing functions, infinite loops, and so on). The same amount of additional effort will allow defects found by code reviews to be placed in the categories of Section 1.6: computational, logic, input and output, data handling, interface, data definition, and data base. This additional information will provide sharper focus for determining where the development process should be revised.

Another increment of effort will result in the defects being classified by severity. Severity is a more subjective matter than classification by type. A four- or three-grade scale is about as fine a system of distinction as can be realized; any more levels lead to too much time spent in making the discriminations. Whatever the number of grades that are established, the intrinsic meaning of each grade must be defined as in the three-grade scale of Section 9.5. The inclusion of severity rankings in the tabulation of defect data permits analysis to be made at more than one level. For example, one can first perform an analysis, by using only the most significant defects, to determine which defect removal techniques are failing to live up to expectations. If there is no clear result from the analysis, the members of the next most severe class are added for a second round of statistical investigation. The objective of this is to put one's resources where they will return the greatest profit.

Collecting defect data from the results of static analysis is not quite so simple as summarizing the logs of reviews. The programmer, on finding a fault, is much more interested in correcting it than in recording it. Still, it should be possible to persuade the programmer to save hard copy reports of detected defects for tabulation at the end of each day or week. If hard copy is impractical, the programmer may be able to find a way to file the reports output to his CRT. Designers of static analysis systems would be well advised to build in a facility for automatic filing of discrepancy reports for the specific purpose of defect collection.

Collection of defect data during active test is quite a different matter, at least for informal, or development, tests for which formal discrepancy or change request reports are not required. When a test does not succeed, the last thing a programmer cares to think about is a bookkeeping procedure. The programmer's attention is totally taken by the need to find the source of the problem. Moreover, once the defect has been located and fixed, the programmer is interested only in confirming the success of the debugging procedure. Short of having an auditor standing next to each tester, any defect collection mechanism that is used must be kept extremely simple.

A "bean-counting" form is about as simple a device as possible. The use of a bean-counting form requires no more of the programmer than that he scratch a hash mark in an appropriate place on a piece of paper. A pair of forms is even better, as, for example, the forms of Figures 10.1 and 10.2.

In Figure 10.1, we see three dimensions of defect collection: identification of the test phase in which the fault was detected, the programmer's assessment of the origin of the fault, and the programmer's judgment of the fault's severity. A single mark is made in the appropriate space in the rectangular table for each defect.

Of the nine defect origins appearing on the form, only the first five apply to the program itself, and some might even argue that the fifth does not.

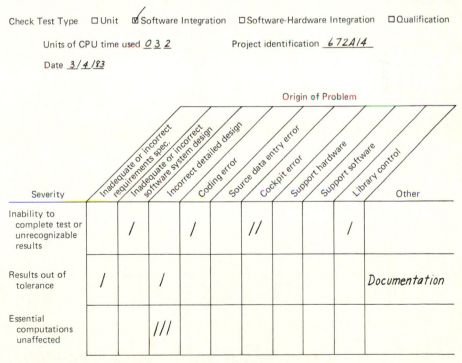

Figure 10.1 Daily test log: defect source and severity.

The last four are included partly to help analyze weaknesses in the test environment and partly to simply account for the incidence of a test failure on that day, something that will be needed for time domain trend analysis used to estimate the amount of testing that remains. There is also an "other" column. There are always "other" categories, whether required to compensate for lack of space or to acknowledge the limits of the imagination of the form's creator. In the illustration, a documentation defect was listed in this column.

As is evident, the day to which Figure 10.1 applies saw a rich harvest of defects: seven program faults and one documentation defect. Unfortunately, there were also three problems (two cockpit errors and a library control problem) that reduced testing efficiency.

Figure 10.2 is the accompanying form. It asks the programmer to classify each program fault by type. The information from this form will be of use in the more finely cut analyses of where improvements in development are most required. Like Figure 10.1, this form contains the date to which the recorded defects apply. The date of either form can be input to a model for estimating the remaining test time, but only the seven defects of Figure 10.2 (which also appear, with others, on Figure 10.1) apply to the subject program.

Figure 10.2 also requests identification of the module to which each fault was traced. This will subsequently be used to identify failure-prone modules.

Project Identification _672A14_   Date _3/4/83_

Module	Fault Type							
	Computational	Logic	I/O	Data handling	Interface	Data definition	Data base	Other
Alpha	/							
Bravo		/						
Charlie					//			
Delta			//					
Echo						/		

Figure 10.2   Daily test log: defect classification.

It is one thing to glibly state that these forms are simple to complete and another to get the testers to agree that their completion will not add an administrative burden to the testing process. The milieu of program testing and debugging tends to be one of confusion, often attended by clutter on every nearby surface. "Where did I put those data collection forms?" "Did I remember to record that last bug?" "Do I want to take the time to figure out what kind of bug this one is?" "Why in blazes am I doing this, anyway?"

What these questions add up to is a requirement for management to motivate,* instruct, and help those who will be filling out the forms. With regard to the last, the best help is to have the person responsible for accumulating the data (a software quality engineer makes an ideal candidate) fill out all the header information before giving the forms to the testers. It also helps to hand out the forms each day so that the testers do not have to store a supply themselves. Indeed, the time to hand out today's forms is also the time to collect yesterday's, thus making certain that programmers do not put off completion of the forms until they have only (erroneously) remembered data to enter.

Other helpful actions include providing clipboards to aid in the control of the clutter problem and commenting on incorrectly completed forms directly they are received.

To motivate programmers to take this data-gathering business seriously, one can appeal to their professionalism. If the programmers understand that one of the principal purposes of the exercise is to improve the process by which they produce programs, including the justification of the cost of new capital expenditures, they will have reasons of their own to cooperate. They should also be told, both in writing and in person — as in an in-house seminar with plenty of opportunity for questions — the whys and hows of the data collection program. Moreover, the same reports provided to management should be made available to the programmers not only to let them see the fruits of their efforts but to satisfy their curiosity concerning the origins of defects, the types of defects, and the effectiveness of defect removal activities.

We have also to take care not to *demotivate* programmers. It must be made clear that the purposes of defect data collection are not those of self-incrimination. To this end, it helps if tabulation is made by personnel not reporting to programming management. Again, software quality engineers can be called upon. The only correlation of the data with individual programmers is that implied by the names of the modules in Figure 10.2,

---

* Management itself may not be motivated. Let the management jury stay its decision on this matter until it has read to the end of this chapter.

and this information needs to be disseminated only for the identification of failure-prone modules. Since by definition (as we shall see in the next section) only a very few modules will ever be labeled "failure-prone," the anonymity associated with collection and tabulation by an outside agent will largely be preserved.

Let us not forget instruction. Forms such as those of the two illustrations appear to be self-explanatory, but questions will arise. Some programmers may have difficulty distinguishing among the fault types of Figure 10.2. All programmers will have questions concerning the broader classes found in Figure 10.1. For example, it will not be obvious to everyone that an incorrectly entered binary patch or the failure to stipulate the correct patch file is a cockpit error, whereas not updating the link file for the identification of the latest patch file is a library control error. Instruction should be in the form of a simple written guide accompanied by verbal tutelage, as in the previously suggested in-house seminar.

There is less of a problem in collecting defect data during formal (e.g., qualification) testing. Assuming all test failures caused by program faults result in diagnoses accompanied by formal change requests, one has only to pluck the relevant information from the request form. The change request will identify documents requiring modification, from which one can ascertain which of the first five categories of Figure 10.1 applies. (Occasionally, however, there will be some confusion between coding and source entry errors.) The description of the change itself will provide the information of Figure 10.2.

For failures during formal test that are not traceable to program faults — that is, failures attributable to the last four categories of Figure 10.1 — we can look to the test log, where test anomalies would normally be excused by notations such as "Loading error — bad disk read."

Summarizing, a thorough program of recording and characterizing defects during the frenetic testing phase is possible, given assiduous planning and implementation effort by management. The effort will be worth it.

10.2 Failure-Prone Modules

One of the profits of a defect data collection scheme is the identification of the elements of a program that need to be replaced in their entirety. Whether we are concerned with individual procedures or several procedures grouped under the name of a single module, many large software systems have at least one module that seems to have been born and bred in misery. There are several possible causes to explain the existence of failure-prone modules: unstable external specifications, change of personnel in the middle of a development phase, a distracted programmer, or a programmer who did not understand the external specifications. Whatever the cause, these modules are so defect-ridden that each corrective action seems only to create as many new defects as it cures.

It happens fairly often that the programmers charged with diagnosing failures during test are aware of these modules. Occasionally, however, little is said for fear of jeopardizing the situation of a fellow worker. Regardless of the relations among the programmers, in large systems, where there are many modules to contribute to test failures, a particularly troublesome module may easily go unnoticed.

Yet it is important to know of them. For reason of the efficiency of the remaining test activity, and possibly the quality of the delivered product, identification of a failure-prone module calls for analysis to determine the quality of the module's structure. This may take the form of a combination of detailed design and code review (in principle if not in form) even if they had been performed earlier or of an audit of the code against its design documentation. (Maybe the reason the module cannot be fixed is that the fixes are relying on obsolete documentation.) A complexity measurement (see Section 7.1) is a valuable input. Analysis may indicate that remedial action is possible. On the other hand, it may reveal that there is nothing for it but to return the module to the drawing board.

What concerns us in this chapter is how one goes about identifying failure-prone modules. Enter defect collection. Given a tabulation of the number of modules contributing N defects, N ranging from zero to the maximum number of defects attributed to any one module, a Pareto analysis* can be performed to detect the modules contributing an untoward share of the failures. That this method can succeed was demonstrated quite some time ago by Albert Endres with data from a system comprising 422 modules.[1] Consider Figure 10.3 for a hypothetical system of some 200 modules. Notice that no defects were found in 41 modules, 1 was found in 35 modules, and so on, until we got down to 2 modules with 18 and 24 defects, respectively.

Now, it may be that the two suspicious modules are much larger than the others or, at the stage of testing that the diagram represents, that these two modules have had much more exposure than most. However, if neither of these tests is met, by inspection we can declare these two to be candidates for failure-proneness, and they should be examined carefully.

One wants to start looking for failure-proneness early enough (say, a third of the way through integration) to avoid wasted test effort, but this invites a hazard. The earlier one analyzes, the greater the likelihood that a

---

* Pareto analysis is a common quality control technique. It takes its name from Vilfredo Pareto, who early in this century performed a much-remarked demographic analysis of the distribution of wealth. His analysis showed that a surprisingly small number of people controlled most of the money.

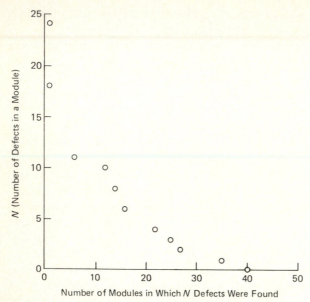

Figure 10.3 Detection of failure-prone modules.

skewed defect distribution is as much the result of unequal exposure to failure opportunities as it is the consequence of inherent module weakness. It may well be that the earliest opportune time to apply this kind of analysis is when integration is 80 percent complete. The software structure and the type of testing one does will provide the necessary clues to determine a reasonable time to start.

In any case, a failure-prone analysis should be undertaken at the conclusion of software integration or top-down testing and (if applicable) at the conclusion of hardware and software integration.

10.3   Estimating Testing Progress

Defect data collection can also be instrumental in estimating the effort necessary to complete the testing of a program. If one knew precisely how many defects were in a program at the start of testing and if a record were kept of the number of bugs removed and the length of time it took to remove them, an estimate could be made of the time required to remove the balance (assuming the estimate took into account the timewise nonlinearity of defect detection and the rate at which new bugs were introduced). However, one does not know the number *ab initio*. Using past experience and size and complexity models, as in Section 7.1, we may be able to arrive at a rough guess (say, ±30 percent) of the number of bugs, but we still have to reckon with both the introduction of new bugs and the rate of defect exposure.

Defect seeding, discussed in Section 9.5, can also contribute to the estimation of test progress. If we knew the seeds to be randomly distributed with respect to the input domain of the program and if we knew the percentage of those that were recovered, we should be able to arrive at some measure of how far testing has to go. Indeed, reliability models (which we shall soon discuss within the context of diminishing rates of defect detection) have been based on seeding. However, it is not clear that they offer any intrinsic advantage over models based on the exposure of real defects. What is clear is that any scheme for estimating progress should be based on some kind of trend analysis, that is, some way of extrapolating in time from the recent history of testing.

Trend analysis.   Trend analysis implies the graphing of some measurable activity against time. Several such activities recommend themselves. One that applies to formal testing is the comparison, in time, of the opening (description of a failure) and closing (defect removed) of program trouble reports (PTRs) or their equivalents. If we see a trend such as that of Figure 10.4, we can feel fairly confident that testing is on schedule, or at least that we can draw linear inferences from the ratio of completed to scheduled tests. On the other hand, Figure 10.5 tells us we are in trouble.

Trends such as PTR closing rates are useful for the synoptic evaluation of progress, and they are included among the "leading indicators" used by ITT Programming to warn of impending problems. However, since both

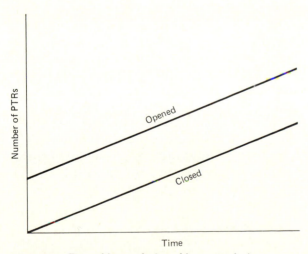

Figure 10.4   Favorable trend of trouble report closings.

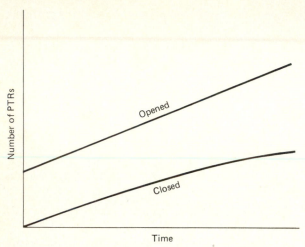

Figure 10.5   Worrisome trend of trouble report closings.

the opening and closing of PTRs are subject to a number of transitory influences, the relation between them tends to be too erratic for quantitative modeling, especially if PTRs enter into the defect removal process only at a time (e.g., qualification testing) when the number of defect detections is too slight for statistical smoothing of the perturbations.

Another trend that lends itself to analysis is the ratio of failed to passed tests,* also one of the leading indicators. For both qualitative and quantitative purposes, the individual trends of both failed and passed tests have interest of their own. From Figure 10.6, one quickly sees that things are working out well.

The curve of the failed tests introduces the trend technique that has received the greatest attention: reliability growth modeling. We shall examine this technique, mostly for its intrinsic value but also to provide a mathematical basis for the term "software reliability," before returning — if briefly — to the subject of simple trend analysis.

Reliability growth models.   Software reliability growth models have evolved in an attempt to emulate the reliability models in use for hardware. The hardware models were a response to the need to predict reliability of operational equipment. Reliability prediction was the impetus for the research on software models also; but for reasons that will be discussed later, the

---

* Alternatively, the ratio of failed to attempted tests or the ratio of passed to attempted tests.

software models appear much more suited to the estimation of additional test effort. Since testing has to do with defect removal, the use of reliability models for this purpose implies a correlation between defects and reliability, and indeed there is one. However, reliability growth models relate more to failure than to defects. This is worth some further exploration.

Reliability and defects. It is reasonable to expect that the reliability of a computer program is an inverse function of the number of defects within the program, and to a large extent it is. However, simply estimating the number of defects in a program does not allow one to accurately compute the program's reliability. We can easily visualize a system having but one defect that is woefully unreliable. For example, imagine an operating system that crashes every time a fumble-fingered user tries to log in with an illegal password. We can also visualize the same operating system, corrected to be tolerant of entry errors, as having a dozen defects resident in a routine that no one has chosen to use. These would have nil effect on reliability.

In short, to model reliability in the sense of a user's perceptions, it is necessary to model the history of *failure*, not the number of defects. This simple principle is not the least bit compromised by incorporating defect counts within the models, since the defects tallied are exactly those that

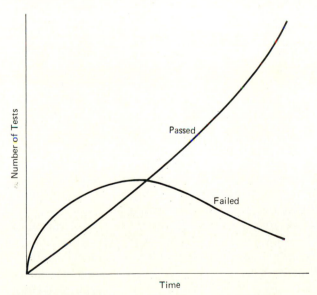

Figure 10.6   Trends of successful and unsuccessful tests.

resulted in failure.* Therefore, they inherently are defects of interest with regard to reliability.

With that, let us now define reliability and its relation to failure:

Reliability function: $R(t)$ = probability of no failure in the interval from 0 to t

Failure function: $F(t) = 1 - R(t)$

More formally, we can define the failure function as the *cumulative distribution function* (cdf) of failures. A more important definition derives from the cdf.

Frequency function: $f(t) = \dfrac{dF(t)}{dt}$

Another common name for the frequency function is the *probability density function* (pdf).

Another function, and one central to most model development, is the *failure rate* or *hazard function,* usually written as $Z(t)$ or $\lambda(t)$, and defined as the pdf of the time to failure, given that failure did not occur prior to t.

$$Z(t) = \frac{f(t)}{R(t)} = -\frac{dR(t)}{dt}$$

Given a hazard function, we can compute the reliability:

$$R(t) = \exp - \left[\int_0^t z(x)\,dx \right]$$

Given these basic definitions, we are ready for a brief survey of some of the models that have been used to describe the reliability of computer programs. The overview that follows is designed to demand no background in reliability theory beyond the above definitions. As a result, it is necessarily shallow. Nor is any attempt made to be comprehensive. However, each model was selected to illuminate another aspect of the use of reliability modeling and its limitations. Several surveys[2–5] of greater breadth or depth are available, and a deeper understanding of reliability theory can be found in books such as those of Lloyd and Lipow[6] and Shooman.[7] For the reader who really wants to dig into the few models that are individually mentioned in the next several pages, it is best to consult the references directly applying to each. In most cases, two references are provided.

Each of the models that follow requires input of the time duration between failures (roughly, the interval between defect exposures). Also, although this is not made explicit by all model builders, each model applies to a program having all of its working parts in place. That is, the model

---

* Somewhat simplistically, at one defect per failure.

parameters are estimated on the basis of only the failures of the fully integrated program or build.

Classical models. The term "classical models" refers to classical, as distinguished from bayesian, probability theory.* Among the earliest models are the Shooman exponential model[8,9] and the Jelinski-Moranda De-Eutrophication† model.[10,11] Both assume that each defect in the program is equally likely to produce failure, but at random times (Poisson process), and that defect removal introduces no new defects. They also assume that the failure rate is proportional to the number of remaining defects and remains constant between failures. Using the notation of Jelinski and Moranda,

$$Z(t_i) = \phi\,[N - (i - 1)]$$

for the time between the $(i - 1)$st and ith failures. N is the initial number of faults and ϕ is a proportionality constant. From this hazard function, the reliability function is computed:

$$R(t_i) = \exp\,[-\phi\,(N - n)t_i]$$

where n is the number of defects removed by the $(i - 1)$st interval.

Observe that in any testing interval — that is, the interval between the time when the last bug was removed and the next failure occurred — reliability decreases exponentially. This is contraintuitive: The longer we await a design failure, the more confident we get about the goodness of the design. On the other hand, it is a natural consequence of assuming a constant hazard rate between failures, a premise that implies that there are more defects to be found and in time they *will* cause failure.

Use of the model entails estimating N and ϕ from the failure history to date. The usual methods of estimating the parameters for this and other models are curve fitting (as in a least-squares sense) and MLE (see Section 9.5). For the Jelinski-Moranda model, the MLE equations are

$$\sum_{i=1}^{n} \frac{1}{\hat{N} - (i - 1)} = \frac{n}{\hat{N} - \left[\sum_{i=1}^{n} (i - 1)X_i\right]\Big/ T}$$

and

$$\hat{\phi} = \frac{n}{\hat{N}T - \sum_{i=1}^{n} (i - 1)X_i}$$

---

* Advocates of bayesian models often use the world "frequentist" instead of classical.
† Suggesting that testing cleanses murky computer programs of bugs, much as remedial pond management reduces the population of algae and water lilies.

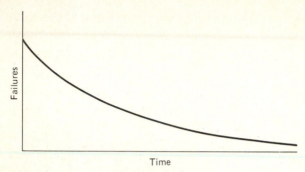

Figure 10.7 Exponential distribution.

where $X_1, \ldots, X_n$ are the elapsed times between successive failures and

$$T = \sum_{i=1}^{n} X_i$$

With $\hat{N}$ and $\hat{\phi}$ calculated, one has all the parameters necessary to plot the exponential decrease of the failure rate as a function of time, as shown in Figure 10.7. From Figure 10.7 we infer that, having selected a failure rate we are willing to settle for (one that may be extremely small but must be finite), we can determine how much test time will be required to achieve it.

Since the model can compute $R(t)$ for this last interval, it is tempting to compute the mean time to failure (MTTF) for the interval. Formally,

$$MTTF = \int_0^{\infty} R(t)\, dt$$

Writing $R(t)$ as $R(t) = e^{-\alpha t}$, $MTTF = 1/\alpha$. For the Jelinski-Moranda model,

$$MTTF = \frac{1}{\phi\,(N - n)}$$

With this we have an indication that we have ventured into troubled waters. MTTF is a single number of venerable importance in the physical world, where random processes govern observed failure phenomena. Destructive molecular migration in electronic devices is random. The rate at which individual atoms of iron combine with oxygen to rust the girders of a bridge is random. We also have systems comprised of so many individual and physically independent parts, each having its own failure pattern, that in the aggregate they, too, exhibit a Poisson failure process that can be summarized by MTTF calculations.

But what can we say of MTTF with regard to computer programs? Can we define a single causal phenomenon that would give MTTF an inherent significance? We can not. The best we can do is draw an analogy to the system of many individual parts and posit that a program of many discrete states may have its failure potential described by MTTF. However, each state is subject to failure only if it can be adversely affected by a defect; and by the time we might begin to get interested in the statistical time to failure, most of the bugs have been purged.

Generalizing, statistical conclusions about computer programs offer the potential of hazard any time a point statistic such as MTTF is used to characterize the failure process. It is more intuitively agreeable to stay with trend conclusions, as evinced by distributions such as $f(t)$, especially when one plots actual failures against the applicable portion of the derived curve to see how closely the experimental results track the model. Another approach to validating the usefulness of a model is to calculate its parameters at several intervals — say, a week apart — as the time to predict the remaining test effort approaches. Using the Jelinski-Moranda model as an example, if the variation in $\hat{N}$ from calculation to calculation is so large as to militate against the usefulness of the conclusions, either it is too early to try to use the model or the model does not adequately describe the failure-fix process.

Many programmers have observed that the failure trend during testing seems more Rayleigh-distributed (Figure 10.8) than exponential; that is, the failure rate increases with time in the early testing period. Perhaps this reflects start-up problems when entering a new phase of testing or the effects of varying staffing levels. In any event, a Rayleigh distribution will result from application of the Schick-Wolverton model.[12]

Except that the failure rate is proportional not only to the remaining number of defects but also the duration of the time between failures, the hazard function for the Schick-Wolverton model is identical with that of the previous model:

$$Z(t_i) = \phi \, [N - (i - 1)] \, t_i$$

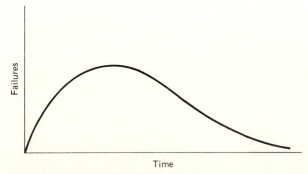

Figure 10.8 Rayleigh distribution.

The increase of hazard with time has even less intuitive appeal than the premise of a constant failure rate, but it does produce the desired Rayleigh function:

$$R(t_i) = \exp\left\{-\phi\,[N - (i - 1)]\,\frac{t_i^2}{2}\right\}$$

Both the Jelinski-Moranda and Schick-Wolverton models assume one fault per testing, or debugging, interval. In actual test experience, as during endurance tests or tests in which failures are not evident until subsequent data analysis, several failures may occur during a test interval. On a suggestion of Myron Lipow, Alan Sukert modified both models to permit detection of multiple bugs in a given debugging period. The modifications affect only the MLE parameter solutions, not the models themselves.

Thus far, the only measure of time we have been concerned with has been calendar time. Yet it is obvious that during an interval of a day, there is more opportunity to experience a failure if the program is running for 8 hours than if it is executed for only 10 minutes. The Musa execution time model[13,14] accommodates both calendar and execution time, the former retained to estimate further test and correction activity. Another departure is that Musa's model allows the introduction of new faults during the period of testing. In yet another attempt to reflect realistic testing conditions, the model does not require that defects be corrected apace with failures, although it does assume a constant ratio of failures to corrections.

Recall that the objective of most of the modeling research was the prediction of software reliability during actual, or operational, use. More will be said about this later. In any case, Musa's model attempts to account for the difference between the stressful testing situation and an operational environment by including a *testing compression factor*. Despite its simple techniques for describing an actual testing milieu, the Musa model has been found to be fairly accurate by several independent researchers and has enjoyed as wide an acceptance as any of the models.

Other classical models have been directed to specific peculiarities of program testing and debugging, going beyond the fairly simple assumptions of the Musa model. One of these is the Trivedi-Shooman Markov model[15,16] which defines sequential sets of "up" and "down" states for the program. The transitions between the states are modeled as a Markov process, with the transition probabilities derived from independent failure and correction rates. One of the noteworthy features of this model is that it takes debugging time into account and, in the process, calculates the availability of the program for further testing. Then there is the Shooman-Natarajan model,[17] which attempts to closely model the disagreeable fact that the debugging process not only removes bugs but injects new ones as well.

The last of the classical models we shall look at is the Goel-Okumoto nonhomogeneous Poisson process (NHPP) model.[18,19] In several respects it resembles the Jelinski-Moranda and other early models in assuming that the failure rate is proportional to the number of defects. However, unlike those models, contrariwise to the assumption that the time to a given failure is independent of the other times to failure, it assumes that the time is dependent on the preceding failure. However, the numbers of failures in nonoverlapped intervals are assumed to be mutually independent. Also, rather than model the initial number of bugs as a fixed parameter to be calculated, it regards the number as a random variable.

A mean value function, m(t), represents the cumulative number of failures and has as its limit a, the mean of the cdf as time becomes undefinably large. The failure rate (or NHPP intensity function) is a continuous, rather than a discrete, function:

$$\lambda(t) = abe^{-bt}$$

where b is a proportionality constant. For finite time,

$$m(t) = a [1 - \exp(-bt)]$$

For determining when one will have removed N′ defects, the model provides the expectation of N′(t), given that n bugs have been found thus far:

$$E \{N'(t)|N(t) = n\} = a - n$$

The equation for reliability — that is, for the next failure's occurring at t — is conditional on the last failure's occurring at s:

$$R(t|s) = \exp \{-a [e^{-bs} - e^{-b(s+t)}]\}$$

Bayesian models. We shall see two features of the NHPP model in the bayesian models: the conditional form of the reliability function and the random, rather than parametric, form of a key variable (in the NHPP case, the initial number of defects). In bayesian models, *prior* probabilities for random variables are postulated from theory or historical data. They are iteratively updated with new data to form *posterior* probabilities. Bayesian advocates claim that, with the acquisition of new data, their models improve in accuracy at a faster rate than do the classical models. This coin has another side that becomes apparent when we look closely at the claim that bayesian models do not require good estimates of prior probabilities. Indeed, there is even a formalized notion of *vague priors.* Successive updates with new data presumably allow a model to converge to a plausible solution, but the replacement of presumptive beginnings with faith in the power of iteration remains disquieting to many.

To clarify this business of priors and posteriors, let us look at Bayes' equation for conditional probability, given in every elementary text dealing with probability. The probability of the simultaneity of events A and B is that of A, given that B has already occurred, multiplied by the probability of B. This is written as

$$P \{A \cdot B\} = P \{(A|B)\} \, P \{B\}$$

and leads to the posterior probability of A, given new data B:

$$P \{(A|B)\} = P \{(B|A)\} \times \frac{P \{A\}}{P \{B\}}$$

This equation can be read as stating that the posterior probabilities are proportional to prior probabilities when multiplied by likelihoods.

One of the earliest bayesian models for software was that of Littlewood and Verrall.[20] It avoids the assumption of a constant hazard rate between failures and attributes to successive execution times the properties of independent exponentially distributed random failure rate variables. It also accommodates imperfect debugging. Like the Shooman-Natarajan model, this extends to the modeling process sources of failure beyond the sources inherent in the program, specifically, the admission that testing is not deterministic.

The failure rate is assumed gamma distributed* with two parameters to be determined. The resulting failure rate trend (the dashed line of Figure 10.9) shows a decrease of failure rate as the time to the next failure increases.

One of their advantages is that bayesian models can reflect the improvement in reliability during intervals unmarred by failure. Although there is no causal basis for the failure rate of a computer program to decrease except upon the removal of a bug, the decrease in failure rate supports one's intuitive sense that the longer a program chugs on uneventfully, the more one tends to rely on it. Of course, intuition also says that when a failure does occur, we quickly lose our faith. A model producing the solid line of Figure 10.9 would reflect this more realistic, if less sanguine, view. (This point has also been made by G. Myers.[21])

Models that assume defects to have equal probability of failure disassociate defects from the structural properties of programs. Nevertheless, some defects present more hazard than do others. This was noted in the

---

* Gamma probability distributions are so named from the familiar gamma function, or generalized factorial, which they incorporate. Like the exponential and several other distributions, the gamma distribution has its own constituency among reliability engineers. It is particularly favored by bayesians, since it can show both increasing and decreasing failure rate (recall that the exponential distribution has a constant failure rate) and is mathematically quite tractable.

discussion of reliability and defects early in this section. Littlewood's *bayesian differential* debugging model[22,23] takes differing hazards into account. Each defect is given its own failure rate ϕ_j. Given that there were N initial defects of which i have been removed, the failure rate of the program is

$$\lambda = \phi_1 + \phi_2 + \cdots + \phi_{N-i}$$

The unknown ϕ_j are treated as a set of random variables Φ_j, each member having its own pdf. That λ is a function of the remaining number of defects recalls a fundamental premise of the Jelinski-Moranda and other early models. Indeed, the Littlewood model may be viewed as a generalization of Jelinski-Moranda.

The pdf of failure at arbitrary time t is modeled as a function of the cumulative execution time during which defects have thus far been eliminated, and also of N, α, and β, the last two being parameters that shape the gamma distribution. N, α, and β are to be estimated from the historical data. The shape of the failure rate curve is the same as that of the dashed line in Figure 10.9, with the failure rate dropping, after each correction, by $\alpha/(\beta + t)$.

The last bayesian model to be taken up is directed at the interesting prospect of an acceptance-rejection criterion for computer programs. The Thompson and Chelson bayesian model[24,25] uses two priors, one for failure rate and a second for the probability that the program contains at least one fault. (We can view the preceding models as having assumed this probability equal to 1.) With this model we return to the presumption of a constant hazard rate between failures; this time, however, it is a random variable with a gamma-distributed prior.

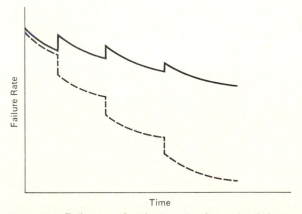

Figure 10.9 Failure trend with piecewise decreasing failure rate.

Let us overlook several of the interesting aspects of this model and go directly to the business of a fail-pass criterion applied some time after no failures have occurred. The posterior distribution function of failure rate λ, given historical failure data H, is formed as a rather complex function of the gamma distribution. Let us denote this as $F(\lambda|H)$. Now consider the lower $1 - \alpha$ limit* on λ. One accepts the program if $F(\lambda|H) \geqslant 1 - \alpha$.

Acceptance or rejection (give up or test some more) criteria can be applied to the failure rate distribution or the reliability computation of any reliability growth model. If we dare to essay a failure-free program, the Thompson and Chelson model seems particularly appropriate for this purpose, since the parameters of the posterior distribution for the probability of *no* defects enters into the computation of $F(\lambda|H)$.

Further remarks on validation and use. Although there have been several published reports attempting to validate or compare software reliability models, individually or in competing groups, independent validation information remains scarce. Perhaps this is as it should be. None of the models is as rooted in causality as we should want it to be, and in the absence of well-grounded determinism, we would tend to be timid about pure statistical validation approaches.†

Simply put, validation based on a small number of programs, however successful the results may appear, is of arguable value if it cannot be demonstrated that the premises of the model did in fact apply to the subject programs and the manner in which they were tested and debugged. One might counter with the proposition that if the Jelinski-Moranda model (for example) proved accurate for a given program, it has been demonstrated that the defects were randomly scattered and that the test data were timewise random over the input domain. However, it is equally possible that neither was random and that the skewed distribution of both defects and applied stimuli had somehow balanced each other.

Summarizing, the validity of a given model is an inverse function of the distance between its assumptions and the conditions under which defect data were collected, conditions related to the program, personnel, tools, and procedures for testing and debugging. In selecting a likely model, one

---

* α is generally taken as the risk of rejecting true hypotheses, in this case, the hypothesis that λ is acceptably low. Statisticians use another measure, β, for the risk of incorrectly accepting a false hypothesis. Typical values assigned to α and β for acceptance testing range between 0.001 and 0.1.

† Examples of misleading statistical conclusions abound. I understand that a brokerage house has observed that the stock market has risen in each year that a team from the preexpansion National Football League has won the Super Bowl. This is known as the Super Bowl Leading Indicator, or some such thing. I recall also, that, over a period of 10 years or so, the correlation factor of the birth rate of Oslo with respect to its wintertime stork population was a convincing 0.95.

tacitly accepts its premises. Pursuing an earlier remark, if a scatter plot of the actual failures with respect to the model's failure rate plot shows correlation *reasonable enough for the intended purpose,* one continues with the model and updates it at frequent intervals (weekly during periods of high defect removal; following each failure during periods of high reliability). If the scatter plot casts doubt on the fit between the model and the circumstances, another model is tried.

One warning attends the use of progressive validation. Certain models are fairly "twitchy," showing considerable variation in the MLE solution from one week to another, although they may in time settle down. (Indeed, under a wide range of operating circumstances, an MLE solution may not even exist.) A striking example of this with regard to the Jelinski-Moranda model was published by Dale and Harris,[26] based on work by E. H. Forman and N. D. Singpurwalla. In the example, MLE produced an estimate of one remaining defect at the end of the third testing interval. By the end of the twelfth interval, after 83 defects had been removed, the estimated remaining number of bugs remained a confident 1.

As a side issue, if one understands the explicit and implicit premises of a model that was unsuccessfully used, analysis of the reasons for the model's unsuitability may lead to a better understanding of one's own test and debug process.

Let us close the discussion of reliability growth models with a remark about their capability to predict operational reliability. This is, after all, what the models aspire to do. Apart from any inherent limitations concerning failure modality (e.g., failure rate directly proportional to the undifferentiated total number of defects), none of the models are capable of fully distinguishing between the effects of program defects and the testing environment. Attempts to compensate for the latter have been made. We have Musa's compression factor and his use of both execution time and calendar time, recognition in the Trivedi-Shooman model of the need to incorporate the time taken to debug, the creation of new bugs in the Shooman-Natarajan model, and imperfect debugging in both Littlewood models. However, the total number of variables during testing that affect the rate at which failures can occur is larger than any one model can represent; indeed, it is doubtful that we can describe some of the variables in a manner that would permit their being adequately modeled to this purpose. Thus, the use of reliability growth models to extrapolate from testing into operation has to be an arguable business.

Trends revisited.   Apart from the insight they help us gain with respect to the meaning of reliability, one has to wonder if reliability growth models are worth it after all. If the data are smooth enough to provide confidence that a reliability model can be properly fitted, the data are also smooth enough to provide a reasonable estimation of how things stand, simply by inspection. Consider the data of Figure 10.10. One can attempt to fit any of a number of models to this record of failure incidence, but the curve, drawn free-handedly and unconsciously giving greater weight to the more recent events, is sufficiently accurate to suggest that little testing remains.

Unless the curve is clearly asymptotic to a line of zero slope, this simple a trend analysis offers a poor *quantitative* conclusion concerning the remaining test effort. Things improve a bit in this regard if one attempts, by using any of the various curve-fitting methods about, to fit the data to some defined curve. However, the very selection of a curve implies the return to reliability modeling, except that now the procedure is bereft of even the slightest pretense of causality.

10.4   Improving Productivity and Quality

The use of collected defect or failure data has thus far been discussed within the reference of single projects and for purposes limited to those projects. However, the data accumulated on a single project — even better, over several projects — can be used to improve the process by which we prevent defects and remove those that were not prevented. Curiously, we tend to ignore the analysis of defect data for this purpose. As Santayana remarked, "Those who cannot remember the past are condemned to repeat it." Defect data allow us to quantify the past, so that we not only remember it but can use it to improve the future.

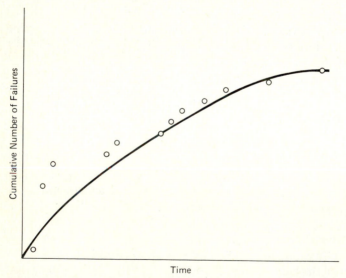

Figure 10.10   Trend analysis by inspection.

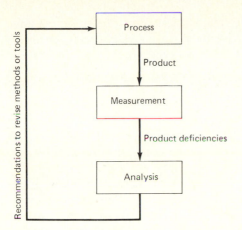

Figure 10.11 Process quality control.

What is suggested here is an analogy to approaches used for many years by the quality control community. There the result of a process is periodically measured, analyzed, and fed back to refine the process. Figure 10.11 illustrates this schematically. If tennis balls are starting to get out of round, it is time to refurbish the machine that produces them. If, on a new production line, the balls are barely within specification, one immediately reanalyzes the choice of machine or examines the way it is being used.

So too with computer programs. If there are too many defects to remove or if one of the removal processes seems not to be as effective as we think it should be, a change in the process is suggested. With regard to computer programming, we would do well to replace the word "process" in Figure 10.11 with "standards." No improvement program can be undertaken without a reasonably stable software production environment. Putting it differently, for computer programming the process *is* the set of standards in use — whether these are in the form of written procedures or implicit in the software development environment (Section 2.4).

If asked, most programming managers will say that they have a good feel for the effectiveness of their standards. But they do not really know. They cannot know without measurement. Except for the correction of grossly ineffective standards, numbers are required.

> For the nature of Number is to be a standard of reference, of guidance, and instruction of every doubt, throwing light on everything unknown.
>
> PHILOLAUS, fifth century B.C.

What the ancients knew, we also know, and we shall start with the use of defect data to improve the defect prevention process.

Defect prevention.   Returning to Figure 10.1, we have the means for identifying the origins of the defects that survived to testing. We also have the logs of requirements, design, and code reviews. Let us assume that we have tabulated the past year's data with the results (after weighting for severity) as in Figure 10.12. A cursory inspection of the graph reveals that the number of requirements definition faults is excessive. Compared with one's competitors, it may be that the number of defects in all of the origin classes is excessive. This is difficult to ascertain, but certainly the process of defining requirements is a target for improvement. Even if most of the requirements defects were detected during the requirements reviews, the rework associated with removal had to have had an adverse effect on productivity.

Analysis to determine the reason for the poor performance during the requirements phase will take further data gathering. This includes interviews with persons associated with the generation and use of specifications produced during that phase and close perusals of the change requests affecting requirements specifications and the logs of the requirements reviews. The last is particularly valuable because, although it cannot ac-

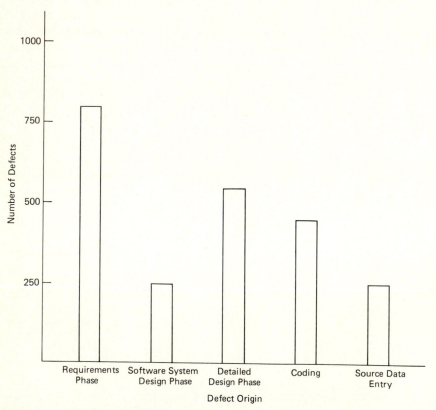

Figure 10.12 Defect source histogram.

count for all requirements defects, it is a concise record of a large number of the defects. Let us assume that it is learned that a great number of the requirements defects were in the form of missing information. Perhaps the people generating requirements definitions need more schooling in what it is that program designers need to know to do their jobs. On the other hand, examiners may learn that on several projects missing information was not available at the time it was necessary (by management fiat) to start the program design. In this case, allusions to the cost of rework may serve as ammunition to discourage management from insisting on unrealistic schedules.

Let us not forget fault modality. By using defect classifications as recommended in Section 10.1 and carried through to testing by Figure 10.2, collected data can be interpreted to shed light on the influence of one's methods on the generation of requirements, design, and code defects.

One may want also to consider comparing projects. Usually, new methods or tools are not introduced across the board. More cautiously, one tries out the novelty on only one of the ongoing projects. With defect data, it is possible to quantitatively determine the effect of innovation on defect prevention by comparing the data for the subject of the experiment with the data of other projects.

And so it goes. The result of data collection and analysis will be an updating of methods, procedures, and tools: new standards defining the responsibility of individuals, new controls on the initiation of work tasks, the acquisition of a new programming design language processor, expanding the capabilities of the static analyzer, improving the editor used for source data entry, whatever.

Defect removal. Analysis to improve the defect removal process is mostly directed at defect detection. We have also to contend with library control mishaps (see Figure 10.1) and the failure to close out corrective actions from reviews, but the greatest profit is to be found in improving defect detection. Again, graphs such as the graph of Figure 10.12 are used, but with the abscissa comprised of defect removal activities. It is obvious that if design reviews catch nearly as many requirements defects as design defects, something needs to be done to improve the EOR of requirements reviews. As a matter of procedure, with regard to defect removal analysis, the first thing one does upon completing the last series of tests for a given project is to tabulate all the detected defects by phase of origin and circumstances of detection, following which the EOR of each defect removal process is calculated.

Weaknesses in defect detection methods are not always as obvious as the example of low productivity for requirements reviews. Let us assume that few defects are found in unit test compared to those found in integration testing. This suggests that the standards for unit testing are inadequate, or are not being followed; both conditions being correctable. However, a certain amount of care applies to the comparison of defect removal EORs. With reference to the data collected by using the form of Figure 10.2, suppose that further analysis reveals that most of the defects found during integration testing were interface defects. Many of them could not have been found by unit testing, no matter how effective one's methods. Similar subtleties can produce deceptive comparisons of various tools or test case selection techniques, especially with regard to the I/O and data base defect classes.

Nevertheless, the data are there for analysis to reveal the existence of real problems and to separate problems that are real from those that are only apparent. The exact steps that are followed in measuring the effectiveness of each defect removal process are determined by the techniques and tools that are used and by the specifics of any interaction among them. For example, the use of coverage instrumentation during functional testing to partly satisfy structural testing standards is a possible source of classification confusion. Only by knowing how the ambiguity was resolved can one determine whether a detected defect should be dropped into the functional or structural hopper (assuming one has established such for bean-counting purposes).

Note, too, the use of supplementary causes of test failure (for example, the last four columns of Figure 10.1) to expose weaknesses in the testing environment. These provide fine-grained information invaluable for improving the defect removal process.

Improving the effectiveness with which defects are removed is, of course, a direct contribution to the improvement of quality, of which more needs to be said.

Other aspects of quality.   We can say more about the improvement of quality; but once we depart from the discussion of defects, we cannot say much that is quantitative. This chapter deals with measurement, and, recalling the remarks of Section 3.4, there are no good measures for most of the attributes of software quality.

This raises the issue of just what it is we mean when we speak of "software quality." Getting to the heart of the matter, we should like to be able to define software quality as the following:

> The quality of a computer program is the measure of its usefulness, suitability, adequacy, and conformance to the requirements set forth for it.

But we cannot define it so because the only one of the bottom line attributes that we can measure is conformance to requirements, and even that is measurable only in the number of clearly recognized defects. We could replace "measure" with "assess or measure," but that begs the question because any assessment is subjective. Perhaps we should yield entirely to intrinsicality and define quality thusly:

> The quality of a computer program is the degree to which the users perceive the program to be suitable, useful, and adequate and the extent to which it conforms to the requirements set forth for it.

If we have to define quality, this may be as realistic as we can get.* In any case, let it be understood that using measurements for a program of defect reduction does not satisfy all of the objectives of a quality improvement program. Of course, the absence of inherently enumerable properties attending maintainability, portability, adequacy of documentation, and the like has not discouraged heroic efforts from various quarters to quantify them:

> Tales of measures of goodness abound.
> (Call them "metrics" to sound more profound.)
> But the one I bewail
> Would put code on a scale
> To determine the comments per pound

10.5 Summary

1. Sources of defect data are the logs or minutes of reviews and walk-throughs, failures encountered at all levels of test, and software change requests prepared during formal (e.g., qualification) tests.

2. Defects should be classified by severity to gain the maximum benefit from analysis.

3. During periods of active test when failures occur frequently, as in unit and integration tests, it is not practical to gather defect data of much depth. Simple bean-counting forms can be employed, however, to collect some useful data on each defect found. The use of such forms must be accompanied by motivation and instruction from management.

4. Counts of the number of defects found in individual modules are a powerful clue toward finding "failure-prone modules." These are program elements that, for one reason or another, remain defect-ridden despite attempts to fix them.

5. During testing, the rate at which defects are found or failures occur tends to diminish with time. Observations of that rate can be used to update one's estimates of the remaining test effort.

---

* For anyone who finds this definition insufficiently succinct, I recommend that of my colleague Capers Jones: "Quality is never having to say you are sorry."

6. Specific targets for observation include the comparative rates of the opening and closing of trouble reports or change requests during formal testing, the time trend of the ratio of failed to passed tests, the cumulative number of failures as a function of time, and the probability distribution of failure produced by reliability growth models.

7. Reliability growth models present several hazards when used to predict operational reliability on the basis of test data, but they do provide a means of forecasting the rate of failure during a period for which the testing conditions remain constant.

8. The various models that have been developed differ from each other in their assumptions of the effects on failure of the circumstances that attach to testing and the population and distribution of defects.

9. Defect prevention can be improved through analysis of the source of defects, leading to modifications of one's methods, procedures, or tools.

10. Similarly, defect removal processes can be improved by measuring the effectiveness of each defect removal operation and subsequently altering those that detect too few of the defects present at the time of their use.

11. Quantitative defect data used for improving defect prevention and removal will lead to higher levels of programmer productivity and product quality. It should be recognized, however, that the treatment of aspects of quality other than defect density requires a broader quality improvement program.

References

1. Albert Endres, "An Analysis of Errors and Their Causes in System Programs," *1975 Internatl. Conf. on Reliable Software,* IEEE Cat. No. 75CH0840-7CSR, pp. 327–336.
2. Robert Dunn and Richard Ullman, *Quality Assurance for Computer Software,* McGraw-Hill, New York, 1981, pp. 305–328.
3. D. Swearingen and J. Donahoo, "Quantitative Software Reliability Models — Data Parameters: A Tutorial," *Workshop on Quantitative Software Models,* IEEE Catalog No. TH0067-9, 1979, pp. 143–153.
4. Computer Sciences Corporation (under contract to IIT Research Institute), *Software Engineering Research Review: Quantitative Software Models,* SRR-1, Data and Analysis Center for Software, Rome Air Development Center, 1979.
5. C. J. Dale, *Software Reliability Evaluation Methods,* Report ST26750, British Aerospace Dynamics Group, Stevenage, September 1982.
6. David Lloyd and Myron Lipow, *Reliability: Management, Methods, and Mathematics,* 2d ed., published by the authors, Redondo Beach, Calif., 1977.
7. Martin Shooman, *Probabilistic Reliability: An Engineering Approach,* McGraw-Hill, New York, 1968.
8. Martin Shooman, "Operational Testing and Software Reliability Estimation During Program Development," *1973 IEEE Symp. Computer Software Reliability,* IEEE Cat. No. 73CH0741-9CSR, pp. 51–57.

9. Martin Shooman, "Software Reliability: Measurements and Models," *Proc. 1975 Annual Reliability and Maintainability Symp.,* IEEE Cat. No. 75CH0918-3RQC, pp. 485–491.

10. Z. Jelinski and P. B. Moranda, "Application of a Probability-Based Model to a Code Reading Experiment," *1973 IEEE Symp. Computer Software Reliability,* IEEE Cat. No. 73CH0741-9CSR, pp. 78–80.

11. P. B. Moranda, "Prediction of Software Reliability During Debugging," *Proc. 1975 Annual Reliability and Maintainability Symp.,* IEEE Cat. No. 75CH0918-3RQC, pp. 327–332.

12. George Schick and Ray Wolverton, "An Analysis of Competing Software Reliability Models," *IEEE Trans. Software Eng.,* vol. SE-4, March 1978, pp. 104–120.

13. John Musa, "A Theory of Software Reliability and Its Applications," *IEEE Trans. Software Eng.,* vol. SE-1, September 1975, pp. 312–327.

14. John Musa, "Validation of Execution Time Theory of Software Reliability," *IEEE Trans. Reliability,* vol. R-28, August 1979, pp. 181–191.

15. Ashok Trivedi and Martin Shooman, *A Markov Model for the Evaluation of Computer Software Performance,* Research report, Polytechnic Institute of New York, EE/EP 74-0111-EER110, under contract to ONR and RADC, May 1, 1974.

16. Ashok Trivedi and Martin Shooman, "A Many-State Markov Model for the Estimation and Prediction of Computer Software Performance Parameters," *Proc. 1975 Internatl Conf. on Reliable Software,* IEEE Cat. No. 75CH0940-7CSR, pp. 208–220.

17. M. Shooman and S. Natarajan, *Effect of Manpower Deployment and Bug Generation on Software Error Models,* Technical Report RADC-TR-76-400, Rome Air Development Center, January 1977.

18. Amrit Goel and K. Okumoto, *A Time Dependent Error Detection Rate Model for Software Performance Assessment with Applications,* Syracuse University, published as Report RADC-TR-80-179 by Rome Air Development Center, May 1980.

19. Amrit Goel and K. Okumoto, "Time Dependent Error-Detection-Rate Model for Software Reliability and Other Performance Measures," *IEEE Trans. Reliability,* vol. R-28, August 1979, pp. 206–211.

20. B. Littlewood and J. L. Verrall, "A Bayesian Reliability Growth Model for Computer Software," *1973 IEEE Symp. Computer Software Reliability,* IEEE Cat. No. 73CH0741-9CSR, pp. 70–77.

21. G. Myers, *Software Reliability: Principles and Practices,* Wiley-Interscience, New York, 1976, pp. 334–335.

22. B. Littlewood, "A Bayesian Differential Debugging Model for Software Reliability," *Workshop on Quantitative Software Models,* IEEE Cat. No. TH0067-9, October 1979, pp. 170–181.

23. Bev Littlewood, "Stochastic Reliability Growth: A Model for Fault-Removal in Computer Programs and Hardware Designs," *IEEE Trans. Reliability,* vol. R-30, October 1981, pp. 313–320.

24. W. E. Thompson and P. O. Chelson, "Software Reliability Testing for Embedded Computer Systems," *Workshop on Quantitative Software Models,* IEEE Cat. No. TH0067-9, October 1979, pp. 201–208.

25. W. E. Thompson and P. O. Chelson, "On the Specification and Testing of Software Reliability," *Proc. 1980 Annual Reliability and Maintainability Symp.,* IEEE Cat. No. 80CH1513-R, pp. 379–383.

26. C. J. Dale and L. N. Harris, "Approaches to Software Reliability Prediction," *1982 Proc. Annual Reliability and Maintainability Symp.,* IEEE Cat. No. 82CH1732-7, pp. 167–175.

Operational Phase

11

Configuration Control

With respect to programming, the operational phase of software is a matter of maintenance and modification. Alterations should be accompanied by fewer gnawing uncertainties than attend work started from scratch. Therefore, programming's M&M should be within the taste of all programming managers. In fact, what promises to be a toothsome sweet frequently turns out to be a jawbreaker.

A strict definition of "maintenance" restricts use of the term to three activities: the removal of defects that escaped previous efforts at detection or removal, the update of documentation to conform to needs that arise during operations, and alterations to permit adaptation to new operating environments. In the latter class we have revisions to accommodate the quirks of a different compiler or operating system, revised user data bases for new installations, and the like. The term is also used by many people to include minor enhancements such as improving the format of workstation menus.

"Modification" is generally taken to mean the addition of new features or functions requiring a substantial amount of programming effort. The word is also used to refer to major rewrites undertaken to improve performance. Modifications include improving the speed of a compiler, adding LIFO to the FIFO capability of an inventory control system, and adding color graphics to a personal computer.

The boundary between maintenance and modification has fuzzy sectors —one person's minor enhancement is another's major improvement, especially if the second person writes advertising copy—which has led many people to lump all changes made during the operational period under the single word "maintenance." Indeed, the inclusive use of "maintenance" is implicit in the word "maintainability," used universally to describe the facility with which programs may—for any reason—be changed.

So much for trying to clarify the muddier waters of programming. Whether maintenance or modification, significant problems are encountered if the program being altered is not a clearly defined product, that is, if the documentation does not agree with the code, if the comments do not accurately describe the code, or if the many installed copies of the program are not clones of the master code files. These are the conditions that lead to jawbreaking. None of this would matter much if code were not so easy to change. However, few products are as easily — and sometimes covertly — altered as are programming products.

Thus, the emphasis is on configuration control during the operational phase. However, if a software system is to remain under control during its working life, it must start out under control. Indeed, the problems attending control are as great during development as afterward, since each removal of a defect permanently alters the state of the software. Accordingly, we shall begin the discussion of configuration control with its genesis during development, starting at a time when the program is defined only by its initial *baseline,* the description of what it is expected to do when it is completely built.

11.1 Baselines

Software baselines, which seem to have had their origin with the military, establish a sequence of unambiguous references to the known properties of a program or system of programs at any time during development or operational life, including the period before any code exists. From the time the need for a program is identified, something is known about it. Initially, that may be no more than a vague notion of what the program is to do: "We need a computer and some software to control the automatic paint spraying apparatus." From then on, the program gradually emerges, and in a controlled programming process it incrementally takes on more concrete definition through a sequence of documentation and code releases. Certain sets of releases constitute the baselines, all of which are subject to change at any time. Changes may reflect necessary or desired revisions of the external characteristics of the software, as in the addition of a new function, or internal matters, such as the removal of a defect. Configuration control is the control of these changes.

The military system of baselines may not be optimum for all programming environments (there are even differences among the military branches), but it has worked for a diversity of projects. A synthesis of the several variants underlies the set of baselines defined by Bersoff, Henderson, and Siegel.[1] This will serve as a good illustration of the formal baselines established for computer programs, except that their "design" baseline will be split into a top-level design baseline and a detailed design baseline, as described by Dunn and Ullman.[2]

1. Functional baseline. The definition of the problem; the basis for agreements between buyer and seller; the description of the product that will be developed.

2. Allocated baseline. The apportionment to specific hardware (if applicable) and software elements of the functions that must be performed. For a development project involving only a single program operating within an existing computer, the allocated baseline is the same as the functional baseline.*

3. Top-level design baseline. For each program or major portion, the overall scheme of meeting its requirements.

4. Detailed design baseline. For each program or major portion, the description of how it will be built.

5. Product baseline. For each program or major portion, its code and the description of that code. The description is an "as-built" version of the detailed design baseline.

6. Operational baseline. The product baseline updated as necessary at any time in the life of the program.

These are the formal baselines. Additional informal baselines are necessary for code and design data during the development period. The scheme of informal baselines will derive from the production method being used. For example, during integration, a group of procedures added as a single module to the evolving system will have its descriptive documentation and source code under some form of control from the time the set of tests directed to the module has been completed.

Returning to the formal baselines, we should recognize that there may have to be several top-level and detailed design baselines for a single software system, possibly to account for division into several subsystems assigned to different development teams or possibly to account for delivery of a succession of builds. The criterion for determining whether to establish a baseline has to do with the fundamental concept of a baseline:

> Regardless of the level of abstraction to which it applies, a baseline defines the descriptions of the properties of a program that must be controlled to provide accurate knowledge of the program in its current state.

---

* That is, unless it is considered advantageous for planning purposes to separate performance requirements definitions for each of the major portions of the program. If this is done, each of these portions (usually subsystems) will then be controlled as a separate item.

That is, at discrete points in the development or operational life of a program, existing documentation and code must be frozen, placed in a master library, and changed only by some established procedure.

The documents involved may take a number of forms. A typical documentation system follows:

Functional Baseline
System specification

Allocated Baseline
Software requirements specification
Interface specification

Top-Level Design Baseline
Preliminary design specification (executive control scheme, component specifications, memory allocations, and so on)
Data base specification
Qualification test specification

Detailed Design Baseline
Preliminary design specification (augmented with more detail)
Design specification for each element
Functional test specifications for module and integration test

Product and Operational Baselines
Design specifications (updated to as-built status)*
Users' manual
Maintenance manual

Each baseline includes the material of its predecessor. As an illustration, once the requirements specification comes under control, it remains under control through successive baselines. This does not necessarily mean that a code change inconsistent with the requirements specification cannot be made without formal authority. For example, if the discovery were made during hardware-software integration that the sense of an external flag was reversed in the specification, the code would be changed to conform to the hardware reality and a change request would be filed to indicate correction of the erroneous description of the flag. In this way, the change request becomes the documentation of a fait accompli.

In addition to the documents listed above, one may also want to include certain planning documents: program development plan, software quality plan, test plans, and the configuration control plan itself. The decision to control these plans depends mostly on whether one requires certainty that any changes made to the plans will be disseminated to all the people who should be aware of them.

---

* Also called product specification.

Before launching into the business of how baselines can be controlled, let us look at the three fundamental reasons for defining baselines when only documentation of the program exists:

- Definition of the current state of the program for use by those about to continue development in a new phase
- Definition of the program in a manner that will permit the results of one development phase to be verified with respect to the results of its predecessors
- Ensuring the accuracy of documentation for the benefit of those who will be responsible for the system during its operational life

11.2   Code Control

Special problems attach to baselines that contain code. For one thing, it is impossible to look at a physical code file and immediately judge its currency. Not only are there no pages marked up in red to indicate interim changes, but not until the header record of the file is displayed is the version or revision status of the file apparent.* Another major problem is that permanent changes to code may be made effortlessly. Simply call the file into the editor buffer and type away. And do it several times a day during the test and debugging periods.

Special problems require special solutions, and a number have been developed for controlling the changes in code files. Common to most of them is a maxim that seems to amount to surrender: Avoid control until the subject code begins to stabilize. What sounds like cowardice is really a sensible approach — provided one does not extend the period of anarchy more than is necessary. There is no need to control code if the code remains entirely in the hands of its author. While a programmer is testing or debugging his procedure or group of associated procedures, the only control necessary is that required for the programmer's own purposes. Almost any mechanism used will work. Indeed, control may not be appropriate at the time the code is handed over to the integration team; the first few hours or days of integration testing may evoke too many changes in the code for external control to be practical. However, when the time arrives for the next set of procedures to be added to the evolving system, it is necessary to place the code under control.

At this point, an audit should be conducted to ascertain whether the design documentation relevant to the subject code has been modified (redlined) to conform to the changes that, rather than bring the code into

---

* Except for code files in the form of punched cards.

compliance with senior design or requirements documentation, actually represent changes in them. This is the easy part. The rest requires tools.

The basic problem of code control is making certain that only the latest (or latest authorized) edition of the code for each procedure is linked with other procedures to form the program that will be tested. One solution demands that each edition have a unique identifier, for example, version 1, revision 16. The compiler automatically passes the edition information, intact, to the header record of the object string. Finally, the link editor examines the edition information before linking to confirm that it agrees with that in the link file. This scheme works well if the link file is itself included among the items under configuration control.

Let us see how this works in moderately difficult circumstances: a two-shift integration operation. The day shift finds a bug in module ALPHA and fixes it, updating the revision code from 16 to 17. They revise the link file to correspond and place hard copy of the file in the current (or "working") archives of the library. When the night crew comes in, there can be no question in their minds about which procedures are the proper ones for testing. If a loading error occurs because the link editor was unable to find ALPHAMOD version 1, revision 17, the programmers will be alerted to the fact that they had tried a load with an old edition, which they can easily confirm by inspection of the hard copy of the link file. This is a much surer way of avoiding testing with obsolete editions than the usual practice of doing no more than expect the night crew to look at the daily activity summary left them by the day people.

Note that the term "module," as used above, may refer to individual procedures or to groups of procedures. If the latter, the amount of bookkeeping is reduced, but at the expense of taking care that the group is always compiled as a unit, that is, that one does not also have the option of compiling a single procedure by itself.

In a variant of this method, the operating system adds a flag to the last edited version of the procedure, deletes the flag from previous versions, and allows the compiler to operate only on source files containing flags. (Programmers can still compile older versions by defining additional compile time parameters, but they cannot do so inadvertently.)

Once we start thinking about mechanized controls for source code and the constituency of "load modules," the executable composite program submitted for testing, we are on the subject of *librarians*. A librarian is an essential part of the programming development environment; for no matter how diligent programmers are in recording the cutting and pasting operations that lead to revised source files, no matter how meticulously revised editions are bound anew by the link editor, library control without tooling amounts to no more than a buckram tiger.

Consider a system of several hundred modules, some of which are likely to be changed on any given day during periods of active test. Although a human librarian will be helpful in keeping track of changes, may even be the funnel through which all source code changes are made, the likelihood of perfect performance over a period of several days is nil. It is far better to have powerful library control tools and to use the human librarian mostly to audit the use of the tools and to make certain that affected documentation also has been revised.*

Recalling the discussion of Section 2.4, the more elegant librarians (e.g., the librarian of Programmer's Workbench[3]) allow one to recreate a procedure as it had existed in any previous edition. Moreover, it has facilities that permit concurrent editions of a procedure to be controlled. During debugging, several temporary variants of a procedure may be required for diagnostic purposes. Once the bug has been found, the capability of recalling the authorized version for repair makes trivial the business of stripping diagnostic code.

Summarizing, code control is the affair of librarians, primarily those found in programming development environments but augmented by those found sitting at desks. With the help of these librarians, the time for code control to become official — that is, to pass out of the hands of the cognizant programmers and into those of personnel associated directly with configuration management — can be delayed until the initial flush of bugs has been removed. At that time, the source files become part of a baseline, either interim or formal.

Patches.   Configuration control specialists reserve for binary patches the same affection that farmers have for droughts. Patches have so often proved intolerably troublesome that from time to time twice-burnt programming managers outlaw them. Yet they are sometimes the only efficient way to diagnose stubborn problems. Moreover, although it is the sort of thing we tend to discuss only with subdued voices, a fair case for testing with patches can be made if the programming development environment cannot support relocatable compilation or for any other reason requires that an entire program be recompiled after a single source statement is changed.

So patches may have to be tolerated, and a way must be found to deal with them. As inconvenient as it may sometimes be, all patches that are to

---

* During development testing, one does not want to go through an official documentation change process for each necessary alteration, but this invites the hazard that the backlog of unrecorded changes will reach the point at which catch-up is impossible. Well before it is reached, the librarian must issue the programming equivalent of overdue fines, even calling on programming management to postpone further testing until the documentation is cleaned up.

be used for a planned test — that is, one designed specifically for the purpose of defect detection or demonstration of performance — must be entered through a patch file. Moreover, that file should carry edition information and be treated by library control just as though it were a standard module. For unplanned tests, as when tracking an elusive bug, one can still stand at the computer console and toggle in patches or use the instruction modification commands of a microprocessor development station. However, these are debugging procedures and should not be permitted for normal tests. Testing with uncontrolled patches is tantamount to testing an undefined program.

It is common practice to periodically (say, every Friday afternoon) wipe the patch file clean by altering the source code, recompiling, and relinking. If necessary, the librarian (person) acts as the enforcer of the practice. However, the persuasive or strong-arm powers of a librarian may be inadequate to the task. A structural approach to forcing frequent cleanup is to limit the size of the patch area in memory. As a side issue, all the tests passed with the recently expurgated patches should be repeated with the revised source code. One can err in translating a patch to source language no less than in translating design data to source language.

Firmware.   Configuration control of code must be carried one step further when the operational memory for a program is a set of ROMs (read-only-memory chips), PROMs (programmable ROMs), or electronically alterable PROMs. Consider an operational situation in which it becomes necessary to replace one of these firmware devices because of electrical failure. This will be possible only if its portion, or *partition,* of the load module is unambiguously known. Ambiguity can be avoided only if the partitioning (alternatively, *mapping*) process is repeatable.

Let us look at the problem with the help of Figure 11.1, borrowed from Dunn and Ullman.[2] Here we see a load module of 3000 16-bit binary addresses transferred to a set of 12 identical ROMs each having 1000 locations containing 4 bits of memory. The way in which the address space of the load module is mapped into that of the ROM array is through the use of a partitioning program. To replace any one of the 12 ROMs, the load module is processed anew through the partitioning program, but only the 4000 bits unique to the failed ROM are delivered to the ROM fabrication facility.* This implies that the partitioning program itself must be under configuration control. Any change made in it may affect the final parti-

---

* In actual practice, it would be more likely that the artwork for the ROM had been kept on file and that these 4000 bits would be used to verify that the correct mask data record was selected and that it is current.

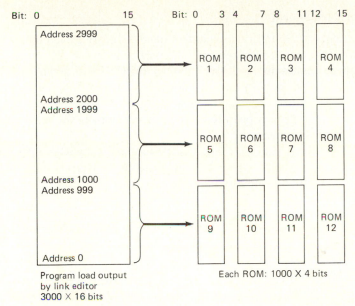

Figure 11.1   Partitioning into firmware.

tioning result. If the partitioning program is deliberately modified — as for improving the efficiency of ROM utilization or to accommodate a different device size — the original version must be saved as part of the program support library peculiar to the programming product for which the ROMs were made.

Before leaving the topic of firmware, let us look at a problem that may seem woefully pedestrian to software people but is particularly vexing to manufacturing people: How can one be certain that the correct firmware device is inserted into its allocated place on the printed-wiring board? Indeed, on the correct *board?* As tiny as these devices are, there are machines that can print tinier, small enough to allow an 18-character label to be affixed to some part of the device's anatomy. One can arrive at a number of useful labeling schemes. For example, four characters can be used to identify the system into which the program is to be embedded, two characters for the major hardware unit or nest of boards, three characters for the board, and two characters for the location on the board. There remain enough characters left over to record the program edition and some ancillary information peculiar to the manufacturing system. The program edition is especially useful if several concurrent versions are to be maintained. With proper labeling, semiconductor devices can be stockpiled in parts bins in the hardware assembly area without creating the hazard that an insertion error will escape the notice of the inspection department.

11.3   Configuration Management

The various elements of configuration control need to be organized into a system. Appropriate paperwork is required to commemorate certain control activities and to ensure distribution of change information. Responsibility for compliance with the configuration control plan must be fixed, and a system of audits to ensure compliance must be worked out. These matters, some of which have already been referred to in passing, are the components of *configuration management* (CM).

Although much of configuration management is taken up with control boards, release and change notices, and the like, the most basic concern is quintessentially mundane: a sensible labeling scheme.

Labeling.   Consistent labeling practices, the sine qua non of code control, are also of inestimable help in relating documents to code and to each other. A labeling scheme that encompasses all controlled material, must have three major parts: *identifier, subject,* and *edition.* These may occur in any order, although edition information is rarely, if ever, the first. The identifier carries the description of the type of configuration item that is labeled. As an example, a two-character identifier field can take the following values:

SF	Source file
RB	Relocatable binary file
LM	Load module
RS	Requirements specification
IS	Interface specification
TS	Preliminary (top-level) design specification
DB	Data base document
DS	Detailed design specification
PS	Product specification (or description)
PD	Pseudocode design data
CM	Configuration management plan
TP	Test plan
TT	Test specification
TR	Test report
UM	User manual
LF	Link file

The subject field refers to the final product or some portion of it. Let us divide it into three subfields so that it can be used as a mnemonic.

Subject::= ⟨program (or system)⟩⟨subsystem⟩⟨module⟩

Given this, a configuration management plan for the program OSVM would be labeled CM OSVM xxxx xxxx *edition.* The two fields of x's mean that the plan refers to all subsystems and modules of OSVM. DS OSVM USER xxxx *edition* is the detailed design specification for the user interface subsystem, and SF OSVM USER PASS *edition* is the source file for the password handling routine of the user interface subsystem.

Alternatively, numbered subject fields are often used in lieu of those employing alphanumeric mnemonics.

Editions may be divided into two parts, one for version level and the other for revision index.

Edition::= ⟨version⟩⟨revision⟩

The version level is updated when a new function is added, when the system is reconfigured for new operating circumstances (e.g., a message switch directed to a different communications protocol), or even to indicate the addition of new modules during integration. The revision index is incremented when a defect has been removed or a minor improvement of the performance has been made. All new versions start with the revision index reset to zero.

In a method as simple as this, one cannot directly correlate the version or revision of a given module with that of the full system. However, one can consult the link file of the executable program LM OSVM xxxx xxxx 02 14 and see that it contains the module RB OSVM USER PASS 01 03, which we know derives from SF OSVM USER PASS 01 03.

Precisely how one sets up a labeling scheme and formulates rules concerning the correspondence of editions among material of different identifiers depends on the type and size of the systems being developed, the number of characters one is willing to use, and — most of all — any conventions already predicated by elements of the programming development environment. Whatever method is used, the key should be consistency between code files and corresponding documents. Thus, the design documentation specific to the source file SF OSVM USER PASS 01 03 should have the same version index, 01, as that file. If correspondence does not exist at every moment during development, it should exist by the time OSVM starts its qualification test. As a second example, if the load module at the start of qualification is LM OSVM xxxx xxxx 02 14, the product specification (which may include material from the design specification of USER PASS) should also be at version level 02, as should the requirements and other documentation descriptive of the complete product.

Note that revision levels may properly be inconsistent, since defects may be removed from either code or documentation without affecting the other.

In this labeling method, we see the code files as the ultimate arbiter, as it were, of version level. Still, one needs to be able to quickly determine the current edition level of not only individual code files but of all documentation as well. This requires a cataloging tool, to which, in a somewhat different context, we shall return toward the end of the chapter.

Configuration management instruments. Three types of events attend the life of a controlled document or code file: its release to the control system, formal requests for change, and formal notification that a change request has been complied with. Much of configuration management has to do with avoiding nonproductive improvised measures of handling and marking these events while at the same time ensuring that unauthorized alterations are not encouraged by cumbersome bookkeeping. Accordingly, it is customary to initiate or record each type of event by using a unique instrument, generally a printed form that reduces the likelihood of incomplete information and incomplete dissemination.

Software release notice. The software release notice (SRN) is the vehicle for placing a document or code file in a baseline. The form used for it should call for its label, the name of the system, the name of the subsystem or component or whatever division of the project is applicable, the date, the person under whose authority the item is released, and a list of job titles to whom the notice will be sent. The form should have room to place the actual names of people next to their titles. For example:

Librarian	D. Dewey
CM manager	I. Control
Project leader	A. Boss
Subsystem leader	D. Capo
Quality engineer	C. Sharp
Test director	B. Thoro
Distribution manager	G. Diaspora

Quite obviously, an SRN applies to any new documentation or code. It should be used also to mark new versions of systems already in operation, normally at the completion of qualification testing of the new version. This will alert whoever is in charge of distribution of code and manuals to take appropriate action.

Software change request. There are two fundamentally different reasons for wanting to change a document or a code file: externally generated causes and internally generated ones. The external reasons generally are seen as changes in the functional or allocated baseline that affect the program design, as by adding a new requirement, altering the interface to a piece of external equipment, and so on. The internal changes are those required to improve efficiency, improve maintainability, purge code no longer used, and remove defects. Whether inner-directed or outer-directed, the first stage in altering controlled material is the generation of a software change request (SCR).

With respect to the immediate interest of defect removal, an SCR is generated when controlled code produces a failure and debugging has found the defect and has found a fix for it. The debugging process is often preceded by another piece of paper, a program trouble report (PTR), that lists the symptom and — if possible without debugging — the portion of the program responsible for the problem. The PTR is often used as the basis for the decision that an attempt should be made to solve the problem, especially during formal testing and the operational period when a confrontation with a defect is often avoided in favor of some sort of work-around. If the decision is to fix the problem, an SCR ensues.

The information contained in an SCR includes the labels of all code files and documents affected by the change, the names of the system and applicable subsystems and components, a description of the change, an estimate of the cost in labor-hours to effect the change, and other versions of the system to which the change should also be made. If the SCR is the result of a PTR, the PTR is referenced, as are, of course, the date and the identity of the requestor.

The SCR goes to a review board, or software configuration control board (SCCB), where the decision is made to proceed with the completion of the requested change.* While awaiting the board's decision, the SCR assumes the status of an interim software change notice (ISCN), lending enough officiality to the change to justify further testing with the altered program.

Software change notice. The last of the CM instruments is the software change notice (SCN), a sort of mini-SRN. It is issued by the librarian when the change has been satisfactorily tested and the correctness of the documentation updates has been verified. In addition to the name of the issuer, the date, and the name of the system, the information on an SCN includes a reference to the SCR that was its progenitor, the labels of all the controlled items that were affected,† and a brief description of the change and its effect, if any, on the baseline performance definition.

For operational systems, a single SCN may affect several different versions distributed at diverse installations. Inclusion of the version labels for each of these implies that the change was tested on each. One of the functions of the SCCB is to look for documentation (as might be supplied by a quality engineer) that those tests were, indeed, made.

The SCN is sent to the SCCB, the author of the PTR (recall that we have

---

* Actually, once an SCR has been written to fix a bug, in contrast to increasing or improving the program's capabilities, the decision to proceed is quite nearly perfunctory. The purpose of the SCCB in this regard is principally to ensure that the status of the baseline is known to all relevant personnel.

† If necessary, both old and new edition suffixes will be provided. For example, if version 2, revision 16 metamorphoses into version 3, revision 0, this information is helpful to people having to sort things out.

followed the change process for the repair of a defect), appropriate programming management personnel, and quite possibly a separate function responsible for the distribution of updates.

Software configuration control board.   We have been referring to the SCCB without stating who sits on it. Although the board's constituency is very much a function of the type of system in which it gets involved, some generalizations are possible. If the systems involve elements other than computer programs, as in embedded software or the software of bundled computer systems, there may be a representative of a configuration control board of greater scope. Programming management will certainly have a seat on the board. If a software quality assurance function exists, it will be represented. A member of either marketing or a program management office may hold a seat, although it will usually be vacant unless the agenda includes consideration of changes in the functional or allocated baselines. The board is rounded out by the librarian.

References to the board's functions in earlier discussions of this section suggest that the board is a decision-making body. This is an overstatement, except in theory. At a project level, one would expect that decisions to authorize work on an enhancement or the repair of nettlesome but not critical problems would be made elsewhere, although the people engaged in those deliberations might well include those who attend SCCB meetings. The real decisions faced by the board are those pertaining to procedural matters. The board's role in configuration management is to make certain that control is maintained. Its composition reflects the purpose of ensuring awareness, not deliberation. The questions that arise are not those of feasibility or selecting the best approach, but those having to do with such matters as making certain that estimates of cost were made, that the documentation associated with a code change was correspondingly altered, and the like. As a result, it is not necessary for the SCCB to meet immediately each time an SCR or SCN has been prepared. It is generally adequate to call for weekly meetings during development, monthly meetings during the first year of operational life, and even less frequently thereafter if few changes are being made.

In short, for the majority of the changes presented to the SCCB — those made to remove defects — the board places its stamp of approval on work already performed, either the actual changes or their associated paperwork.

For outer-directed modifications, we have quite a different matter. Enlarging the scope of the project, whether by the addition of new functions, requirements of portability, or whatever, has to do with cost and schedule. For outer-directed changes, the SCCB may be charged with advising management that they have been estimated in accordance with established procedures, or it may even be given the authority to make the final decision. A board meeting dealing with such matters may be called at any time for the specific business at hand. Moreover, its composition may differ (as by the addition of someone from the marketing department) from that required to sanctify changes already made.

Outer-directed changes often blur the distinction between configuration control as practiced during development and control as practiced during the operational period. It is more the rule than the exception that major alterations of the requirements specification start to crop up well before the first release of the finished project. For that there are a number of reasons: a new business-dictated mode of operation, a change of the supplier selected for interfacing hardware, the need to match the competitor's newly announced features, and so forth. They may begin as early as the design phases and continue to play their special brand of havoc even during qualification testing. Without a diligently pursued system of control, programmers may soon find it difficult to be certain of the external specifications they are supposed to be working to.

The need to accommodate protean requirements specifications gives new meaning to the word "baseline." We usually think of the control of various concurrent versions as being a problem of, say, a telephone switch customized to each of 100 different exchanges, an operating system now at version 3 but with some customers stoutly maintaining loyalty to version 1, or a computer-aided design system for semiconductor chips required to operate with a variety of graphic front ends. But how about an embedded program for a large instrumentation system? As an illustration, here is a typical situation faced by military contractors: Version 1 was qualified at the contractor's plant. But even as it was being qualified, two contract change notices were received. While these were being worked into version 2 (for incorporation in serial no. 2 of the full system), version 1 was being modified during field tests. Baseline documentation reflects version 1, revision 0; the program that actually demonstrated its usefulness is version 1, revision 1; and back at the laboratories, the programming staff is readying version 2, revision 0 for installation in all subsequent systems. Little do they know that it will be modified in its field test even while the first field-tested system continues to undergo the military's year-long evaluation of effectiveness or that two more contract change notices are on the way to permit the system's installation on additional types of ships or aircraft.

All of this can easily get out of hand. The SCCB more than pays its way by assiduously monitoring the p's and q's of configuration control.

11.4   Control of Installed Variants

Whether or not concurrent sets of requirements definitions existed before any code became operational, for large systems they will almost certainly develop during the operational period. Then they will be realized as concurrent operational baselines. In the sense that afterthoughts occur with less frequency as the distance from the conceptual phase of a project increases, control is somewhat less difficult during the operational period. On the other hand, more of the outer-directed changes will result in permanent diversity of baseline content, and this creates a new set of problems. That is, at a given moment, several versions of a system may be extant and have to be maintained. Moreover, the various versions will be at different revision levels.

The situation only gets worse with time and with the maturation of the system ("evolution" may be the more appropriate word) and that of the (by now) several operating systems under which it is installed. Consider a defect found in version 4, revision 19 of an operational system. The decision is made to fix the problem. Even before the repair is made, an investigation is undertaken to determine which of the other versions have the same problem. This may not be as simple as ascertaining which of the others have the same version-revision level as the faulty module found in version 4, revision 19 of the system. The same defect may exist in other editions of the module. In some variants of the system, the module may have been boarded up by having its call removed. For example, to improve throughput, an input error–checking routine may be blocked off for systems connected to hardware devices that contain their own error checking. It is also possible that other parts of other variants of the system have code that compensates for the bug or simply cannot be affected by it. For example, in version 4, revision 19, the module at fault may, under some circumstances, fail to provide an adequate time-out before accepting a user command. Version 4, however, is the only interactive version; all the others are batch.

In addition to determining which versions of the system are affected and how they should properly be tested, we have also to consider the high cost of regression testing of operational software. Although the practice has certain obvious disadvantages, one may wish to determine if it is more prudent to leave any of the variants alone.

All of this bothersome business adds up to the necessity of unambiguously knowing the exact composition of each installed system: its modules, including any installation data bases, and their editions. Only with this can a proper investigation be made to determine the effect of the change on each and the manner in which it needs to be verified. An analogy is found in the industries where the number of articles produced per year is in the tens of thousands and includes a great diversity of variants. Consider the plight of Starka Motors. Starka manufactures only compact motorcars, all of which use the same chassis. It would seem that a Starka is a Starka. However, some are sedans and some are coupes; some have automatic transmissions and others not; some have jersey upholstery and others have leather; and so it goes. How does Starka know exactly what goes into each product?* By cataloging, that's how.

Somewhere there is a master catalog that identifies each component of each car produced by Starka — which version (AM or FM radio, power or manual steering) and which revision code. The information is used for inventory control, production control, even sales support. What software producers need to do is to consider each software shipment as a product just as generic as a Starka and, further, maintain a "top assembly drawing" listing each component (and its edition) in the shipped product. Alternatively, they could permit no two shipments to have the same edition number if they vary by a single byte and maintain a top assembly drawing for every edition. Neither solution is an obstacle for software producers who use the same kind of data management system that motorcar producers use. Indeed, that is the practice of many software producers. It is less common, however, to find a software producer who uses a tool that also recalls the full set of documentation (including edition information) that can be correlated with each set of operational components. Since the kind of cataloging tool referred to is really a tree search system — with the top leaf the name of the system — it is not much different from the bill-of-material explosion system used by Starka for production control, and there is no reason the information cataloged for each leaf cannot include its associated documentation.

Distribution. Rigidly controlled configuration records are nowhere more important than for the distribution of the right updates to the right installations. This is a problem faced by firms whose business is selling operating systems (including computer manufacturers), those that sell volumes of applications systems, telecommunications manufacturers who have sold various versions of a basic programmable switch, and all others who have a large geographically distributed user base. There are times, of course, when a supplier of a given software product announces that only one version will be supported, and then gets away with it. But even that supplier is likely to sell many different software systems; so if the problem of controlling the distribution of updates to variants is solved, the equally important job of supplying updates of the right product to the right customers still exists.

The obvious solution is that a data base information system is required.

---

* It may be argued that this is not a representative case of support for operational products, since the illustration is of a production process. However, both the production phase of motorcars and the operational phase of computer programs immediately follow the period of product development. Besides, wait until Starka has to recall all those cars equipped with power brakes manufactured to Specification Control Drawing A1357908642 Rev. R.

Of course, even if we can now be assured that the right mailing list is compiled for the distribution of a new release, there remains the problem of knowing that the mail room did not drop the ball — or perhaps more appropriately, diskette or card deck. What is called for here is an extension of the quality control system to include distribution: records to be completed in the mail room and then matched to those in the data base, instant access by users to a caring voice if something goes wrong, and so on.

We need not worry about the mail room if downloading through a network controlled by the user data base coupled to a master librarian is possible. However, this is scarcely the general case. If the last step of distribution is usually bereft of mechanization, one does not always have to be as resourceful as do some:

> There's a trawler far out in the sea
> Steered about by a clever PC.
> Version five came one day
> In an odd sort of way:
> On the back of a tired manatee.

11.5 Summary

1. Maintenance and modification (in common usage, the former word often subsumes the latter) operations require exact information about the program being altered. Configuration control is directed to the accuracy of that knowledge.

2. Baselines are controlled collections of information concerning a program — initially just documentation, but later including code. All development work constitutes a departure from the previously established baseline.

3. Code is more difficult to control because it is not as easily inspected as documentation is. Effective control is possible only with auditable library control tools.

4. Patches should be confined to patch files, which can be controlled much as any module can be.

5. Programs that take the operational form of firmware require an extension of the library control system to account for the partitioning into firmware devices and the correct placement of each.

6. A uniform labeling scheme for documentation and the several forms of code is essential to configuration control. Such a scheme must include provisions for identifying successive editions.

7. The principal instruments used to control software are release notices for new material or new versions, change requests, which indicate the

scope of effort to make a change and its impact on baseline material, and change notices, which are used to disseminate the new status of a baseline.

8. These instruments are used by control boards, who have the ultimate responsibility to ensure management of the change process.

9. In the later stages of development and throughout the operational period, the configuration management machinery must cope with concurrent authorized versions. A workable approach is to consider a system as a generic product particularized for each variant by a list of the components (and their editions) that it comprises.

10. Control of concurrent baselines has also to be carried through to the distribution process to ensure that each installation gets the updates it needs and none other.

References

1. E. Bersoff, V. Henderson, and G. Siegel, "Software Configuration Management: A Tutorial," *Computer,* vol. 12, January 1979, pp. 6–14.
2. R. Dunn and R. Ullman, *Quality Assurance for Computer Software,* McGraw-Hill, New York, 1981, p. 134.
3. Evan Ivie, "The Programmer's Workbench — A Machine for Software Development," *CACM,* vol. 20, October 1977, pp. 746–753.

Chapter

12

Maintenance and Modification

The opening paragraph of Chapter 11 noted that, from a programming point of view, the operational phase of software is the business of maintenance and modification. And a very expensive business it is. Two-thirds of all programming costs are spent in improving, adapting, or recycling existing software. The largest software consumer of all, the U.S. government, is said by the Government Accounting Office to spend $1.3 billion a year on M&M. This appears to be the most conservative of several estimates, some of which indicate that $4 billion per year may be closer to the truth. The high cost may be attributed to the huge inventory of software that now exists and needs continued support, but that cost is exacerbated by the unique problems that beset operational support. This chapter explores those problems and discusses their solution.

Before addressing the problems in detail, let us note that the direct cost of changing programs is scarcely the only M&M cost. The rest of the cost is directed toward changing associated documentation and testing the changes — testing to determine not only that the desired result was achieved but also that undesired side effects were not obtained in the process.* We rely on configuration control to reduce the cost of updating documentation while at the same time increasing the likelihood of preserving the correctness of documentation. We rely on effective defect removal procedures and tools to reduce the cost of testing while simulta-

---

* As an example of the cost division, *Aviation Week & Space Technology,* April 19, 1982, quotes a software specialist in Collins' air transport avionics division as saying that 80 percent of the cost of change is expended on documentation and verification. This may, however, be an extreme imposed by the certification requirements of the Federal Aviation Administration.

neously providing confidence that changes do work and that the software system has not been debased.

Analogously to the development of new programs, the methods and techniques for M&M defect removal are strongly influenced by those used for designing and coding changes. Accordingly, we should start by looking at the overall milieu of maintenance and modification.

12.1 Maintenance and Modification: A Process of Iteration

We do not have to look very long at maintenance and modification programming. In principle, it is quite nearly the same as that for new programs. The same set of procedures, the same techniques, and the same tools can be used. Each program change during M&M is an iteration of the development process, and for large systems there will be many such iterations.

> The endless cycle of idea and action,
> Endless invention, endless experiment,
>
> T. S. ELIOT, *Choruses from the Rock*

When attention is paid to M&M, it is usually within the reference of "invention": adding new features, adapting to a new user operating environment, even removing latent defects in a deliberate and controlled manner. Unfortunately, "experiments" do enter into M&M as well, especially when attempts at finding the source of a problem have failed or when one tinkers blindly to improve performance. This chapter, of course, deals with methods that have been devised to avoid the nonproductive toying with operational programs that has been all too prevalent.

Recalling the configuration management instruments of Chapter 11, modifications to an operational system (as distinguished from maintenance) generally made are in response to a software change request (SCR) initiated, perhaps, by actions within the marketing or contracts department. Once a project is approved, addenda to the requirements documentation (alternatively, technical statements of work defining new features or redefining existing ones) are released by a software change notice (SCN). The addenda are to the modification project precisely as the requirements specification was to the original project. The subsequent phases of the modification project continue the analogy. If one wants to use the offices of configuration management to the utmost, the top-level design to implement the modification is first released as an SCR to the design documentation and then released with an SCN after the top-level design review. The same process can be used to control the detailed design and code associated with the modification.

Apart from minor enhancements, maintenance (as distinguished from modification) activities do not start with an SCN to the requirements documentation. Indeed, if the removal of latent defects has no effect on the design documentation, the most senior controlled item against which an SCR is prepared will be the source code. Nevertheless, however far back into the documentation hierarchy it reaches, maintenance, like modification, replicates the development process.

If both maintenance and modification are processes that iterate development, they are equally capable of producing the same kinds of defects one finds in the level 0, revision 0 editions of programs. Indeed, many observers believe that M&M are more prone to defect production than the development of new programs. Part of the reason is that the M&M programmers often have poorer programming environments to work with. The worst case is found where maintenance is performed at an installation facility lacking the testing and debugging tools available in the laboratory, especially if the operational computer is not the computer on which much of the development was accomplished. We see this in point-of-sales systems, instrumentation systems, engineering design systems, and similar installations in which a "vertical" system was delivered by an original equipment manufacturer (OEM). At the laboratory, the OEM had a mainframe computer running a modern software development environment. In the field, there may be nothing but the target processor itself.

Nowhere is this situation more acute than in the military. Recent policy changes have encouraged the services to perform their own software maintenance on computer-driven military systems. A given base or post, however, may have dozens of systems to maintain, some of which include more than one kind of computer. It is impossible for the maintenance programmers to have at their disposal the same software development environments that all of the original programming teams had. This is one of the prime motives behind the recent initiatives by the Department of Defense and its agencies to standardize on instruction set architectures (ISAs) and programming languages.*

Although not universally true, the quality of M&M programmers also contributes to defect production. Since M&M involve less conceptual thinking, conventional wisdom has it that M&M are a good place to train entry-level people. No few programming managers believe it a safe place to assign their less able experienced people, as well. Yet, what is it we expect of an M&M programmer? We expect the programmer to understand the

---

* Ultimately, the goal is to have but one language, Ada, for which there will be well-tooled environments available on several common host machines. More, shortly.

logic of another, often with inadequate documentation of that logic. We expect each M&M programmer to be responsible for a part of an operational program that may have been the product of a large number of development programmers. At certain locations (of which the military illustration is the prime example), we expect the programmer to be proficient in a number of programming languages, to have some understanding of the workings of a number of integrated systems, and to know the innards of many computer architectures.

This is scarcely a proper assignment for any but the more capable and experienced programmers. The staffing problem joins that of maintenance programming environments in lying behind the military's demand for commonality of programming languages and ISAs. Meanwhile, unfulfilled expectations of M&M programmers exist at many military installations as they will continue to exist in industry, especially in companies unable to standardize on target processor architectures and languages.

A third cause for the error-proneness of M&M programming has already been alluded to: poor documentation. We have both inadequate documentation and documentation that is inconsistent with the code to consider. The latter is a problem for the configuration control specialists to contend with, and the former is the responsibility of programming managers, starting during the development phase. Nevertheless, although we now know the solutions, there is a great body of code out there that is poorly supported by paper.

Summarizing, maintenance has not only to deal with latent defects traceable to the original development activity but also with defects produced during subsequent modifications and — recursively — maintenance.

For a better understanding of the task of defect removal during M&M, we should like to know more about the defects found during the operational period. Unfortunately, few systems have been analyzed. Software managers (including this one) generally feel that the distribution of these defects with regard to type does not differ much from that found during development, except that the need for defenses against invalid input often is first recognized during operation. A study undertaken by Robert Glass shows that of the 100 defects examined in each of two large projects, the largest class (30 percent total with good correlation between the two projects) was omitted logic, defined as the absence of necessary segments or statements.[1] These, of course, would include omitted validity checks. Of the others of Glass' categories for which the total number of reported defects were significant and for which we see some correlation between the two projects, regression defects accounted for 8.5 percent and documentation defects for another 8 percent. Both of these are defect types we would most expect to be evident among operational programs; the former simply because it reflects the error-proneness of maintenance, and the latter because the documentation is now being used by persons other than its authors.

12.2   Program Characteristics Favorable to Maintenance and Modification

What we know of operational defects is largely what our common sense tells us. Common sense also leads us to the recognition of the characteristics of programs that makes the programs maintainable. Above all, we look for programs that exhibit logical simplicity — failing that, at least clarity. The earmarks of simplicity and clarity include modularity (true functional modularity, not arbitrary segmentation) and a hierarchical control structure, restrictions on each module's access to data, structured data forms, the use of structured control forms, and generous and accurate annotation.

Much has been said of the technical members of this set in earlier pages. Of good annotation, there are several features that must be included. First, the header information for each procedure should provide a concise statement of the procedure's external specifications, including a description of its input and output data. Each section of the procedure should be introduced by comments identifying the section's relation to the external characteristics. Finally, comments within each section should relate groups of statements to the program's documented description. This last is automatically achieved by using design language statements as source code comments.

Although it is less significant, consistent indentation practices are allied to annotation as a technique to make listings more easily understood by maintenance programmers.

The language of the source program makes an obvious contribution to the clarity — or lack thereof — of programs. Assembler languages are the most difficult to read; compiler languages that support structured programming are the easiest. Beyond these familiar canons, the relation of other language features to clarity is more subjective; often it is a matter of the programmer's amount of experience with the language judged.

Apart from clarity, languages can exert structural influences on maintainability. As a prominent example, we can look at some of the attributes of Ada, a language designed with maintainability as its foremost objective. Ada's separation of the interfaces of a procedure from the procedure's implementation encourages modularity in the sense of information hiding. The versatility with which programmers can declare data types is not only conducive to self-documentation; it inhibits maintenance programmers from misusing existing variables. The ability to compile packages separately further encourages functional modularity.

To what extent Ada succeeds in reducing maintenance errors is still unknown. Indeed, there are those who, fearful of the misuse of Ada's generics and the richness of its language, feel that it may have an adverse effect. In the balance, however, it is hard not to believe that Ada will be beneficial to M&M.

What is the language that has the least maintainable qualities? Many programmers will agree with Jean Sammet, who, after positing that languages that are most suitable to providing good documentation are the most useful for the long haul and that languages that provide ease of programming have the greatest short-haul use, remarked, "The two languages which I think are the extreme ends of the spectrum . . . are COBOL for ease of reading and maintenance and APL for ease of writing, but hardly ease of maintenance."[2]

12.3 Other Influences on Maintenance and Modification

Perhaps even more important than the programming language is the software development environment. One looks for the same kind of features available to the development programmers, with even greater emphasis on the cataloging and retrieval facilities for documentation. As noted in Section 12.1, for programs that must be maintained at a number of sites, transportability of the development environment may be a problem. Often, the computers available at the operational sites are different from those used for development; they are even different from each other. Returning to Ada as a paradigm, we see the Ada programming support environment (APSE) having, at its core, an interface (KAPSE) between the APSE and the host machine and host operating system. Thus, the development environment for a given system will be available to the programmers who have to maintain it, provided a KAPSE has been developed for their host system.

Given that maintenance and modification is an iteration of development, if the development environment is available for M&M, it follows that one would want to employ for M&M the methodology used for development. This includes the identical set of measures for defect prevention and the identical set of practices for defect removal. Under those circumstances, we should expect a marked reduction in the tendency to produce defects through M&M and a corresponding improvement in the ability to detect and fix program bugs. This sunny situation will come about only through management actions during the development phase. In addition to stipulating criteria for modularity, programming standards, documentation, and controls, management should specify a maintenance support plan calling for the delivery of the development, test, and debug tools used for the zeroth iteration of the program (the development project). The corollary to this is that the software development environment must be under a configuration control regimen quite nearly as exacting as that imposed for the operational program.

With the introduction of management attitude, we return once again to the initiatives of the Department of Defense and the service branches in promoting software maintenance. Putting together all of their innovations, we find common documentation standards (courtesy of the Joint Logistics Commanders' Computer Resources Group), language commonality (especially the promotion of the DOD's own Ada), a transportable software development environment (APSE, courtesy of the Ada Joint Program Office), and commonality in instruction set architectures (a thrust of the deputy undersecretary of defense for embedded computer resources). Thanks to management awareness and action, the prospects for future M&M of military systems are bright. Producers of *all* programmed systems would do well to draw upon the decisions of the military's programming management. The most important influence on maintenance and modification, as on most matters in both government and industry, is that exerted by management.

At the present time, most M&M is performed by the supplier of the software. This applies to military systems as well as all other generic types of software. However, this does not mean that M&M is performed by the same people responsible for the original development. Nor do we necessarily find the maintenance programmers colocated with the development staff. Although maintenance performed at installation sites has been used to illustrate the most severe problems, many of the issues raised in that context apply when support is centralized also. The model for an operational support facility that will underlie the balance of this chapter is that currently most common: a maintenance facility belonging to a software supplier but organizationally (and perhaps geographically) separate from the development facility.

12.4 Reporting Defects

Repair of defects accounts for the majority of all the work assignments undertaken by M&M programmers. This is not to say that the bulk of programming time necessarily is spent on defect repair, since a major modification will require much greater effort than a repair. Rather, the statement simply means that when the year's accomplishments are totaled, defect removal operations outnumber all the other achievements.

The removal of a defect from operational software starts with its report from a user installation, which is where we shall start. Chapter 11 introduced the program trouble report (PTR), a generic name for the form used to report anything from a recurring system crash to a bit of confusing machine-user dialog. PTRs may also be used to report documentation defects, although separate forms for them also are used. The PTR documents its author's perceptions of improper program behavior. It may or may not contain the author's own thoughts about the source of the problem. That depends on who the originator is. If the PTR is initiated by a field service engineer, it may include quite a bit of preliminary sleuthing; if prepared by the manager of a text-processing office, probably none. In either case, as well as all those in between, the emphasis of the PTR must be placed on describing the *symptoms* of faulty service in the operational environment.

Software users are generally as adept at describing problems as most of us are when talking with our automobile mechanics.

"I can't start the engine when the car is parked uphill. It has happened twice."

"Does the starter crank it in the usual way?"

"I guess."

"Does the engine cough at all?"

"I couldn't tell. Both times I got stuck it was raining so hard I couldn't hear anything but the raindrops pelting the car."

Unfortunately, the authors of PTRs are usually unknown to the maintenance programmers, which precludes, or at least delays, the kind of dialog that led our mechanic to dismiss the uphill business as a meaningless coincidence. Even though subsequent telephone conversations are helpful, the burden of operational problem reporting falls on the PTR. To assure the most accurate reporting possible, the PTR form will have to serve as a built-in guide to its completion. Information that the form should explicitly request includes

- Name of person and installation reporting the problem.
- Telephone number.
- Date
- Identification of the faulty program, including its edition.
- Identification of the computer and operating system. (If the problem is in the operating system, the form should note that the correspondent should supply the names of programs or functions run under it at the time the problem is evinced.)
- Subsystem or major module at fault, if known.
- Symptom and approximate number of times it has been observed.
- Any recurring operational circumstances that attend the problem; for example, "Problem occurs whenever we back up master file directly after inputting a new transaction; that is, without first calling for any reports."
- Any relevant hard copy produced by the system.

- Any change in operating conditions prior to first incident; for example, "Problem with operating system started after we added a modem and a call-up terminal."

Analysis of the information on the PTR may lead the maintenance programmer assigned to it to request additional information. For example, for problems having to do with abnormal halts, the request may be made to copy the contents of the machine registers or to take a dump. If the user is unsophisticated, instruction in the use of procedures to acquire the needed data may be necessary.

12.5   Analysis of Defect Reports

In the case of software for which there are many installations, there is fair probability that the maintenance programmers have seen earlier reports of the problem. The time required to diagnose, repair, retest, and distribute the correction generally is long enough to permit the bug to have been shared by many installations. But someone has to report it first, and that person, more often than not, will be asked to supply additional information, as noted in the preceding section. If the problem looks sufficiently severe, or if the user is a favored customer, it may even merit a visit from a support programmer of one title or another. The on-site investigation may impress the user with the quality of service, but the user had best be prepared to concede the machine time required by the visitor.

For the convenience of both users and maintenance programmers, the maintenance facility is the preferred place for diagnosis. The extent to which diagnosis is possible depends on the degree to which the problem can be recreated remotely from its source. This, in turn, depends on the quality of the description of the problem (which, in the aggregate, improves as more users discover and report the problem), and the capability of the programming environment to simulate operational conditions. The latter is problematic when the subject software is embedded in an operational system. Apart from the issue of support tools discussed earlier, outside-world simulators may be adequate to the task. Their adequacy, however, will rarely exceed the simulation capability enjoyed by the original programming team, and often as not, the original programmers had inadequate tools. Worse, if the system is an old one and was developed on contract for a small number of copies and if the development environment was not contracted for as a deliverable item, the test bed used by the development programmers will no longer exist.

Section 12.3 observed that managers acquiring a custom system should call for the delivery of development tools. Increasingly, the purchasers of custom software are learning this, but millions of lines of code were written before it was understood. A large percentage of that code is still being used. The delivery of the tools does not necessarily imply that the purchaser intends to use them himself. This is simply his insurance that they will be there, if needed, for *someone's* use. Perhaps they will be lent to the original software supplier for his diagnosis of a problem. On the other hand, the supplier may have gone out of business or the warranty (if any) may have expired and the supplier's cost estimate for diagnosis and repair is considered excessive. With the tool set in hand, the owner of the operational system has the option to either ask an independent software shop to take on the job or do it himself.

In any case, the capability — or at least the potential — of recreating a failure in the laboratory does not exist if no one has a test bed to provide a reasonable verisimilitude of the operational environment. For embedded software, this not only means that diagnosis in the laboratory may be impossible but further implies that maintenance programmers on field assignment may have to bide their time for days or weeks while awaiting a repetition of the set of circumstances that caused the reported failure. Let us take a computer-controlled braking system for a commuter rail system as an example. After three reports of staccato braking action, programmers take to riding the train to monitor both the computer and the operational conditions (the approximate number of passengers, speed, grade, and so forth). After 20 days of riding back and forth, memorizing the signs along the right of way, and kibitzing the poker games in the cars, the programmers are rewarded by an incident similar to the incidents that had been reported. The problem is diagnosed, but at a monstrous price.

Expanding on an earlier remark, the elaborate test bed prepared for development either must be maintainable throughout the operational life of embedded software or should be capable of being assembled anew. The latter is costly, and it must be reckoned early in the determination of the cost of support for the entire life cycle.

Returning to the more general topic of this section, several separate activities may attend the receipt of a trouble report. We can summarize them as follows:

- Attempt to correlate with other trouble reports.
- Assess severity.
- Decide whether to repair.
- Attempt to recreate the problem in the maintenance facility.
- Attempt to diagnose the problem solely by analyzing the program. (This is analogous to debugging without obtaining further experimental data.)
- Make on-site inspection to diagnose problem.
- Fix problem.

Of these, the first three are the only ones that apply to all program trouble reports. Thus far, the assessment of the defect's severity and the issues that attach to deciding whether to try to remove it have been ignored. We shall turn to them now.

12.6   To Fix or Not to Fix

The most obvious factor influencing the decision is that of the defect's severity. Section 9.5 defined three levels of severity in an example of acceptance criteria. For the disposition of field defect reports, four levels may be more suitable:

1. Defect renders system so unreliable or unsuitable as to preclude further use.
2. Defect forces major* restrictions of the system's use.
3. Defect forces minor* restrictions of the system's use.
4. Defect creates operational difficulties but no restrictions of use.

If the judgment is made that level 1 applies, the decision-making process has concluded. Examples of level 1 defects are frequent crashes of a time-sharing system, a paper mill control system that allows excessive pollutants to flow into the river, a printed-wiring-board layout program that generates an abundance of short circuits, an electronic funds transfer system given to crediting transfers to the wrong bank, and a cryptographic military communications system that garbles more messages than not.

Level 2 defects usually result in a decision to fix. They include the inability of a telephone switch to handle peak loads within acceptable connect times, the inability of an airborne rocket launch system to handle certain likely tactical situations, an automated office network that loses all but the first two unread pieces of electronic mail, an accounting system that improperly handles Schedule D of the IRS 1040 form, and a spacecraft oxygen monitor that gives frequent but incorrect warnings of insufficient oxygen reserve.

Although most level 2 defects are eventually removed, their removal may take some time. We would expect that most of the defects of the first three levels will be reported within the first few months of operation of new or recently modified software. This implies a relatively dense PTR population. We would further expect that the number of level 2 defects will exceed

---

* The use of the words "major" and "minor" are clear clues that a subjective judgment is involved. The easiest rationale to use is one based on defect tolerability with respect to the program's application. For example, an intermittent system crash is intolerable in a space vehicle navigation system. On the other hand, intermittently inaccurate steering outputs can be tolerated because the system will self-correct in a short time. Contrariwise, intermittent crashes are tolerable in a batch payroll system, as long as they do not occur too frequently, but intermittent inaccuracy may lead to either bankruptcy or wholesale staff resignations.

the number of level 1 defects. Accordingly, any given problem of level 2 may have to wait its turn to be addressed. Still, these problems are severe enough that, once solved, a fix is likely to be distributed immediately to all users. Not so with the next level, where it may be reasonable, if there are many corrections, to batch them for release to users.

Level 3 defects, for which workarounds are generally possible, tend to straddle the fix-forget fence. Here are some examples: An airline reservation system frequently releases previously assigned seats, thereby requiring reassignment at the gate; a telephone switch intermittently refuses to accept conferencing directives; a general sort routine used in batch operations loops interminably if the input file is already in sort order; an autopilot takes excessive time to stabilize after being switched from heading mode to the tracking of ground transmitters; a control system for a bottling plant frequently requires manual intervention to add a few more bottles to those metered into the filling queue; and an accounts payable system occasionally draws checks for amounts approaching the gross national product.

All of these have backup modes of operation or produce errors that are easily found. Even the last example is not terribly serious, as long as it happens infrequently, since outlandishly large drafts are bound to be caught by cursory manual inspection. The defect is likely to be fixed in one of these events:

- The maintenance people have little else to do at the moment.
- The defect will have an adverse effect on the product's marketing prospects.
- The defect has annoyed a large number of voluble users.
- The defect is easy to correct.

These considerations are weighed against others. The defect may not be a candidate for further attention if the judgment is made that its removal is likely to create new defects — a comment on the state of the program's structure or the currency of knowledge about that structure — or if it is felt that the cost of repair outweighs the tangible value.

Level 4 defects are the ones computer users put up with most of the time. They entail no restrictions on the use of the software. Nevertheless, from the producer's point of view, they are not to be dismissed. Even in the absence of more severe defects, the sum of these annoyances may tarnish the system's reputation. Among level 4 defects are those affecting documentation: misleading logic documentation (a problem for the maintenance programmer) and confusing or missing user documentation (such as omitting one of the steps to get from here to there). Faulty program operation includes a computer game that sometimes leaves a piece of the destroyed spaceship on the face of the monitor, a process control system that needs to be reinitialized when switched on at the start of each day (not because of the memory medium, but just because that is the way it was designed), a bank teller network that has an arbitrary way of assigning priorities to workstations, and an office automation system that requires an excessive number of steps to get to one subsystem from another (say, from text processing to letter transmission).

That these are minor defects in terms of their impact on users does not mean that they are necessarily easy to correct. Thus, many are known and documented but are left untouched. Documentation corrigenda may cost more to distribute than the labor cost of the corrections themselves. Considerations of program faults may be governed by the previously remarked fear that the software structure may be less tolerant to further change than the users are to the things that need changing.

Independent of severity, cost, and program maintainability, a fourth factor, namely, warranty, will be decisive in the contemplation of certain repairs. Software warranties, once unknown, are appearing in increasing number. Warranties replace the intangible issue of goodwill — at least with regard to the supplier's postdelivery commitment to the customer. Warranties can also serve to explicitly limit the supplier's responsibility. Apart from the more obvious advantages this offers him, the software producer also gains the opportunity to more accurately reckon support costs at the time a new product is being conceived.

Warranties raise a troublesome issue for the software sales — usually for contracted developments — in which the customer is delivered the source code as well as a working program load. Both customer and developer must now contend with the effect of any changes made by the customer. Not only may such changes introduce new defects, they may also make it harder for the supplier to locate and remove defects of his making. One solution calls for the supplier — possibly in concert with the customer — to attempt to recreate a reported problem by using a copy of the system as it was delivered, a copy held by the producer in its pristine state. If the problem can be demonstrated to exist in that copy, the supplier fixes at no cost. If not, the customer either pays for the correction or decides to live with the problem.

We must recognize that, ultimately, the customer pays for the warranty. Thus, both seller and buyer would do well to define the types of defects for which the seller will be liable. The simple examples on preceding pages of severity grades are no substitute for language specific to the subject programmed product. Even then it is difficult to bound the seller's obligation in a way that will exclude the need (or opportunity) for subjective judgments. It remains that goodwill and the desire of both parties to enjoy a continuing, mutually satisfactory business relationship will affect the decision to fix or not. The warranty serves as the formal reference within which decisions are made.

12.7 Postponing Code Death

One of the more popular myths one hears is the one that has programs gradually degenerating to the point that they have insufficient economic value to warrant updating. A cursory look at the facts belies this:

- That the accountants wrote off the program in 5 years does not affect the program itself.
- Programs do not decompose or wear out.
- Users adapt to level 3 and level 4 bugs. Having once adapted, along with their reluctance to undertake a new learning process, they tend to resist the importation of a new system.

What does cause obsolescence, however, is one of the following:

1. The loss of efficiency that attends workarounds eventually makes the acquisition of a new program, presumably one in better shape, attractive.
2. The program must be updated to be used at all, but there is no one to perform the update.
3. Dozens of previous changes have so destroyed the program's structure that the likelihood of succeeding at a necessary modification is nil.

The first of these has so strong an analogy to the replacement of other capital assets that it needs no explanation. For both the other two we have any number of reasons why a program must be updated if it is to continue in use. Here are some examples: The payroll system must be expanded to handle one more deduction, since the state is about to impose a new payroll tax. The aircraft autopilot must be modified to conform to the control surface interaction of a new jetliner. The central telephone switch must further segregate and record time charges to comply with revised tariff regulations. To keep up with the response time enjoyed by competitors, the batch analysis systems of a brokerage house must be placed on line. Now that the hardware designers have expanded the robot's degrees of freedom from four to six, the software must be so enriched.

The second of the three sources of obsolescence is really a family of causes. A software producer may be unwilling to update a program because he feels that the market for the update is insufficent to make the diversion of programming labor worthwhile. Whether a homegrown system or a system acquired from a supplier, it is possible that the one person who has maintained the program these past 5 years is no longer with the firm and has left little, if any, useful documentation. It is even possible that there is no one to update the program because there is no one left in the firm who knows the language of the program or wants to learn it. Look about a programming shop working in PL/1 and C and try to find a programmer willing to undertake a 1401 Autocoder update.

The third cause of obsolescence returns us to the substance of this chapter. Maintenance and modification practices must be directed to forestalling the degeneration of the program's structure. A quick change plastered onto a program without regard to program structure will jeopardize the longevity of the program. Place a condition branch in module ALPHA so that it calls the new routine OMEGA for the new condition, have OMEGA directly call the modules subordinate to ALPHA, alter these modules so that their return to OMEGA is based on conditions different from those that predicated their initial design, and one has the new structure shown schematically in Figure 12.1.

The proper way to do things is to figure out how ALPHA, ALPHA1, and ALPHA2 work and then modify all three as necessary or even replace the group. However, it is quicker to implement the illustrated approach of recklessly breaking into the code so that new functions can be designed apart from those that had existed. Since programming follows the line of least resistance, the pasted-on change is the more common to find. Unfortunately, it takes few modifications of the kind illustrated by Figure 12.1 before the cost, schedule, and resulting behavior of a modification can no longer be estimated. This is, of course, only one of many ways in which maintenance and modification can sabotage program structure.

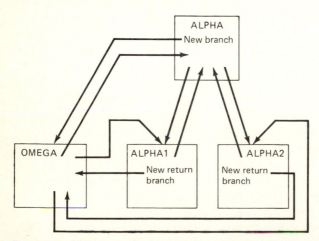

Figure 12.1 The aftermath of an attack on program structure.

The solution is obvious: Maintenance management must insist that all alterations follow the programming precepts that attended the original design. Similarly, maintenance management must take care to maintain the documentation used by its programmers. Also, complete regression testing must be undertaken with each software release. It may, however, be permissible to release the new edition before the completion of regression testing, subject to recall if adverse effects turn up in the completion of the tests.* In general, it is fair to say that the M&M programming standards must be as well thought out and religiously followed as those used by development programmers.

At some point, of course, every program will be retired from active service. Even then, however, if its language is not yet archaic and its structure not too badly ravaged, it may be possible to reuse some of its parts or to reengineer them to fit into the new system. Whether that is worth the effort depends on the size of the subject parts. A complete subsystem of a functionally decomposed program may well lend itself to reincarnation in a new system.

To determine the potential for retreading code, an inspection of the text should be performed. Unfortunately, this is not quite so simple as determining the number of *goto's,* the number of *no-op's,* or the number of comments of the genre, "From here to line 1560 is from the original program. We don't know what it does or if we need it any more but we were afraid to take it out." These counts help, but they should be accompanied by broader measures of structure, such as the complexity calculations of Section 7.1.

Whether or not a satisfactory structural measure of aging is possible, we should not want to consider the reusability of a subsystem that does not perform well. Unfortunately, it is even more difficult to take a measure of performance for the purpose of gauging either the viability of a complete system or the reusability of a component. To the extent, incomplete as it is, that we can equate reliability with software middle age, a reliability model for operational programs might be useful. The closest approach to this is Cheung's model, which attempts to measure reliability with respect to a user environment.[3] By using techniques similar to those of Littlewood's semi-Markov[4] and stochastic models,[5] this model requires the user to know the operational transition probabilities between module pairs and the reliability of individual modules. These are not the most common data available, although Cheung does provide techniques for their estimation.

Reliability, of course, is but one aspect of the remaining usefulness of

---

* One must remember, also, to update the set of regression tests that will be used in the future to account for the changes just made.

either programs or their parts. It is as clear that we should like to be able to reckon the remaining economic life of programs as it is that we do not really know how to do so. This would seem fertile ground for new research. Certainly we should be able to do better than the simplistic counting measures alluded to two paragraphs earlier. Or perhaps not:

> There's a model in use so I'm told
> For the rate at which programs grow old.
> It counts no-ops, and then
> It divides through by ten,
> And the quotient's the last version sold.

12.8 Summary

1. Properly performed maintenance and modification activities represent iterations of the programming development process.

2. To a large extent, management control of maintenance and modification can be exerted through the configuration management machinery.

3. Many maintenance programmers, especially those working at installation sites, are under the burden of having to work with programming environments inferior to those used by their development counterparts while at the same time having to maintain proficiency in a variety of systems (some of which are poorly documented), computer architectures, and programming languages.

4. The difficult conditions of maintenance programming result in the commission of an untoward number of errors.

5. With regard to the properties of programs that abet the work of maintenance programmers, simplicity and clarity are the most important.

6. The initiatives of the Department of Defense and its service branches in standardizing languages, computer architectures, documentation methods, and programming environments constitute a noteworthy attack on maintenance problems.

7. The initiation of the removal of a defect from operational software starts with a program trouble report. Since this is the source document for a maintenance project, printed forms should be used to guide the preparation and ensure the inclusion of all relevant information.

8. The removal of a reported defect reintroduces the issues that attend debugging, but only after it is possible to recreate the problem. That is often a difficult task at a maintenance facility.

9. It may make good sense not to attempt to remove a defect. In the absence of warranty obligations, the factors that influence the decision

include severity of the defect's effect on operations, reputation of the product, the number of users affected, and the estimated ease of removal.

10. Software warranties offer advantages to both seller and buyer. However, it is necessary to carefully spell out the seller's obligations if the buyer modifies the product.

11. The rate at which programs become obsolete has to do not only with changes in programming practices and the operational environment but also with the state of preservation of the program's structure. If the structure remains in good shape, even though it is uneconomical to modify the whole program, parts of the program may be usable directly or be capable of reengineering for use in the program's successor.

References

1. Robert Glass, "Persistent Software Errors," *IEEE Trans. Software Eng.* vol. SE-7, March 1981, pp. 162–168.
2. A. Perlis, F. Sayward, and M. Shaw, *Software Metrics,* The MIT Press, Cambridge, Mass., 1981, p. 110.
3. Roger Cheung, "A User-Oriented Software Reliability Model," *IEEE Trans. Software Eng.* vol. SE-6, March 1980, pp. 118–125.
4. Bev Littlewood, "Software Reliability Model for Modular Programming Structure," *IEEE Trans. Reliability,* vol. R-28, August 1979, pp. 241–246.
5. Bev Littlewood, "A Bayesian Differential Debugging Model for Software Reliability," *Workshop on Quantitative Software Models,* IEEE Cat. No. TH0067-9, October 1979, pp. 170–181.

List of Initial-Letter Abbreviations

AI	artificial intelligence
APSE	Ada Programming Support Environment
ATP	acceptance test procedure
AUT	automated unit test
BNF	Backus-Naur-Form
cdf	cumulative distribution function
CE	concurrent Euclid
CM	configuration management
CPU	central processing unit
CPT	chief programmer team
CRT	cathode-ray tube
EDP	electronic data processing

EOR	efficacy of removal
FIFO	first in first out
GRC	General Research Corporation
HIPO	hierarchy plus input-process-output
HOS	higher-order software
ISAs	instruction set architectures
ISCN	interim software change notice
ISDS	integrated software development system
IV&V	independent verification and validation
JAVS	Jovial Automated Verification System
KLOC	thousand lines of code
LIFO	last in first out
LOC	lines of code
M&M	maintenance and modification
MLE	maximum likelihood estimate
MSEF	Microprocessor Software Engineering Facility
MTTF	mean time to failure
NCSS	noncomment source statements
NHPP	nonhomogeneous Poisson process
N-S	Nassi-Schneiderman
OEM	original equipment manufacturer
pdf	probability distribution frequency
PDL	program design language
PET	program evaluator and test
PROM	programmable read-only memory
PSL	problem statement language
PTR	program trouble reports
PWB	Programmer's Workbench
REVS	requirements engineering and validation system
ROM	read-only memory
RSL	requirements statement language
SADT	structural analysis and design technique
SCCB	software configuration control board
SCN	software change notice

SCR   software change request

SQA   software quality assurance

SREM   software requirements engineering methodology

SRI   Stanford Research Institute

SRN   software release notice

TBD   to be determined

TEM   test effectiveness measure

VHLL   very high level language

V&V   verification and validation

Index

About the Author

Robert H. Dunn's twenty years of programming management experience encompasses engineering, data processing, real-time, and scientific systems. He is currently Manager of Programming Quality for ITT Programming. A well-known lecturer on programming quality issues, he has represented the industry on select government planning teams, and he is coauthor of the book *Quality Assurance for Computer Software* (McGraw-Hill).